PELHAM
GRENVILLE
WODEHOUSE

VOLUME 1
"This is jolly old Fame"

"A masterpiece. An enthralling analysis of
PGW's writing and humour".
Sir Edward Cazalet, PGW's grandson

"Despite Wodehouse's antipathy towards critics, Kent's first volume demonstrates just how much the thick-skinned of us have to explore in his work. The term "sweetness and light" has notable literary origins in distinctly literary works, stemming from "dulce et utile" (literally "sweet and useful") from Horace's *Ars Poetica*, by way of Jonathan Swift and Matthew Arnold. The words symbolize not just a Victorian gentility but a classless curiosity, and love for fellow man. Wodehouse's work should perhaps be seen in this vein, useful tonic to the darkness in the world, and more poetry than plot. It is therefore excellent news that we await two more volumes of Paul Kent's work that can help us to unpick that poetry and try to better understand the source of that "sunlit perfection".
Eliza Easton in the *Times Literary Supplement* (TLS)

"It's amazing after the many thousands of words written about PGW that there can still be anything new to say – but Paul offers many fresh thoughts and assessments, expressing them most effectively and entertainingly".
Murray Hedgcock, author of *Wodehouse at the Wicket*

"[A] delightful work, complex and full of revelation throughout. And yet for me, the best part of reading this is the tone that somehow simulates Wodehouse's in an academic work".
Gary Hall, Editor of *Plum Lines,* the quarterly journal of the Wodehouse Society

"Kent slides open a sash window, blowing fresh perspective into those stuffy establishment rooms full of recycled opinion".
***Wooster Sauce*, journal of the P.G. Wodehouse Society (UK)**

"A remarkably clear appreciation of the special qualities of Plum's work. I can recommend it highly".
Neil Midkiff, webmaster 'Madame Eulalie's Rare Plums' Wodehouse site

"This is the sort of thinking and writing the world of Wodehouse appreciation needs – and gives the rest of us plenty to talk about".
Honoria Plum, 'Plumtopia' blog

"The book is great . . . most excellent."
Thomas Langston Reeves Smith, past President, The Wodehouse Society (US)

"I really think [Paul] has produced a terrific and original study of PGW's work, and [the book] makes a lot of points and connections which are new to me".
Tony Ring, Wodehouse scholar and co-author of *The Wodehouse Millennium Concordance* (8 vols.)

"Such a breath of fresh air".
Karen M. Shotting, past President, The Wodehouse Society (US)

PELHAM GRENVILLE WODEHOUSE

VOLUME 1
"This is jolly old Fame"

PAUL KENT

Leapfrog Press
New York and London

P.G. WODEHOUSE 1881-1975
HUMOURIST
NOVELIST
LYRICIST
PLAYWRIGHT

So reads the simple inscription on the memorial stone unveiled in London's Westminster Abbey in 2019, honouring the greatest comic writer of the 20th century. Sir Pelham Grenville Wodehouse KBE (also known as "Plum") was all these things, writing more than 70 novels, 300 short stories, over 200 song lyrics and more than 20 plays in a career spanning eight decades. Over 40 years after his death, Wodehouse is not just surviving but thriving all  over the world, so far being translated into 33 languages from Azerbaijani to Ukrainian via Hebrew, Italian, Swedish and Chinese. There are also established Wodehouse societies in the UK, the USA, Belgium, Holland and Russia. His books are demonstrating the staying power of true classics, and are all currently in print, making him as relevant – and funny – as he ever was.

ABOUT THE AUTHOR

Vice-Chairman of the P.G. Wodehouse Society (UK), Paul Kent has published a trilogy of literary biographies on Wodehouse, as well as *What Ho!*, ten short pamphlets on Wodehousean themes. He is currently preparing two companion volumes that look at Plum's literary influences and dramatic work, respectively *Plum's Literary Heroes* and *Wodehouse at the Theatre*. All are available from TSB (https://www.canofworms.net/shop)

Pelham Grenville Wodehouse
Volume 1: "This is jolly old Fame"

© 2023 Paul Kent

9 8 7 6 5 4 3 2 1

Published in the United States by Leapfrog Press, 2023
Leapfrog Press, Inc
www.leapfrogpress.com

First published by TSB, 2019

TSB is an imprint of:

Can of Worms Enterprises Ltd
7 Peacock Yard
London SE17 3LH
United Kingdom

www.canofworms.net

Cover design: James Shannon
Typesetting: Tam Griffiths and James Shannon
Index: Zoey James

Printed and bound in the United Kingdom

ISBN: 978-1-948585-27-9 (paperback)

British Library Cataloguing in Publication Data
A catalogue record for this book is available from the British Library

Library of Congress Cataloging-in-Publication Data
A catalog record for this book is available from the Library of Congress

An index and bibliography for this and subsequent volumes
can be found online at: www.canofworms.net/pgwindex

The Forest Stewardship Council® is an international non-
governmental organisation that promotes environmentally appropriate,
socially beneficial, andeconomically viable management of the world's
forests. To learn more visit www.fsc.org

I really am becoming rather a blood these days… [In] a review of a book in the *Times*, they say *"The author at times reverts to the P.G. Wodehouse manner"*. This, I need scarcely point out to you, is jolly old Fame. Once they begin to refer to you in that casual way as if everybody must know who you are all is well.

P.G. Wodehouse

A POTTED LIFE OF P.G. WODEHOUSE

1881	October 15	Birth of Pelham Grenville Wodehouse at 1 Vale Place, Guildford, Surrey
1894		PGW first attends Dulwich College, London
1900		Receives his first payment for writing: from *Public School Magazine* for an article entitled 'Some Aspects of Game-Captaincy'
1900	September	Starts work at the Hong Kong and Shanghai Bank, London
1901	July	First real short story published in *Public School Magazine*, entitled 'The Prize Poem'
1901	August 16	First contribution to *Globe* newspaper
1902	September 9	Resigns from the HS Bank
1902	September 17	First article for *Punch* magazine, entitled 'An Unfinished Collection'
1902	September 19	First book published, *The Pothunters*
1904	April 16	First visit to the USA
1904	August	Appointed Editor of the 'By The Way' column at the *Globe*
1904	December 10	First published lyric, 'Put Me In My Little Cell', sung in *Sergeant Brue* at the Strand Theatre, London
1906	March 6	Employed by Seymour Hicks as the resident lyricist at the Aldwych Theatre
1906	March 19	First meets future collaborator Jerome Kern
1906	August	First novel for adults, *Love Among the Chickens*, published
1907	December 6	Joins Gaiety Theatre as lyricist
1909		Second visit to USA, where he sells short stories to *Collier's* and *Cosmopolitan*
1911	August 24	First play, *A Gentleman of Leisure*, opens in New York
1913	April 8	First play in London, *Brother Alfred*, flops
1914	August 2	Returns to New York
1914	August 3	Meets Ethel Rowley, née Newton, an English widow, at a New York party
1914	September 30	Marries Ethel Rowley and inherits her daughter Leonora
1915	March	Appointed drama critic of [US] *Vanity Fair*
1915	June 26	First appearance of Lord Emsworth and Blandings Castle in the serialisation of *Something New* (*Something Fresh* is U.K. title) in *Saturday Evening Post*
1915	September 18	Jeeves makes his first appearance, in the story 'Extricating Young Gussie' published in *Saturday Evening Post*
1916	September 25	First Bolton, Wodehouse & Kern musical comedy, *Miss Springtime* debuts in New York and is moderately successful

1919	June 7	First Oldest Member story, 'A Woman is Only a Woman', published in *Saturday Evening Post*
1923	April	First Ukridge short story, 'Ukridge's Dog College', appears in *Cosmopolitan*
1926		PGW elected a Fellow of the Royal Society of Literature
1926	July	First Mr Mulliner story, 'The Truth About George', appears in *Strand* magazine
1930	June 1	Starts first contract with MGM in Hollywood
1933	August	First instalment of the first Jeeves and Bertie Wooster novel, *Thank You, Jeeves*, published in *Strand*
1934	January 19	Successfully challenges in court the U.K. Inland Revenue's attempts to claim more income tax on his earnings
1934	June	Settles in Le Touquet, France
1935	June 3	Buys Low Wood in Le Touquet
1936	June 26	Awarded medallion by International Mark Twain Society
1939	June 2	Invested as D. Litt at Oxford University
1939	September 3	Britain declares war on Germany
1940	May 21	PGW, Ethel and animals try to leave Le Touquet in the light of the German advance, but their car twice breaks down
1940	July 21	Start of PGW internment by Germans in camps successively at Loos Prison (Lille), Liege, Huy and Tost (Upper Silesia)
1941	June 21	PGW released from internment and taken to Berlin
1941	June 26	PGW makes the first of five radio broadcasts for fans in neutral USA
1941	July 15	'Cassandra's' BBC radio broadcast of a vituperative attack on PGW, calling him a traitor
1943	September 11	PGW transferred to Paris
1944	May 16	Death of PGW's step-daughter Leonora
1947	April 27	PGW and Ethel arrive in US on SS America
1952	March	Ethel buys a house in Basket Neck Lane, Remsenburg, Long Island, New York, close to Guy Bolton's home
1955	December 16	PGW becomes an American citizen
1960	January 27	PGW elected to the *Punch* table
1961	July 15	BBC broadcasts 'An Act of Homage and Reparation' by Evelyn Waugh
1965	May 27	BBC TV series *The World of Wooster* begins transmission
1967	February 16	BBC TV series *Blandings Castle* begins transmission
1974	November	PGW's last complete novel, *Aunts Aren't Gentlemen*, published in the U.K.
1975	January 1	PGW knighted by Queen Elizabeth II, his wife Ethel taking the title Lady Wodehouse
1975	February 14	PGW dies in hospital

CONTENTS

Author's Note

In this book, I will try to deliver a tour of Wodehouse's genius that, were he to read it, would not elicit such comments as "ghastly", "rot", and "perfect perisher". Hence the absence of his particular bugbear, footnotes — except for the lonely but wholly necessary example located at the foot of the first full page of text.

Preface
P. G. Wodehouse in the 21ˢᵗ Century

P. G. Wodehouse needs no introduction.
Ogden Nash

Paper has rarely been put to better use than printing Wodehouse.
Caitlin Moran

All humour should really aspire to the condition of Wodehouse.
Jonathan Coe

P. G. Wodehouse is the gold standard of English wit.
Christopher Hitchens

Wodehouse, all in all, is lasting astonishingly well.
Philip Hensher

In 2015, three of Pelham Grenville Wodehouse's best-loved comic characters celebrated their 100th birthdays. Back in the *annus mirabilis* of 1915, Bertie (yet to be surnamed "Wooster") and Jeeves respectively crawled out of bed and shimmered onto the page in the short story 'Extricating Young Gussie', and Clarence Threepwood, ninth Earl of Emsworth bumbled onto his in *Something Fresh*.[1] Their creator was 34, King George V occupied the British throne, the British Empire peaked at around 23% of the planet's land mass, 63% of the U.K.'s population would die before it reached 60, the London *Times* cost one (old) penny, and women in England were yet to be given the vote.

But as Wodehouse's writing started to catch fire, so the Edwardian world that informed it was being brutally swept away by the Great War; and as his fame reached its peak in 1939, a second global conflict would conclusively destroy what little was left, while temporarily marking him out as a traitor to his country. For the remaining three decades of his creative life, Wodehouse was to plough a lonely, even

---

1 The novel was given a different title – *Something New* – in America. This annoying habit, which affects dozens of PGW's publications, is the bane of anyone writing about Wodehouse, and has begat millions of necessary but bothersome explanatory footnotes – including, of course, this one. Suffice to say, I will be using the British titles (and dates of publication) in what follows, except where the context demands that I don't. This is the final footnote in this book.

1

unique, literary furrow, but one still rich in recognition and achievement. He died in America, age 93, on St Valentine's Day 1975, a pipe and tobacco pouch to hand, working on his latest novel. An exile who hadn't set foot in the land of his birth for 36 years, the British Government awarded him a KBE just weeks before his passing, belatedly making him a Sir.

Given that Wodehouse's world was deeply anachronistic for most of the time he was creating it, the fact that Bertie, Jeeves, Lord Emsworth and others in his comedy cavalcade have passed their centenary is on its own a remarkable feat and a cause for celebration. More important, however, is that, having survived this long, the books in which they appear are demonstrating the staying power of true literary classics, having somehow managed to sail through the choppy waters of time and geography, manners and modes. What keeps them afloat – and not merely a *succès d'estime* – is, of course, the ease with which they continue to make readers laugh in spite of the seismic social, cultural and political changes that have taken place since their creation, and for this we must credit their author's unique sense of humour and his remarkable facility for writing elegant, memorable and timeless prose. As fellow novelist A. N. Wilson observed in 2011:

> Popular English fiction of the twentieth century did not have much of a shelf life. J. B. Priestley, Angela Thirkell, Warwick Deeping, Dorothy L. Sayers. It is hard to think of anyone reading them now, except for curiosity value. Bring the list up to date – with John Fowles or Kingsley Amis – and you see the same thing happening; they are crumbling before your eyes, like exhumed bones exposed to ultraviolet. Not so P. G. Wodehouse, who is now bought and read more than ever.

Although it's a broad-brush claim, there's plenty of evidence that Wilson could have cited if he'd wished to support it. For Wodehouse (or "Plum" as he's regularly known – a shortening of his first name "Pelham") is not merely surviving but quietly thriving. This most English of authors has been translated into more than 30 languages, from Azerbaijani to Ukrainian via Hebrew, Italian, Japanese and Mandarin. There are sizeable, well-established Wodehouse societies in the U.K., and the USA, Belgium, Holland and Russia actively promoting his legacy. A 99-volume uniform edition of his complete works is currently in print and at the time of writing has sold well over half a million copies. There are reports that India's young professionals binge on marathon Wodehouse quizzes. And if you subscribe to internet news alerts mentioning 'Wodehouse', you will find dozens of references to his writing pinging into your inbox every week from newspapers, magazines, websites and blogs from just about every corner of the world.

But it wasn't always like this: for the longest time, it seemed he was both hopelessly unfashionable and criminally undervalued. In the 1990s, American critic and Pulitzer Prize winner Michael Dirda ruefully noted in the *Washington Post* that Wodehouse "seems to have lost his general audience and become mainly a cult author savoured by connoisseurs for his prose artistry". The Indian novelist and politician Shashi Tharoor called for "a long-overdue Wodehouse revival in England", having noted "how low [his] fortunes...had sunk in his native land". Quite how low is evidenced in a 2001 tome purporting to provide an overview of 'Literature in Britain Today', which casually filed Wodehouse under "minor humourists and stylists".

Two decades on, that situation has improved considerably, thanks to a number of timely rear-guard actions fought by fans, publishers, and Plum's literary estate, helped along by the curious, capricious machinery that governs the ebb and flow of literary reputation. Copywriters need no longer draw on ages-old praise from Hilaire Belloc that he was "the best writer of our time...the best living writer of English...the head of my profession", for new generations of public figures now regularly mint their own superlatives. Leading the charge, Stephen Fry and Hugh Laurie – to many the definitive small-screen Jeeves and Wooster – have respectively hailed him as "the finest and funniest writer the past century ever knew" and "the funniest writer ever to put words to paper". And there are plenty more testimonials where those came from; in fact, Wodehouse's fan club, past and present, might just be one of the most heterogeneous of any author, numbering public figures as diverse as Queen Elizabeth the Queen Mother, Richard Dawkins, Ken Dodd, Caitlin Moran, A. J. P. Taylor, John Peel, Iris Murdoch, Tim Rice, Billy Connolly and Lemmy out of Motörhead. Countercultural icon Lou Reed once asked for "some Jeeves novels to read on the Eurostar". Two members of the Rolling Stones are reputed to collect Wodehouse first editions. Figures from left and right of the political spectrum have lauded him, from George Orwell and Tony Blair to Bill Clinton and Christopher Hitchens.

Fellow writers J. K. Rowling, Terry Pratchett, Douglas Adams, Kate Mosse, Kazuo Ishiguro, Philip Pullman, Salman Rushdie, J. B. Priestley, V. S. Pritchett, Neil Gaiman, Bill Bryson, and even Bertolt Brecht all swear or have sworn allegiance – and this splendidly diverse gene pool seems to be continually replenishing itself as time marches on.

Quite why Wodehouse has proved such a literary evergreen is not such an easy question to answer as it might first appear. Even Lord David Cecil, who deemed Plum's work "triumphantly good", confessed, "I find it hard to isolate and define the exquisite and elusive qualities which make his art memorable". If one of the most lauded Oxford Professors of English couldn't manage it, the project starts to look like a pretty tall order.

We can, of course, begin by simply pointing to the fact that Plum is funny – often painfully so. And, yes, he can write just about anyone, comic or serious, under the table. But that's far from being the whole story – at least in my own reading experience. This is where things really do start getting exquisite and elusive, for over the years something shadowy and ineffable, yet undeniably real and life-enhancing, has grown in my appreciation of Wodehouse that exists *other than* and *apart from* the whimsy, nostalgia and escape that serve as such excellent introductions to his world. The whole is somehow greater than the sum of the parts. Precisely what that is will, I hope, be more evident – both to you and to me – by the time we part company, having thoroughly inventoried the great man's genius. But it may have to remain, in the poet George Herbert's luminous paradox, "something understood", even though it's the main reason I'm writing this book. Because in order to take Wodehouse at all seriously, we have to somehow peer behind and beneath the laughter without destroying the humour – which, while not impossible, is fraught with problems. As Cecil rightly remarked, "the man who writes seriously of comic things easily appears ridiculous". So in the course of this book, I promise to continually bear in mind that my primary role is to try to enhance the laughter rather than explain it.

I will also be on my guard against the opposite predisposition: the assumption that Wodehouse is so evidently funny, the humour speaks for itself without any need of further explanation. We fans must acknowledge that plenty of people are resistant to Plum's work on the grounds that it is just plain silly or anachronistic or formulaic – and they are, of course, perfectly entitled to their opinion, for it is all these things. Others make the more troubling point that Plum's obliviousness to the real world means that we have to make special allowances for him, to exercise some sort of positive discrimination in order to enjoy his writing. I would counter this with Wodehouse's own observation that "To be a humorist, one must see the world out of focus. You must, in other words, be slightly cockeyed". We as readers are at perfect liberty to buy into this cockeyed vision or not, as indeed we do (or don't) with every other writer who trades in fiction. If we don't and then experience difficulty detaching Plum's world from the one we daily inhabit, we close many doors to fruitful investigation (and of course to pleasure) by worrying whether this askew perspective can be viewed as being in any way relevant or useful. If, on the other hand we do, and demand that Wodehouse's fiction should be examined solely on its own terms, we risk marginalizing his achievement. Either way, we deny ourselves a rounded appreciation of what Wodehouse was up to.

And so it is the ambition of this book to attempt to justify, in as balanced a way as possible, how Wodehouse *earns* the superlatives that are showered on him, and why his work can stand its ground against just about any writer, past or present, and in whatever genre – in short, why the world he created fully deserves to pass into the pantheon of literature that exists beyond fashion and history. Broadly speaking, the first volume, subtitled *This is jolly old Fame*, focuses on the origins and development of his mature writing style in the first quarter-century of his publishing career. The second, *Mid-Season Form*, will examine the worlds he created with it; and Volume 3 (*The Happiness of the World*) will mop up Any Other Business in a series of stand-alone essays.

With a writer as prolific as Plum, any kind of career retrospective can prove daunting. In his novel *Summer Lightning*, we're told: "There is about a place like Blandings Castle something which, if you are not in the habit of visiting country-houses planned on the grand scale, tends to sap the morale"; and in *Heavy Weather*, the distinctly non-U chorus girl Sue Brown remarks that, having arrived there, she feels "like a puppy that's got into a cathedral". In the same way, the grand scale of Wodehouse's complete *oeuvre* can make the reader feel somewhat small and inadequate; there's so much more than Bertie and Blandings, the two series for which he is best remembered but which together account for less than a fifth of his total wordage. Trying to get your head around all – or even a fraction– of the whole shebang, risks cranial meltdown. There are the golf stories, Mr Mulliner's bar-room tales, Ukridge's many misdemeanours, the Drones, the Bodkins, the school stories, the theatre and Hollywood novels, and dozens of one-offs totalling over a hundred separate volumes. On top of that, there are the song lyrics, plays, journalism and letters. Doing full justice to Plum's prodigious output is the most effortless and pleasant form of servitude I know of, yet faced with this mountain of reading, it's all too tempting to draw broad-brush, premature conclusions from a few casual encounters. Yes, Wodehouse did write a lot of silly stories about dotty earls, but there's far, far more to him than that, as I hope this book will either confirm or reveal.

In many ways, there's never been a better time to attempt this kind of evaluation, since only very recently has (almost) the full range of Wodehouse's output become available in stable, readily accessible texts. Until now, trying to survey a career spanning over 70 years has entailed spending sanity-threatening years in libraries and archives far from family, friends and natural light. Fortunately, no more: over 90% of the necessary material is currently piled high on, under and around my desk, or can be accessed with a few clicks.

For this luxury, I owe a considerable debt of thanks to those who diligently completed the preparatory spadework so I didn't have to: Richard Usborne, David Jasen, Benny Green and Frances Donaldson, who were among the first writers to take Wodehouse's comic vision seriously; Wodehouse's most recent biographer, Robert McCrum; Sophie Ratcliffe, the diligent compiler of Plum's correspondence; David Campbell of Everyman, who heroically oversaw the 15-year Uniform Edition project; website impresarios Neil Midkiff and the late Terry Mordue; the good folk over at madameulalie.org for their indispensible bibliographical work; Honoria Plum's invaluable and thoughtful 'Plumtopia' blog; my fellow members of The P.G.Wodehouse Society (U.K.) Tony Ring and the late Norman Murphy, not only for their good fellowship but for their many years of dedication to writing, compiling and publishing fascinating and essential Wodehouseana; and Barry Day, who has collected Wodehouse's theatrical lyrics into a single, handsome volume. Presiding over them all is Sir Edward Cazalet, Wodehouse's step-grandson, who steers the literary estate with skill and charm, and whose constant generosity makes books like this possible. Finally, four special mentions: to Elin Murphy, whose all-seeing eye spotted hundreds of mistakes in the original manuscript, and who is the most through and brilliant editor a writer could wish for (any remaining errors are all my own work); to Amanda Reynolds, who urged me to join The P.G Wodehouse Society in 2008; chairman Hilary Bruce, who charmed me into it; and my schoolfriend Howard Marsden-Hughes, whose loan of *Psmith in the City* when we were 12 was the spark to the flame.

Thanks, everyone.

Paul Kent, London 2019

Introduction
"Getting Back to Comedy"

P.G. Wodehouse…didn't talk about Art, he created it, for comedy is art as well as tragedy and drama.
Look & Learn magazine, issue 692, 19 April 1975

If human culture had to get along without P. G. Wodehouse or Goethe, we would be a lot better off without Goethe.
Alan Coren

One of the most blissful joys of the English language is the fact that one of its greatest practitioners ever, one of the guys on the very top table of all, was a jokesmith. Though maybe it shouldn't be that big a surprise.
Douglas Adams

To write something light, brilliant and frothy is incredibly hard. Anyone can write a serious, miserable book.
Caitlin Moran

The object of all good literature is to purge the soul of its petty troubles.
P. G. Wodehouse, Summer Lightning

In the 1912 short story 'Rallying Round Old George', Reggie Pepper experiences a sudden and unaccustomed attack of philosophy:

> I spent the afternoon musing on Life. If you come to think of it, what a queer thing Life is! So unlike anything else, don't you know, if you see what I mean. At any moment you may be strolling peacefully along, and all the time Life's waiting around the corner to fetch you one. You can't tell when you may be going to get it. It's all dashed puzzling.

Within three years, Reggie would quietly morph into Bertie Wooster, who regularly observes how Life – and its Rich Tapestry – can indeed be annoyingly unpredictable. And for those trying times when the stuffed eel-skin of Fate catches us unawares on the back of the head, or we have "drained the four-ale of life and found a dead mouse at the bottom of the pewter", we can always turn to the works of P. G. Wodehouse. That's what his novels and stories seem to be *for*, to comfort and lift his readers' spirits in times of perplexity. More than any other reason for reading him, that's the one I've heard most frequently down the years, and the one most regularly quoted on his dust jackets to this day: "Reading Wodehouse", states Sebastian Faulks (who rebooted Jeeves and Wooster in his authorized tribute *Jeeves and the Wedding Bells*) "made me look on the bright side" despite being "rather a gloomy kind of chap". "[T]o have one of his books in your hand", echoes author Caitlin Moran, "is to possess a pill that can relieve anxiety, rageiness, or an afternoon-long tendency towards the sour". Journalist Charlotte Runcie writes how, as a student driven to despair by Great Literature, she would turn to Wodehouse, "pick a story, dive in and immediately feel the gloom lift". In 2018, a set of short story anthologies branded "Wodehouse Pick-Me-Ups" hit the bookstands, for "those moments when you're in need of a small dose of joy". And so on.

Cheering people up is no bad thing to be remembered for. As the narrator of *Something Fresh* observes, the gift of humour is twice blessed, both by him that gives and him that receives:

> As we grow older and realize more clearly the limitations of human happiness, we come to see that the only real and abiding pleasure in life is to give pleasure to other people.

And here comes that sentiment again in *Summer Lightning:*

> Happiness, as solid thinkers have often pointed out, comes from giving pleasure to others.

Wodehouse dedicated almost 75 years of his professional life to doing just that, arguably better – and certainly with greater application – than any other writer before or since. For he never deviated from the path of that ambition, no matter what Life threw at him. If, as he once wrote, "the object of all good literature is to purge the soul of its petty troubles", the consistently upbeat tone of his 100 or so books must represent one of the largest-ever bequests to human happiness by one man, at least in literature. This has made Wodehouse one of the few humourists we can rely on to increase the number of sunshine hours in the day, who can help us to joke unhappiness and seriousness back down to their proper size. This being the case, it is tempting to draw comparisons between

"Getting Back to Comedy"

Aline Peters's habitual disposition and that of her creator:

> As a rule something had to go very definitely wrong to make her depressed, for she was not a girl who brooded easily on the vague undercurrent of sadness in Life. As a rule she found nothing tragic in the fact that she was alive. She liked being alive.
>
> *(Something Fresh)*

Most of the characters Plum encourages us to care about have a similarly robust outlook. When we first meet Lord Emsworth in *Something Fresh*, we are told that "Nature had equipped him with a mind so admirably constructed for withstanding the disagreeableness of life that, if an unpleasant thought entered it, it passed out again a moment later". And while not everyone in Wodehouse's world is so admirably hardwired for happiness, the majority are possessed of an enviable lightness in both their outlook on the world and the ways they navigate themselves around it.

This 'lightness' is going to crop up rather a lot in what follows, since it offers a useful entry point to both Wodehouse's comic sensibility and the way his books work their magic. All the reader needs to bring to the party are an ability to suspend his or her disbelief and a developed sense of the ridiculous. That's it. Plum provides the rest, and he works hard, damned hard, to win us over to his perspective. For his lightness does not arrive by chance and is not easily won, but there it is, dependably weaving its way through and around his plots, dispelling any shadows, spreading its disinfecting warmth and throwing wide the gates of his world to everyone. Like Galahad Threepwood, who manages to fish out an unlikely yarn to suit every occasion, "all members of the human race were a potential audience for his stories".

Not every writer's work shares this natural buoyancy, of course. Like Plum's famous comparison between a Scotsman with a grievance and a ray of sunshine, it has never been difficult to differentiate between tragic and comic sensibilities in literature: the former insists that life's default setting is dark and stormy, whereas the latter aspires to Bertie Wooster's chipper morning mood at the opening of *Stiff Upper Lip, Jeeves:*

> I marmaladed a slice of toast with something of a flourish, and I don't suppose I have ever come much closer to saying "Tra-la-la" as I did the lathering, for I was feeling in

mid-season form this morning. God, as I once heard Jeeves put it, was in His Heaven and all was right with the world. (He added, I remember, some guff about larks and snails, but that is a side issue and need not detain us.)

In *Spring Fever*, Wodehouse calls this "the Pippa Passes outlook on life" after the poem by Robert Browning that Bertie mangles in this quote, and on many other occasions. Pippa herself is wont to wander innocently through the streets of her home town, singing as she goes:

> *The year's at the spring,*
> *And day's at the morn;*
> *Morning's at seven;*
> *The hill-side's dew-pearled;*
> *The lark's on the wing;*
> *The snail's on the thorn;*
> *God's in his heaven—*
> *All's right with the world!*

And, in their way, that's exactly what Wodehouse's novels do, spreading sweetness and light (another of his favourite phrases) as *they* go. Some of us actively seek out that breezy style in our choice of reading matter; others, by contrast, prefer to languish in what Plum describes as "grey studies of hopeless misery, where nothing happen[s] till page three hundred and eighty, when the moujik decide[s] to commit suicide" ('The Clicking of Cuthbert'). Whatever our disposition, the choice is ultimately ours, and everyone is happy – each in his or her own way – for literature is a broad church with something in it for everyone.

Despite their difference in mood, neither tragedy nor comedy appears particularly incompatible with the other. As the narrator of *The Adventures of Sally* comments, "There are few situations in life which do not hold equal potentialities for both tragedy and farce". There's a good example in *Pigs Have Wings* as Wodehouse, riffing on Aristotle's well-known definition of tragedy in literature, details "the macedoine of tragic happenings in and around Blandings Castle, designed to purge the souls of a discriminating public with pity and terror". On this occasion, our tragic hero is George Cyril Wellbeloved, Lord Emsworth's former pig man, who may indeed be said to have "plumbed the depths", being barred from drinking beer by his new employer, Sir Gregory Parsloe-Parsloe. "There is no agony", we are told, "like the agony of the man who wants a couple of quick ones and cannot get them". And although George Cyril is not exactly King Lear ("it would...be inaccurate to describe him as running the gamut of emotions, for he had but one emotion"), it was for situations such as these that the genre of tragicomedy was invented. Shakespeare, Wodehouse's all-time literary hero, was forever blurring the distinctions between tears and laughter: death stalks many of his comedies, while comedy routinely invades even his blackest scenes. Consider that ultimate Scotsman with a grievance, Macbeth: right after he's murdered Duncan, Shakespeare inserts the Porter's bawdy comic turn to give us a bit of light and shade before the serious carnage gets going. And makes it fit perfectly.

Wodehouse, as if to mirror the compliment, seamlessly introduces Shakespeare's tragedy into his 1938 comic novel *The Code of the Woosters*:

> Bertie: Jeeves...I can't make up my mind. You remember that fellow you've mentioned to me once or twice, who let something wait upon something? You know who I mean — the cat chap.

> Jeeves: Macbeth, sir, a character in a play of that name by the late William Shakespeare. He was described as letting 'I dare not' wait upon 'I would,' like the poor cat i' th' adage.

> Bertie: Well, that's how it is with me. I wobble, and I vacillate.

Bertie is, of course, no assassin. He simply has been blackmailed into purloining a silver cream jug in the shape of a cow, but can't quite steel himself to commit the crime. Once you've read this exchange, however, I defy you to completely erase the memory of Bertie's forgetfulness when you next see the Scottish Play performed: Macbeth will forever remain "the cat chap" no matter how hard you try to remind yourself he's actually a blood-boltered serial murderer. It's a brilliant example of comedy's power to subvert. And, of course, Bertie is also the unwitting butt of our humour by making the flawed comparison in the first place, as the tragic sublime meets the comic ridiculous.

Guided as much by his temperament as his literary preferences, Plum quickly realized which of the twin masks he was destined to wear, with comedy emerging as the unequivocal winner very early on his career. But this doesn't imply that he was anti-tragedy or couldn't appreciate its power to move. Far from it, judging by the countless times he quotes from Shakespeare's matchless collection: *Hamlet* and *Macbeth* are the clear winners, but *Othello* regularly pops up when jealousy enters his plots; *King Lear* proves useful for bad weather, bad temper and termagant aunts; and even the relatively obscure *Timon of Athens* gets the odd mention. However, in Wodehouse's view, while comedy could quite easily go it alone without tragedy, that equation was not true in reverse: robbed of the leavening and redemptive power of laughter, tragedy was one big downer that nobody in their right mind would want to read or watch. And so he's keen to point out that while Shakespeare may have been the master of misery, The Bard regularly channelled his lighter side.

Plum demonstrates this in an essay from his 1932 collection *Louder & Funnier*. Francis Bacon – the author of the plays regularly attributed to Shakespeare – is dragged into a theatre manager's office for a script conference, where he finds the new "dramatic fixer" (one William Shakespeare) already in residence. The young interloper proposes some drastic changes to Bacon's first draft of *Hamlet* to jolly it up a bit, to which Bacon takes considerable exception:

Bacon: His sufferings drove him mad.

Shakespeare: Not in any play I'm going to have anything to do with his sufferings didn't...I'll do better than that. I'll make him pretend to be crazy. See? Gives a chance for comedy.

Theatre Manager: So it does – I told you this boy was clever. You see, Mr Bacon, we've got to think of the matinée girl. The matinée girl doesn't like loonies. You've got to consider every angle in this game.

Shakespeare: Coming back to this comedy angle, I'll write in a scene where Hamlet kids the two 'Varsity boys.

Theatre Manager: That'll be fine, it'll go down well on Boat Race night.

Summarily dismissing the matinée girl's preferences, Bacon unwisely refuses to put his name to the amended version, allowing Shakespeare to cop all the credit – and thus was *Hamlet* snatched from the jaws of literary oblivion by the insertion of some much-needed comedy. So much so that Bertie Wooster reckons it's "not a bad show" if "a bit highbrow" (*Much Obliged, Jeeves*).

Seriously, though, could you possibly imagine *Hamlet* robbed of what lighter moments it has, with hour upon hour of wall-to-wall gloom? Well, nor could (the real) Shakespeare. And Plum certainly couldn't. Alert to the comic possibilities of just about anything, he too had "improved" Bacon's classic in 1907, recasting the opening scene for the American market by gee-ing it along a bit:

> Hamlet: Say, fellers, about this yer spirut.   [Enter Ghost]
>
> Ghost: Say, Hamlet…I'm your pop. Your step-pop murdered me.
>
> Hamlet: You don't say?
>
> Ghost: Sure. Poured poison in my ear. I was easy fruit. Say, Hamlet, it's up to you.
>
> Hamlet: Sure.

Russian literature was another matter, however, and Plum regularly uses it as shorthand for writing that is wilfully, monotonously, even perversely gloomy. In *Jill the Reckless*, the good-hearted and usually cheerful Freddie Rooke is going through a bad patch:

> Freddie experienced the sort of abysmal soul-sadness which afflicts one of Tolstoy's Russian peasants when, after putting in a heavy day's work strangling his father, beating his wife, and dropping the baby into the city reservoir, he turns to the cupboard, only to find the vodka bottle empty.

Jeeves is apparently a fan of this kind of stuff, but the narrator, clearly himself a humourist, admits the grand gloom of "the great Russians" lies beyond his literary capabilities, making him painfully "conscious of one's limitations":

> Gloom like his calls for the pen of a master. Zola could

have tackled it nicely. Gorky might have made a stab at it. Dostoievsky would have handled it with relish. But for oneself the thing is too vast.

Plum's is not intended as serious literary criticism (he had no fewer than three copies of *War & Peace* in his personal library which appear to have been well-fingered by *someone*). Rather, it's a gentle, deflationary insistence that human life, as detailed in literature, does not routinely have to default to "something that might have occurred to Ibsen in one of his less frivolous moments" (*Summer Lightning* - and yes, Plum was the proud owner of two copies of *The Plays of Ibsen*).

For the most part, however, Wodehouse was seriously predisposed to happiness, and if we take at face value his unequivocal statement to fellow novelist Denis Mackail that "a writer just sits down and writes", it's clear that comedy was what Plum wanted – and perhaps needed – to write. They were, quite simply, a natural fit. At the very start of his career in 1902, he jotted down a telling entry in the first of his commonplace books, as part of an idea for a future short story that never got written:

> The girl and the man had begun to write a novel together. She had wanted to end it unhappily, having ideas about ART; and objections to the conventional (happy?) ending; he had insisted on it ending happily, being a mere mortal in excellent health and spirits.

The 21-year-old Wodehouse ends the synopsis with the girl admitting she was wrong. And if, with his whole writing career before him, he had similarly pondered which direction it should take, he had clearly arrived at the same conclusion, for he *was* that "mere mortal" blessed with "excellent health and spirits" for whom considerations of "ART" [sic] came a distant second to enjoying the few dozen summers we are alive on this planet – and to sharing that enjoyment with his readers.

Now here comes the rub: Wodehouse, in that short paragraph, alludes to the fact that ART – and those who picture it in the upper case – more often than not defaults to unhappiness, misery, bad luck and trouble. Or, at the very least, high seriousness. Those whom he would later to refer to as "the writing people" as distinct from "the general public" often assume comedy to be the cultural lightweight of the literary family, which, were it sufficiently ill-advised to pick a bare-knuckle fight with tragedy, would inevitably be the one to stagger from the contest with two black eyes and a cauliflower ear. And because it's not sufficiently beefy in the gravitas department, it's a regular assumption among such folk that comedy shouldn't – indeed *can't* – be the genre of choice for the writer who wants to create a worthwhile legacy. The novelist, critic and Wodehouse fan Philip Hensher helps flesh out the argument, underscoring three of its main wrinkles as they've developed over time:

> The tenets of criticism generally hold now that a Great Writer deals with solemn subjects; that he writes with difficulty, and exiguously; and that his chosen genre will not be comedy.
>
> ('The Music of the Language', *Spectator* 14 December, 2002)

Wodehouse, of course, doesn't fit any aspect of that critical template *at all*: in *Ice in the Bedroom* he has the writer Leila Yorke remark that all it takes to write "an important novel" is to "cut out the plot...shove in plenty of misery and whine on for at least six hundred pages". It's easy, she says: "I can do it on my head". But does that mean that simply because he chose to accentuate the positive to the virtual exclusion of the negative, Plum is automatically scratched for the Great Artist Handicap? Sir John Mortimer, creator of that sublimely droll barrister Rumpole of the Bailey, also noted the absence of a level playing field among literary genres, and in a 1998 after-dinner speech remarked with reference to Wodehouse, "It is a serious fault in our approach to literature that we do not take comedy seriously", before agreeing that "[a]nyone on a wet Tuesday afternoon can write a tragedy".

Mortimer wasn't encouraging us to get all po-faced and sober about comedy, nor was he suggesting that that a *sunny* Tuesday afternoon is the perfect time to toss off a comic masterpiece. Rather, he wanted to remind us that, just like "serious" writing, comedy can be a massive slog – and take a great deal of Art – to get right. And you don't have to delve far into Wodehouse's letters to discover this. Plum would routinely jettison tens of thousands of words he'd written if he felt his story was "going off the rails"; sometimes, he confessed, the ratio of 'binned' to 'kept' would be as much as 4 to 1. An even more sobering statistic is that on his death, he left a staggering 183 pages of notes plotting the future course of his final unfinished novel at the age of 93. But this meticulousness was a price worth paying because, as Mortimer reminds us, comedy doesn't only give us a laugh, it can open up "an insight into the whole of our culture". After all, laughter is every bit as cathartic as crying, and it's helpful to understand the impulses that drive us – all of us – to both. No one's glass is half empty all the time – or one would hope not – so surely we should allow comic literature to play a full and active role in our search for happiness, rather than patronizing it as mere light relief, a temporary distraction, or the literary equivalent of popping an antidepressant.

Nonetheless, Wodehouse recognized that his chosen genre was the Cinderella of literature, and on one notable occasion his sense of injustice uncharacteristically spilled over into something approaching sourness and even self-pity. In the essay 'Some Thoughts on Humorists', (which you can find in his 'Autobiography with Digressions', *Over Seventy*, published in 1957, or thoroughly revised as 'A Note on Humor' in 1966's *Plum Pie*), Wodehouse's characteristic tone of ironic self-deprecation is, at times, pretty low on the irony, for he really does appear to be genuinely and deeply puzzled about *why* some people are so down on humour. (These benighted souls are known as "agelasts", and Jeeves's favourite philosopher, Baruch Spinoza – who is said only to have laughed when watching spiders fight to the death – was a fully paid-up member of the club.) Even in his final completed novel, 1974's *Aunts Aren't Gentlemen*, Plum has the severe Vanessa Cook admonish Bertie, who is at this point her fiancé:

> [T]hat silly laugh of yours, you must correct that. If you are amused, a quiet smile is ample. Lord Chesterfield said that since he had had the full use of his reason nobody had heard him laugh. I don't suppose you have read Lord Chesterfield's Letters To His Son?

Bertie has to reply with a joke, even though he's blissfully unaware he's doing so ("Well of course I hadn't. Bertram Wooster doesn't read other people's letters").

Here, just a year before his death, Plum is reinforcing the utterly serious point he makes in his essay about the lifelong marginalization of the humourist. It begins at school – public school in his case (a term that in England usually refers to an independently run, single-sex, fee-paying institution). If you tried to be funny in such establishments, you'd quickly be branded a "silly ass"; attempting satire, you'd be referred to as "the funny swine" – and not in a good way, for it was more than probable you'd end up being "scorned and despised and lucky not to get kicked". Fortunately, Wodehouse wasn't bullied, probably because "I weighed twelve stone three and could box", but other nascent entertainers of slighter build weren't so lucky and would most probably switch to writing "thoughtful novels analysing social conditions" or, even worse, as he speculates in *Cocktail Time*, "thoughtful stud[ies] of conditions in the poppet-valve industry", having had their sense of humour bludgeoned out of them. The result? "You are short another humourist" and the world loses another chance to laugh.

In these hostile circumstances, the apprentice humourist did well to keep his mouth shut. As Wodehouse writes in his 1905 school story *The Head of Kay's*, such boys would be forced to censor themselves "for fear of appearing ridiculous": Jimmy Silver, for example, "hid his real feelings as completely as he was able", a survival mechanism necessarily adopted by "most people with a sense of humour". Now and again, he will "express himself in a melodramatic fashion", by which Plum means a sort of jokey, blustering roundaboutness designed to scramble the bully's radar. This kind of stylized delivery often carries over into adult life and is a feature of many of Wodehouse's male leads who are comfortably into their mid-20s. In *Spring Fever*, for example, the "always merry and bright" Mike Cardinal has to explain to his future wife Teresa Cobbold that the mannered way he talks is a form of "protective armour". "You think I'm not sincere because I clown", he complains; but even then, Teresa still has difficulty with the idea that it's possible to have strong and sincere feelings and be less than reverent in expressing them at one and the same time. The trouble is that when Mike needs to "change the record" and come over all serious – he can't. It's a facet of learned behaviour that will never leave him, just as it couldn't leave his creator. Indeed, that melodramatic manner was the *fons et origo* of Bertie's storytelling skills, arguably Plum's single most noteworthy literary achievement.

Having left school, the humourist's next career milestone is to get himself a paying job that involves making people laugh. He then becomes the licensed jester, "a sort of comic dwarf" who capers about the castle of "the king or prince or baron…shaking a stick with a bladder and little bells attached to it". Violence is once again a feature of his profession, for "when he dares to let out a blast" he is often greeted "with a double whammy from a baseball bat" or "a half-brick in the short ribs". Fortunately, on this occasion the blows are metaphorical, a sort of permanent Catch-22 inside which the humourist must ply his trade:

> In order to be a humourist, you must see the world out
> of focus, and today, when the world is really out of focus,
> people insist that you see it straight. Humour implies
> ridicule of established institutions, and they want to keep
> their faith in the established order intact.

In most of its manifestations, comedy is subversive and therefore not
to everyone's taste, especially when it strikes a little too close to home
or challenges long-cherished values. As a Shakespeare devotee, Plum
would have been reminded of King Lear's Fool, a teller of inconvenient
truths who is regularly threatened with a beating: "Truth's a dog that
must to kennel", he informs his wrathful master. "He must be whipped
out, when Lady Brach [false flattery] may stand by th' fire and stink".
Such employers may expect the humourist to make them laugh, but
the world is by its very nature a serious place where laughter is often
inappropriate ("Fiddle while Rome burns, would you?"). So, as a performer who always aims to please, the humourist averts his gaze from
the serious stuff – and is then accused of being trivial. It seems he can't
win, and he ultimately finds himself, through no fault of his own, "apart
from the herd…the eczema on the body politic", the regular Aunt Sally
for people's "touchiness". Poking fun at even the most trivial targets can
set them off: "dogs, diets, ulcers [and] cats" can furnish a convenient
axe to grind for those who wish to scold the humourist for mocking the
things they hold most dear. Even the bane of Wodehouse's life – facial
hair – can be pressed into service for this purpose, despite its tendency
to "destroy one's view of Man as Nature's last word". Watch your step,
he advises, for "[w]herever you look, on every shoulder there is a chip,
in every eye a cold glitter warning you, if you know what is good for you,
not to start anything". Without of course knowing it, Plum was anticipating keyboard warriors of the Twittersphere by over half a century.

The logical conclusion of this less-than-serious set of observations
is that while tragedy has an all-areas backstage pass in Life's Great
Pageant, comedy needs to station itself behind the red velvet rope and
mind its own business. The humourist must be taught to behave himself
in a way that those lucky all-licens'd tragedians do not. Paranoia comes
to stalk his imagination, emboldened by the sort of learned thesis Plum
quotes from in his 1966 rewrite, 'A Note on Humor', which chases the
impulse to laughter deep inside the human brain. According to the

eminent Austrian psychologist Doctor Edmund Bergler, laughter represents a deviation from the human genome itself:

> Laughter is a defence against a defence. Both manoeuvres are instigated by the subconscious ego. The cruelty of the superego is counteracted by changing punishment into inner pleasure. The superego reproaches the ego for the inner pleasure, and the ego then institutes two new defences, the triad of the mechanism of orality and laughter.

"What do you mean, you don't know what he means?" asks Plum. "Clear as crystal" – before proceeding not to analyse what he's quoted. Well, for what it's worth, I think he's saying that the battle for the right to be funny isn't so much fought with fellow schoolboys, regal employers, hostile critics or fans of face fungus, but is actually taking place in our own heads: *a part of our brains – the superego – is actively conspiring to stop us finding life funny*. Which reduces Plum to blank incomprehension: "Attaboy Edmund!" is all he can reply, from some point hovering between his sense of the ridiculous and utter exasperation.

This constant hostility from enemies both within and without, seen and unseen, can take its toll on the humourist:

> He frets. He refuses to eat his cereal. He goes about with his hands in his pockets and his lower lip jutting out, kicking stones and telling himself that the lot of a humourist is something that ought not to happen to a dog.

In the earlier version of the essay, Wodehouse imagines the effect this constant assault on humour would have on Beachcomber of the *Daily Express* (the humourist J. B. Morton), who provided one of the "few scattered chirps" of Plum's kind of comedy in his daily column. But in the 1966 rewrite he makes the more sobering point that continual rejection can push the humourist towards disillusionment and misanthropy, what he calls the "sick humour" practised by '60s bad-boy comedian Lenny Bruce – "and the trouble about being like Lenny Bruce is that the cops are always arresting you, which must cut into your time rather annoyingly".

This sickness was perhaps most keenly reflected in contemporary drama, for which Plum had very little time – "[N]obody", he lamented, "has laughed in a theatre for years" – and theatre was much the poorer for it. At this point in the article, he might well have been reacting to the news that the previous year, at London's Royal Court, Edward Bond's *Saved* had courted notoriety (and got it) by including a scene in which a baby has its face rubbed in its own faeces before being stoned to death in its pram. What, he must have thought, was either joyous or life-enhancing about *that*?

> If only the boys would stop being so frightfully powerful and significant and give us a little comedy occasionally, everything would be much brighter. I am all for incest and tortured souls in moderation, but a good laugh from time to time never hurt anybody.

Wodehouse had first remarked on the drift towards seriousness back in 1949, in a letter to his school chum and lifelong friend Bill Townend: "Two musicals have just opened and both might have been written by Ibsen in one of his gloomier moods". (Frustratingly, he omitted any details as to which they were.) In the mid-1950s came a new wave of plays written by John Osborne and his cohort of Angry Young Men, one of whom pops up in 'Jeeves and the Greasy Bird', in which an uncomprehending Bertie seeks clarification from Jeeves:

> "What's he angry about?"
> "Life, sir."
> "He disapproves of it?"
> "So one would gather from his output, sir."
> "Well, I disapproved of him, which makes us all square."

At around the same time, audiences were treated to the doggedly realistic 'kitchen sink' dramas of Arnold Wesker et al, and from France via Samuel Beckett came the Theatre of the Absurd, neither trend exactly over-cheerful. Plum bracketed them together in 1962's *Service with a Smile*, in which the narrator comments unfavourably on productions by "the Flaming Youth Group Centre" that typically "bring the scent of boiling cabbage across the footlights and in which the little man in the bowler hat turns out to be God".

Wodehouse was more exercised by this topic than this gentle satire might suggest, his dramatic muse being wired rather differently.

Accentuating the negative and eliminating the positive was to tout a wilfully incomplete vision of the world, one for which he was having to over-compensate by pedalling furiously in the opposite direction. Viewed from a historical perspective, this was all a bit tragic, as if these young and thrusting writers had suddenly been robbed of their right to laugh *unconditionally*, or were perhaps scared to, for fear of being thought lightweight. "After all", Plum writes, "people are very serious today, and the writer who does not take them seriously is viewed with concern and suspicion". The other, less generous explanation was that they were seeking to bully their audiences, travelling to the extremes of human behaviour in order to flaunt their rebel credentials and épater le bourgeois. In this context, any humour could only be of the blackest, desperately ironic kind; if and when it came, laughter was nervous or even faintly masochistic, as audiences were goaded into laughing at something they knew they shouldn't find amusing.

Plum would have none of this; why should you need a reason to laugh? To think about *why* you were laughing? Laughter to him was spontaneous, healing, joyous, and definitely *not* intended to make audiences feel awkward, challenged, queasy or – worst of all – guilty. And this wasn't just the embittered bleating of an old dramaturg well past his sell-by date: there was a principle, and an ageless one, at stake here. It was a theme he'd addressed in print almost sixty years previously, when, in 1907, he published a poem satirizing the productions at the very same theatre – then simply known as The Court – that was to stage *Saved* two generations later. In the opening stanza, Plum focuses on the sort of audience the venue habitually attracted:

> They're Pioneers of Progress; they're the Devotees of Art;
> They're the men with bulging foreheads: they're the race
> of souls apart:
> No ordinary drama can rely on their support:
> It is Culture – yes, sir, Culture – that they ask for at the Court.

And what are Culture and Art, those precious pearls adorning humanity's crown, made to deliver? An unalloyed diet of gloom and, in Plum's view, cheap sensation in the form of the odd obscenity. The Court's audiences are in fact so gloomy, "[t]hey enjoy tuberculosis as a humorous relief". Plum, now well into his satirical stride, continues:

> How they love it when a character brings out a gleaming knife,

Or kicks the prostrate body of his unoffending wife!
Such events come all too seldom, and such scenes are all
too short
For the reckless, ruthless audience you meet with at the Court.

This kind of depravity was borderline tolerable if confined to a single auditorium, but in Plum's view the canker had infected the entire West End. In 1905 he had written a poem entitled 'Too Much Hamlet', in which he complains of the ubiquity of tragedy:

A pleasant farce with music would, I thought be to my mind,
But not a single pleasant farce with music could I find.
At every theatre which I sought men answered with a bow,
"We've given up on farces. We are playing Hamlet now".

Though Plum yielded to none in his admiration for Shakespeare (and *Hamlet* in particular), things were getting out of hand. There wasn't enough light and shade in the repertoire for those who simply wanted to be entertained. Culture was doing its damnedest to make sure that nobody could have a good time, and even earlier than this, Plum had poked fun at those who, like George Bernard Shaw, thought that "everyone ought to train for a fortnight before going to see a play" so that they could fully appreciate its worthiness:

Let me plan a little programme
Which is sure to make you fit
To appreciate a drama that is tragic.
Run a dozen miles each morning,
Put the gloves on for a bit,
And you'll find the treatment acts on you like magic.
In a week or so you may
Witness any tragic play.

Unfortunately, this seriousness also could also infect writers of musicals – even the good ones, as Wally Mason admits in 1920's *Jill the Reckless:*

"I've been writing musical comedies for the last few years, and after you've done that for a while your soul rises up within you and says, 'Come, come, my lad! You can do better than this!' That's what mine said, and I believed it.

Subsequent events have proved that Sidney the Soul was pulling my leg."

Once again, artistic ambition – and worth – is equated with a move in the direction of seriousness, as if this is somehow the natural order of things. Even actor-managers aren't immune: in the same novel, Plum describes one such impresario, Sir Chester Portwood, hitherto a purveyor of "light comedy of the tea-cup school":

> His numerous admirers attended a first night at his theatre in a mood of comfortable anticipation, assured of something pleasant and frothy with a good deal of bright dialogue and not too much plot. Tonight he seemed to have fallen victim to that spirit of ambition which intermittently attacks actor-managers, expressing itself in an attempt to prove that, having established themselves as light comedians, they can...turn right around and be serious.

No harm in stretching yourself a bit. But why, Plum seems to be asking, must progress always involve the elimination of laughter? What was so wrong with giving audiences an easy time? It was a theme much on his mind at the turn of the 1920s, and he returned to it in a 1920 article for the US *Vanity Fair* magazine. Ingeniously, he included the same paragraph twice, but with different codas, highlighting the case for plays that entertain and dramas that challenge respectively. Here's the basic premise:

> The public today, let us remember, is composed of people who have just been suffering the strains of a war. They have had to pay out all their savings in income-tax. Living is expensive. There has been an awful lot of snow, and in all probability they have come out without their rubbers [*wellington boots*].

Then comes the first conclusion:

> What do they want? Distraction. Give them light, pleasant, gentle, mild plays and watch them bite.

And the second:

What do they want? Distraction. They want to go to the theatre and see people worse off than themselves. Give them, therefore, strong, tense, gloomy, tragic plays where the fellow goes home with his feet wet after paying his income-tax and finds that his wife loves another, the maid has given notice and the cat has been at the cold chicken.

Both are equally valid, but there can be no doubt which version Plum favours, both artistically and, it appears, financially ("watch them bite"). After all, if you couldn't seek a couple of hours' respite from your troubles in a theatre, where on earth *could* you go? Radio was only just starting up, and TV was still 25 years in the future.

Plum was nothing if not consistent in his viewpoint, and despite the wobbles in those two later articles, he managed to hold on to his remarkable composure and expressed the hope that one day the twin bubbles of Misery and Seriousness would burst, writers would start reintroducing comedy alongside those "solemn subjects", and audiences would once more start "looking and behaving not like bereaved relatives at a funeral but as if they were enjoying themselves". In the meantime, he would persevere in carrying the torch for happiness and entertainment, whether what he was doing was judged to be Art or not.

This brings us to the second item on Philip Hensher's list of what constitutes Great Art: the insistence that all Great Writers were miserable (a) because they were forever writing about those "solemn subjects", and (b) because writing was a form of exquisite torture. The Great Writer is pictured as fighting for every word, wringing his art from the depths of an angst-ridden psyche, so much so that his productivity isn't likely to be great ("exiguous", as Hensher expresses it), only infrequently squeezing out, like Wodehouse's Rodney Spelvin, a "slim volume of verse bound in squashy mauve leather". Once again, Plum found himself outside the tent: because he published so much, he must have either lacked a sense of quality control, or not paid his subs to the gods of literary suffering. Either way, his work had to be second rate.

With Plum's superhuman work ethic, you can see how this particular prejudice might rankle. Although we have considerable evidence of just how hard he *did* have to struggle to perfect his writing (see Chapter 9), he was temperamentally as far from considering himself a butterfly broken on the wheel of his art as it was possible to be. He satirized this incongruity in 'Fore!', a sort of Preface to *The Clicking of Cuthbert*, his first collection of golf stories from 1923:

> This book marks an epoch in my literary career. It is
> written in blood…
>
> As a writer of light fiction, I have always till now been
> handicapped by the fact that my disposition was cheerful,
> my heart intact, and my life unsoured. Handicapped, I
> say, because the public likes to feel that a writer of farcical
> stories is piquantly miserable in his private life, and that, if
> he turns out anything amusing, he does it simply in order
> to obtain relief from the almost insupportable weight of
> an existence which he has long since realized to be a wash-
> out. Well, to-day I am just like that.
>
> Two years ago, I admit, I was a shallow *farceur*. My work
> lacked depth. I wrote flippantly simply because I was
> having a thoroughly good time.

Happiness had made for shallowness in his writing, but then he took up
golf, and thanks to its unlikely ministrations, both Plum and his art were
baptized into a whole new world of pain. Like Figaro, he continues, "I
can smile through the tears and laugh,…that I may not weep…[like]
the clown jesting while his child lay dying at home…Leave me to my
misery", he begs.

Newly armed with this tragic sensibility, Plum was all set to become
a Great Writer. Or he would have been, if the passage wasn't soaked in
bucketfuls of his trademark irony. If anything, his output at this stage
in his career was getting funnier, brighter and more accomplished with
each publication. Trying to beef up comedy's cultural stock by claiming
it offset some sort of secret sorrow just won't work in Plum's case, even
taking into account the setbacks he suffered at Fate's hands throughout
his long life. But this hasn't stopped his most recent biographer, Robert
McCrum, from having a go, despite Plum expressly warning against it.
As broadcaster Danny Baker remarks in his autobiography *Going to Sea
in a Sieve*:

> P. G. Wodehouse noted in his own memoirs that being
> a contented and happy child is not what readers want
> from an autobiography. They look for darkness, regret
> and conflict, a glimpse of the wounded infant propping
> up the vindicated adult survivor.

This is probably the Plum sentence Baker is remembering, from *Over Seventy*:

> The three essentials for an autobiography are that its compiler shall have had an eccentric father, a miserable misunderstood childhood and a hell of a time at his public school, and I enjoyed none of these advantages.

Plum's childhood was, absolutely, characterized by an almost total absence of parental love and, later on, incredible disappointment at not being able to follow his older brother Armine to Oxford University. But did these setbacks impact significantly on his art? Remarkably, no, they didn't – except, perhaps, that they might have contributed to his steely determination to be a success. Charles Dickens may have made great literary capital out of his childhood privations in the blacking factory, but Plum didn't follow suit, and wouldn't for the rest of his life. In a letter to Townend from 1945, written when he still wasn't sure if he'd be prosecuted for treason, and the year after his beloved stepdaughter Leonora had died suddenly, age 39, he demanded: "Do you find that your private life affects your work? I don't". And, quite amazingly, it didn't.

Pick any of the biographies, even McCrum's with its Freudian glosses, and you should come away with a portrait not of a wounded animal but of a man possessed of an almost superhuman psychological robustness which occasionally borders on dullness and even insensitivity. Plum's boss at *Vanity Fair*, Frank Crowninshield, was perhaps surprised that his star drama critic was actually "a stodgy and colourless Englishman…self-effacing, slow-witted and matter of fact" – a rather different proposition from what he might have expected, having read Plum's sparkling prose prior to meeting its author.

Next, try the letters: nothing much to see here, either. Brisk, business-like, capable of deep affection and loyalty, a tad Eeyorish occasionally, the odd flare-up of anger or sentiment – but no self-pity. An impressionistic by-the-by: at least as far as his work is concerned, Plum's attention is most often directed towards what's happening in the present, or with his future plans. The past is most decidedly past: time and again in his letters to Bill Townend or Leonora, he remarks that a particular novel or a story is "the best thing I've ever done" – invariably the one he's just finished. And there's absolutely no reason to believe he didn't genuinely mean it. His own home library contained a far-from-exhaustive collection of his own work, as if what had gone before no longer interested him.

Now read the novels and stories, and if you're looking for the tears of a clown, you'll be sadly disappointed, because there simply aren't any. He would never have dreamed of saying to his audience, "I've suffered for my art – now it's your turn", nor would he have solicited their pity. To do so would be discourteous, betraying his vision of how comedy worked, and even what it was *for*. Comedy could only be about the story, the whole story and nothing but the story – no ifs or buts and *absolutely* no distractions. Serving which end, as he tellingly points out in the 1921 rewrite of *Love Among the Chickens*, "The dark moments of optimistic minds are sacred". And so the front ranks of his characters are stuffed with orphans and aunts rather than children and their parents, not because he's sending out a coded message about his childhood isolation, but because they work better in comic situations. Imagine if Bertie's comments about Aunt Agatha were actually aimed at his mother – not so funny, then.

So, while the act of writing *was* a cathartic and even a therapeutic process for Wodehouse (as it is for absolutely every other writer), it did not represent an unburdening. Rather, it was the working *out* of a creative compulsion, not the working *through* of his personal problems. A writer who writes "by nature", he remarked to Bill Townend, does it for no other reason than:

> ...the pleasure of turning out the stuff. I really don't care if the books are published or not. The great thing is that I've got them down on paper, and can read and re-read them and polish them and change an adjective for a better one and cut out dead lines.

Call me credulous, but I for one believe him – not least because indulging in literary paranoia doesn't make Wodehouse any funnier, and actually *is* the drag on his humour he insisted it was. Thus, my Wodehouse can never be McCrum's "laureate of repression", because with a writer as scrupulous as Plum, if something isn't there, it does nobody any favours to supply it on his behalf. We just have to take his own statement that "I have always accepted everything that happens to me in a philosophical spirit" at face value, and leave it at that.

But it's once the fruits of the humourist's art are published that his problems really begin. In "these grey modern days", Wodehouse writes, humourists must learn to live with the fact that they are "looked down on by the intelligentsia, patronized by the critics and generally regarded as outside the pale of literature". He could console himself that such people, in Bertie's words, "notoriously enjoy the most frightful bilge"; but like his own creation Rosie M. Banks, he had to reconcile himself to the fact that he was one of those popular authors who was "neglected by the reviewers yet widely read" and would therefore never make it onto Literature's top table. "I have always been alive to the fact that I am not one of the really big shots", he wrote. "Like Jeeves, I know my place, and that place is down at the far end among the scurvy knaves and scullions".

That said, he didn't do too badly for favourable notices, certainly until 1939, but it seemed the higher the brow of the reviewer, the deeper the frown. Perhaps the most outspoken anti-Wodehousean was Queenie Leavis, who, in her influential 1932 treatise *Fiction and the Reading Public*, zoned in on Wodehouse as the anti-Christ for hogging all the limelight and keeping worthier writers from being noticed. "For the first time in the history of our literature", she snorted, "the living forms of the novel have been side-tracked in favour of the *faux-bon*" – which is incorrect on several different counts, but anyway… With breathtaking arrogance, she reserved particular scorn for those educated people who had gone on record as enjoying Wodehouse – they should have known better. Their crime? To seek enjoyment rather than enrichment from their reading, because this, she snorted again, was the hallmark of "a second-rate mind".

Next in to bat was the cultural commentator Cyril Connolly, who was determined to bring the upstart Wodehouse down a peg or two for the simple crime of being amusing. And, of course, popular. In his 1938 semi-autobiography *Enemies of Promise*, he lambastes Plum as a mere "humourist" whose fate must be to "either cease to be funny, and so lose his entertainment status, or abandon his integrity and, aesthetically stunted, continue to give his public what it wants". Which means (I think, for Connolly is not the clearest writer, particularly when he's far from gruntled) that Wodehouse's powers will inevitably wane, and/or that he will have to churn out stuff that he no longer finds funny simply to please his audience. He then backs up his argument by quoting (unattributed) a line from John Webster's so-preposterously-miserable-it's-funny 1613 tragedy *The Duchess of Malfi*, "for all our wit / And reading brings us to a truer sense / Of sorrow". This characterizes humour as the stuff of youth, because age, learning and your choice of reading matter will force you to the conclusion that living is no laughing matter. If you then insist on eking out your career as a humourist, you're either delusional, a liar or a hypocrite, so removed from reality that you've no idea how miserable the world actually is, or you know that the world *is* miserable and you're pretending it's not. Wodehouse, Connolly assures us, belongs among the latter, one of those writers who "repeat themselves with profitable resignation". And he meant it to sting.

It's here we arrive at the main thrust of this Introduction: literary criticism – which is a significant branch of the Culture industry – has thus far failed Wodehouse miserably; that is, when it has deigned to notice him. And this has long hindered a true appreciation of his achievements not just as a great comic writer, but as a great writer and Artist, *period*, as the novelist Colin MacInnes presciently claimed in 1960 in an essay for *The Twentieth Century* magazine. Indeed, it is sobering to remark that so far in the 21st century, while it may have been rising elsewhere, Wodehouse's stock seems to have fallen among some of the guardians of our culture.

An example: back in 1941, at the height of Wodehouse's fame and immediately before his fall from grace, the *Concise Cambridge History of English Literature* had lauded him as a writer who had "enriched the national mythology with...universally-known figures", which boded well. But by the 2006 edition, his appearances are limited to just two passing mentions and a footnote that essentially reduces his stature to that of a guilty pleasure. That attitude perhaps explains why over 15,000 books have been written about Franz Kafka's doomy masterpieces, and only about 50 or so on Wodehouse. This denial of his cultural significance is a sad reflection that in his home country, at least, comedy regularly falls victim to that most British of inherited diseases: snobbery. And more particularly, intellectual snobbery.

For this we must thank the critical habits of mind encouraged by the Modernist movement, with which Wodehouse's career travelled in parallel, and which he lost few opportunities to ridicule. Unfortunately, the contempt was mutual: his comic confection never stood a chance against those guys (and gals) who practised literary criticism as if it were deep-level excavation. As the outraged Rodney Spelvin – he of the exiguous muse – complains in 'Rodney Fails to Qualify':

> "Only last week a man, a coarse editor, asked me what my sonnet, 'Wine of Desire', meant." He laughed indulgently. "I gave him answer, 'twas a sonnet, not a mining prospectus."

And he got off lightly. Among Modernist critics, the deeper the seam, the more meaningful the meaning – and the more intrusive the conceptual machinery necessary to dig it out. So now literature had to be both grisly *and* difficult, which made the humourist's job even harder, particularly if, as Bertie remarks in *The Mating Season*, his readers are "up on their hind legs, yelling for footnotes" – which, elsewhere, Plum describes as "obscene little fly-specks scattered about all over the page". He was never going to deliver *that* kind of stuff in a million years.

I could play the outraged Wodehouse fan all day, settling scores with those who have misguidedly ticked him off for not being Marcel Proust – but we'll park things there, since their viewpoints, to which they are of course entitled, are their own punishment. And yet they do matter, being part of a much more prevalent, though utterly different, mindset. Take, for example, the startling neighbourliness of Leavis et al's arguments with that of a present-day out-and-out Wodehouse fan like journalist and publisher Sam Jordison. Writing in *The Guardian* in 2014, and having selected *Leave It to Psmith* as the subject of that paper's monthly online reading group, he felt slightly guilty when the following post arrived in his inbox:

> I have been wondering where you would take this reading group for the book, which although very enjoyable, isn't particularly nuanced or layered. What you read is all you get.

In other words, there's nothing in the book to get your teeth into, and Jordison is forced to agree that "most of the novel's pleasures lie on the surface" before asking himself, "What scope does it leave for literary inquisition?" and starting to actively look for things he might say about, well…what it's about:

> When we first meet Psmith, is it important that we are treated to the sight of "a very tall, very thin, very solemn young man, gleaming in a speckless top hat and a morning coat of irreproachable fit"? If this were Shakespeare I'd be looking for great significance in the similar descriptions that run throughout the book. But in Wodehouse, it just seems too much like over-explaining the joke, like attaching too much weight to an admirably light book. I think it's probably safest to assume that the only thing that really

matters is that these sartorial notes are funny and help conjure up that magical inter-war world. Safe not least because burrowing any deeper would put us firmly into the camp of the poets and poseurs that Lady Constance Keeble has started to inflict on her poor old brother at Blandings Castle.

Aye, there's the rub: writing about Wodehouse, we owe it to our subject to know when it is appropriate to pry and when to leave well alone. Although Sam has a gut feeling that there's "a strong case for reading more into Wodehouse's books", he can't seem to get started, justifying his reticence by using that well-known metaphor coined by an anonymous writer in *Punch*, "to criticise [Wodehouse] is like taking a spade to a soufflé", which signifies that Plum's comic confection is too light, fluffy, and delicate to withstand the ministrations of a garden implement. And he's in good company, for the supine Stephen Fry agrees: "You don't analyse such sunlit perfection, you just bask in its warmth and splendour". QED, Queenie would argue: literature cannot live on soufflés alone, and it requires something more meaty and satisfying in its dinner pail if it wishes to remain healthy. I suspect she wouldn't have approved of people who do too much basking, either. But whichever direction it arrives from – and however well-intentioned its proposers – I have to say I find this argument slightly patronizing and, I'm afraid, a bit complacent.

But then again, we have to guard against the opposite tendency as exhibited by Barry Phelps in his 1992 book *P.G. Wodehouse: Man & Myth*, when he claims that Plum was "a complex, subtle, paradoxical and phenomenally intelligent intellectual" – a generous compliment that would have had its subject running for the hills. Once again, we need to apply the litmus test: Plum *was* pretty damned bright and well-read, but does our knowing that make him any funnier? No, is the short answer. And nor does the knowledge that in a single sentence Plum manages to shoehorn in "a pun, a mangled cliché, a simile, a double irony and two synthesized images". This is simply trying too hard and looks to me like a slightly desperate form of apologism. No, if we want to set the record straight, the first thing we're going to have to do is lock our spades in the shed and find another way of doing this.

Both Jordison and Fry strategically duck the issue of depth by falling back on that good old Wodehouse standby: the sheer brilliance of the writing. Jordison's eminently sensible decision to choose *Leave It to Psmith* for his reading group can therefore be justified on the grounds that it constitutes a masterclass in the use of English. But surely his winning ways with words can't be Wodehouse's *only* Unique Selling Point? For although his facility is utterly inimitable, it's a talent he necessarily shares with every other writer of quality and distinction, or they wouldn't be writers of quality and distinction. Expanding the argument outwards slightly, Philip Hensher very plausibly (and correctly) tries to argue for the "mystery" of Wodehouse, which, of course, cleverly absolves him of the necessity of explaining himself further. But need that mystery ultimately reduce everyone writing about Wodehouse to awed silence, or adopting that perennial fallback of copying and pasting favourite passages into miscellanies?

The answer is, of course, No, or I wouldn't be writing this book – and the solution is actually very simple, although it's unlikely to win any prizes for originality. Really, there's no need to wheel in literary criticism's heavy mob, who will tie Plum's work to a chair and beat it with a rubber hose until it confesses to something it didn't do. Nor will deep-level mining equipment prove necessary, or even a hand trowel. Because, by adopting the simple expedient of reading even a few Wodehouse novels with reasonably careful attention, there appear scores of themes and recurring motifs which, considered together, add up to something that is both significant and, ultimately, revealing – so much so that very soon after I started to reread all Wodehouse's books in the chronological order of their publication, it very quickly became obvious that there was sufficient material for more than one volume.

So it's high time we got started.

Before we take that joyous dive into Wodehouse's work, I'm going to bring this introduction to a close with perhaps the most dotty and eccentric celebration of Plum's writing that has ever taken place: the awarding of his honorary D. Litt on 21 June 1939 at Oxford University – the institution that he was prevented from attending due to his father's lack of the necessary. On this occasion, the recipient, to quote Plum himself, was not one of those "dull, stodgy birds whose names are quite unknown to the public but who seem to get honours showered on them", but a bestselling comic novelist whose work was not remotely intellectual. As such, Plum's elevation beyond the realms of the *faux bon* was to prove a tad controversial: E. C. Bentley, a fairly congenial bloke most of the time, complained that it was a betrayal of literature to confer that D. Litt "upon one who has never written a serious line" and encouraged its removal. Ironic, perhaps, given that Bentley was himself a humourist, popular author and inventor of the clerihew, but the dons held their nerve, and the ceremony went ahead as planned.

At the annual Encaenia (literally "dedication festival"), the university's Public Orator customarily delivered a salute to the honorands – only this time, things were slightly different. The then incumbent, Cyril Bailey, rose to the commemoration of this slightly unorthodox appointment by nominating Bertie Wooster, Jeeves, Mr. Mulliner, Lord Emsworth, Empress of Blandings, Psmith and Gussie Fink-Nottle in a speech that was cheered to the rafters, despite being composed and delivered in Latin hexameters. This was followed by the degree presentation itself, with the Vice Chancellor of the University, George Stuart Gordon, adding these words, also in Latin, about their creator:

> *Vir lepidissime, facetissime, venustissime, iocosissime, ribidundissime te cum turba tua Leporum, Facetinarum, Venustatum, Iocorum, Risuum, ego auctoritate mea et totius Universitatis admitto ad gradum Doctoris in Litteris honoris causa.*

Which means more or less:

> Wittiest of men, most humorous, most charming, most amusing, full of laughter, by the authority vested in me and the entire university, I hereby admit you and your whole crowd of witty, humorous, charming, amusing, uproarious creations to the degree of honorary Doctor of Letters.

On one notable occasion Plum did wonder whether Oxford had dressed him up in borrowed robes, but the mood passed quickly. "I had a great time at Oxford", he wrote, despite only managing a mumbled "Thank you" when a speech was demanded at the celebratory dinner later that day. And, yes, the whole process was rather silly and self-regarding, particularly to modern sensibilities or those who write "thoughtful novels analysing social conditions". But no one can claim it wasn't appropriate; for without that particular brand of English whimsy, Wodehouse could not have written what he did and kept us so royally entertained for the last hundred or so years, somehow surviving all the slings and arrows that should, in all reasonable probability, have silenced our laughter but which – thank goodness – haven't.

Plum ended his 1966 article on humourists with an optimistic pre-diction – one that had a challenge cheekily appended to it. Misery, he implied, is just a phase our civilization is going through, and although "[t]he process of getting back to comedy" might be at first "very grad-ual", the sound of laughter, though "eerie" at first, might quickly rise to a crescendo as people "get into the way of it". Happiness will inevitably win through just as it always has, and to those who insist on raising the question "Why do we laugh?" as if it represented a form of culturally inappropriate or even deviant behaviour, he predicted that "[o]ne of these days", someone is going to square up to them with the simple response, "'Why shouldn't we?'"

Chapter 1
A Brief Circumnavigation of Wodehouse

There is no surer foundation for a beautiful friendship than a mutual taste in literature.
'Strychnine in the Soup'

"I do not approve of these trashy works of fiction. How much more profitably would your time be spent in mastering the contents of [Wodehouse on the Niblick]. This is the real literature."
'Jane Gets Off the Fairway'

"No novelists any good except me. Sovietski – yah! Nastikoff – bah! I spit me of zem all. No novelists anywhere good except me. P. G. Wodehouse and Tolstoi not bad. Not good, but not bad."
'The Clicking of Cuthbert'

Wodehouse was always a man with a mission:

> From my earliest years I had always wanted to be a writer. I started turning out the stuff at the age of five. (What I was doing before that, I don't remember. Just loafing, I suppose.) (*Over Seventy*)

From that tender age, and for the next 88 years, Wodehouse amassed a formidable oeuvre that made the majority of his fellow writers appear like loafers. *Quite* how much he produced is difficult to determine accurately, what with the different English and American versions of his novels and stories; the rewrites, reworkings, self-plagiarism, and collaborations; the bewildering array of publishers, magazines, and periodicals he worked for (sometimes under a pseudonym and sometimes unsigned); and that's before we touch on the song lyrics, plays, poems, and journalism which pose even more formidable problems. Nevertheless, there have been some heroic attempts to give this bibliographer's nightmare some kind of order, not least from Neil Midkiff, whose remarkable compilation of Plum's "short stories, short-short stories, humorous essays in story form, and narrative verse" totals (at the time of writing) "639 magazine/newspaper appearances, 11 first appearances in books, and well over 400 collected appearances in books of 407 basic stories appearing under 499 distinct titles". It's a sobering statistic and, as Neil put it, his "daunting task" isn't over yet. (If you'd like a simplified Plum bibliography, you can do no better than visit The P.G. Wodehouse Society (U.K.)'s website (www.pgwodehousesociety.org.uk) and have a gander at Tony Ring's clear and concise listings.)

That said, it's perhaps disappointing – but entirely understandable – that so much of Plum's literary reputation has been built on such a small corner of his prodigious output. If you set out to read an author's entire corpus, it's possible to get a rounded picture of Virginia Woolf's novels, stories, and journalism in fairly short order; but with Plum, even if you read one volume a week, it'll take two years – and a lot more sleuthing. It therefore comes as no surprise that there are so many of what his grandson Edward Cazalet calls "hidden gems" in the catalogue: books that are every bit as worthy of attention as Jeeves and Wooster and the Blandings saga, but are unjustly neglected even though, at the time of writing, they all happen to be in print. This is, quite simply, because there's more than enough familiar material to sate most appetites. By the end of Plum's innings, he'd amassed a total of 11 Jeeves & Wooster novels and 39 short stories; 11 Blandings novels and nine short stories; one Ukridge novel and 19 short stories; 21 Drones Club short stories; and so on. But what of all the rest? *Ice in the Bedroom* or *Do Butlers Burgle Banks?* tend to get crowded out in this exalted company.

Then there's the erratic trajectory of Plum's early career to navigate. As we'll see, he wrote in so many styles and genres, it proved difficult for his early adopters – not blessed with search engines – to grasp just who Wodehouse was, where they could find his stuff, and what they could expect from him. By 1920, however, when Plum was approaching 40, he reckoned he'd finally become a sort of stand-alone cultural presence, proudly writing to his stepdaughter Leonora:

> I really am becoming rather a blood these days… [In] a review of a book in the *Times*, they say "The author at times reverts to the P.G. Wodehouse manner". This, I need scarcely point out to you, is jolly old Fame. Once they begin to refer to you in that casual way as if everybody must know who you are all is well.

It really had taken that long – the best part of two decades as a published author – to perfect the Wodehousean "manner" to the point where it was efficiently doing what he required of it; for him to use it consistently across most of his output; and, most importantly in sales terms, for the reading public to recognize he was the go-to guy for light comedy. And, just as importantly, he had needed to get this clear in his own mind before his fictional world could truly blossom. Let's not forget that by 1920, Wodehouse only had a single Blandings novel under his belt (*Something Fresh*), and just one Jeeves and Wooster collection (*My Man Jeeves*); the golf stories were only just starting to appear, and he had only recently christened the Drones Club. So what we now understand as "Wodehousean" was very much in a protean state of becoming, even in his own imagination. As he wrote to Bill Townend in 1928:

> The only way to get a book public is to keep plugging away without any long intervals. They don't know you're writing until you've published about half a dozen. I produced five books which fell absolutely flat, and then got going with *Piccadilly Jim*. And when I say five I mean seven...all the time I must have been creating a public bit by bit.

For 'five' or 'seven' read considerably more than that: if Plum's *Piccadilly Jim* argument is correct, and I believe it (roughly) is, he had actually published around *20* volumes when this notional stage was reached. While with the benefit of hindsight, *we* might be able to detect a steady progression in the quality of his writing, or that he'd passed such-and-such a milestone, Plum was too busy writing – and following the money – to notice. There had been no blinding Damascene revelation when everything suddenly and joyously came together: rather, "jolly old Fame" – the public endorsement of his talent – had crept up on him from behind and gently whispered in his ear.

Before we go any further, I'm not in the least suggesting that until he reached this entirely hypothetical, moveable feast of a watershed in or around the early 1920s, everything he had previously written should be dismissed as below par or as some kind of extended apprentice-ship – because it absolutely shouldn't, despite what certain Wodehouse scholars have proposed. I think we can generally agree that something *consolidated* itself in his writing during this period of his life, and we are quite justified in pointing to particular texts as being pivotal in Plum's development. But it doesn't necessarily follow that his creative imagina-tion suddenly upped its game or his approach significantly altered – the evolution of Plum's *voice* is slower, more incremental, and unfortunately far more complicated than that. In any case, his *voice* was only the first of three key elements that needed to come together if Plum was to start building his own trademarked fictional world. He also needed to find suitable *subject matter* and, perhaps most difficult of all, a distinctive writing *style*. We might say that in those early years, he was labouring under the curse of the truly gifted – the ability to turn his hand to anything without any significant failures – that made choosing a particular path so much more difficult.

This makes the early period of his career hard to write about in any kind of sequential fashion. You may have noticed on the contents page that the dates prefacing each chapter don't form an elegant, sequential chronology but stutter backwards and forwards in time like a particularly errant series of *Doctor Who*. That's because there was a lot going on in Wodehouse's aesthetics during this early period in his career as he first dabbled, then mastered, and then grew successful in, a number of different genres *simultaneously*. With this book being necessarily cast in a linear form, I am forced to tease them out one at a time. So if you can picture what follows not as a story but as a survey of individual headwaters and tributaries that gradually flow into one another to form a river, it will give a clearer idea of how Plum's writing began to mature.

The first time Wodehouse ever saw his name in print was probably in the pages of *Chums* magazine, from whose editor the ambitious student writer had sought some career advice. This was the published reply to "Mr Wodehouse, of Dulwich" who had asked, in May 1898, how he might set about becoming a journalist:

> One can become a journalist, Mr Wodehouse, only if Providence has willed it. The first requisite is, not only that a man shall be able to write about the things he sees and hears, but that he shall be able to write about them in such a way that other people will be interested in his work…the kind of work he thinks he can write best.

All of this was sage advice: write about what interests you in the way you're best suited to write it – and don't, whatever you do, ignore your audience. These were three principles the 16-year-old Mr Wodehouse not only heeded but would take with him to the grave. The following year, his formal baptism into the world of letters took place when he succeeded his brother Armine as one of the five editors of the Dulwich College magazine *The Alleynian*, to which he contributed several pieces, some credited, some not. But even before that, according to his study mate Bill Townend, he had written "a series of plays after the pattern of the Greek tragedies, outrageously funny, dealing with boys and masters", which haven't yet come to light, although one lives in hope.

From the very outset, and operating on the principle that "the more mud you sling some is bound to stick", Plum threw himself into composition, becoming something of a writing machine. While still a student in February 1900, he received his first-ever pay cheque for a literary work: a 10/6d (52 pence) prize from *Public School Magazine* for the essay 'Some Aspects of Game Captaincy' (later reprinted in the collection *Tales of St. Austin's*). Baby steps quickly turned to giant, ambitious strides: by the time he resigned from his first (and only) formal job outside writing, at the Hong Kong and Shanghai Bank in September 1902, and turned fully professional, Plum had placed no fewer than 80 items in a variety of publications ranging from *Tit-Bits* to *Sandow's Magazine of Physical Culture*, netting him a total of £65 6s 7d (£65.33). "For a beginner", he commented with characteristic understatement, "I was doing pretty well". And there was never, he tells us, a better time to embark on a literary career, what with the number and variety of publishing outlets available to the "industrious young hack" on the make:

> The dregs, of whom I was one, sat extremely pretty circa 1902. There were so many morning papers and evening papers and weekly papers and monthly magazines that you were practically sure of landing your whimsical article on 'The Language of Flowers', or your parody of Omar Khayyam somewhere or other after say thirty-five shots.

'The Language of Flowers' *was* duly sold – to the *To-Day* magazine, netting him 18/4d (£0.92). It was an article that clearly stuck in his memory, as he references it in *Cocktail Time*, published nearly 60 years later ("Isn't there a language of flowers? I'm sure I've read about it somewhere", says Uncle Fred).

And so from his "horrible lodgings" in Markham Square, Chelsea SW3 (now one of London's most exclusive neighbourhoods), Plum tirelessly fired off manuscripts and received sheaves of rejection notices ("I could have papered the walls of a good-sized banqueting hall") while rejoicing in his increasingly regular successes. He allowed himself very little in the way of leisure and knuckled down to writing in practically every spare moment he had – a compulsion that would not leave him for most of his life: "I wrote everything in those days", he remembered, "verses, short stories, articles for the lowest type of weekly paper". And he wasn't always enamoured with the quality of what he produced: "Worse bilge than mine may have been submitted to the editors of London in 1901 and 1902, but I should think it very unlikely". You can read about this early phase of Plum's career in Chapter 2 of *Over Seventy*, where it is crisply rehearsed.

Anyone writing about aspiring literati during this period is bound to draw on George Gissing's seminal novel *New Grub Street*, published in 1891. A landmark in English realism, it contrasts the fortunes of two literary hopefuls: Edwin Reardon, a novelist who can't lower himself to write commercial trash, and the worldlier Jasper Milvain, a young, hard-working journalist who will knock out just about anything for money. Reardon, Milvain informs his sister, "isn't the kind of man to keep up literary production as a paying business... Those people will come to grief" – a remark which will prove sadly prophetic. "He is absurd enough to be conscientious, likes to be called an 'artist', and so on. He might possibly earn a hundred and fifty a year if his mind were at rest".

There are no prizes for guessing which man the young Plum inclined towards, although he combined aspects of both. From this early stage in his career, he clearly regarded his writing as a commodity to be bought and sold rather than a lofty calling – although he seems to have avoided the less attractive aspects of Milvain's studied cynicism. By coincidence, Gissing and Wodehouse shared an agent for a short while – James Brand Pinker (whose surname Plum borrowed for the curate of Totleigh-in-the-Wold, Harold P. 'Stinker' Pinker) – but there the parallels end. One of Gissing's central themes was the degree to which literature was being harmed by the very world of commercial publishing Wodehouse was to thrive in, whereas for the most part the younger writer seems to have rather enjoyed the ducking and weaving. Oddly, Plum waited nearly 60 years before having it out with Gissing in print: while one of the characters in 1961's *Ice in the Bedroom* judges him "a fine writer", Leila Yorke, herself an author, reckons his "stark...and significant" novels are "as grey as a stevedore's undervest". And this is no stray comment. Rather militantly for him, Plum returns to the theme of arty realism no fewer than four times as the plot progresses. But then again, as he turned 80, his literary arteries had hardened somewhat: in print, at least, he was happy to favour those among his characters who were commercial writers rather than boho-wannabes. Back in the 1900s, however, he was still hedging his bets as to how his own career would turn out.

Plum didn't have to wait long before his hard graft produced the desired results – and rather more than Edwin Reardon's £150 p.a. Less than two years after leaving the bank, having heard his first published song lyric being performed to laughter and applause on the London stage, he was moved to write in his private ledger "This is Fame". It was 1904, and Plum would never look back. He was already a successful writer-about-town, and he liked how it felt.

There is a strong sense that Wodehouse actively willed this success to happen, and never seriously lost faith that it would. Beneath the joshing of a mid-1899 letter to Eric George, he informed his school friend that the magazine of a rival public establishment, Tonbridge, had referred to him as "the school Lorryit [Laureate]. S'blood!", before signing himself "P.G. Wodehouse-Shakespeare". A later missive to the same correspondent boasts, "I have a brain that could fill 3 papers with eloquence wit and satire if needs be", and he later recalled that at least on the page he had "the most complete confidence in myself. I knew I was good". Self-belief didn't appear in short supply when he began to compile his ledger of 'Money Received For Literary Work' in 1902 (but which records income from 1900 onwards), which he prefaced with a song lyric from WS Gilbert:

> *Though never nurtured in the lap*
> *Of luxury yet, I admonish you*
> *I am an intellectual chap,*
> *And think of things that would astonish you.*

That same year, he predicted to school friend Bill Townend, in a bravura, only slightly ironic dedication hand-written in a copy of *The Pothunters*, that the novel represented the "first fruits of a GENIUS at which the WORLD will (shortly) be AMAZED (You see if it won't)". Four years on from this prophecy, he had graduated to being a paid author on two continents, trousering (by his own calculations) £505 1s 7d (£505.08) in 1906 and £527 17s 1d (£527.86) the following year. His income was rising "like a rocketing pheasant", those totals including moolah from seven novels, one novella, and a collection of short stories – and this at a time when the average wage in British manufacturing industries was around £40 *a year*.

I've chosen to emphasize this ambitious, driven *practical* side to Plum's personality in part to re-balance the impression Robert McCrum conveys in his biography that Wodehouse spent his early years chewing his nails over Freudian issues arising from his almost parentless child-hood and his forced exile from Oxford. Of course, Plum may well have nursed private griefs – it would be unnatural if he hadn't, and hard work is often cited as an effective distraction from inner pain. But Plum's was a practical, can-do intelligence that refused to dwell for any length of time on disadvantage, the unfairness of life, or what might have been. Whether he considered himself damaged or not, Wodehouse wasn't going to waste time wallowing in self-pity. The moments when he did, at least in writing, are scarce as hens' teeth, and are confined to several references about the iniquity of working in a bank, which had wasted the daylight hours of two valuable years that could have been better spent laying the foundations of his future career. He also wasn't over-enamoured with some of his editors, probably for much the same reason; but these were to prove minor annoyances in an otherwise positive, cheerful and fulfilled outlook. Thus, if he lacked a close family, he would be happy in his own company; if he didn't have enough money to pursue his ambitions, he would earn it; if he didn't have connections, he would make them. And so he did: in comparatively short order, quietly and determinedly, he cast himself as a forward-thinking doer rather than a backward-looking victim. Even the denial of his university place is purposefully recycled as the central plot device in 1910's *Psmith in the City*, and his brief description of Mike Jackson's disappointment on hearing the bad news must rank as among the most poignant scenes he ever wrote.

For much of this period, he was employed by *The Globe* newspaper as a freelance editor and contributor to its daily column 'By the Way', for which he wrote hundreds of humorous paragraphs and dozens of poems. Crossing to New York for a visit in 1904, he quickly cottoned on to the vast commercial potential of the American literary market, and was among the first writers, British or American, to purposely cultivate a transatlantic perspective and writing style: a series of boxing stories, featuring the recurring character of Wyoming-born Kid Brady, and the novel *A Gentleman of Leisure*, later adapted for the Broadway stage in a production starring Douglas Fairbanks Sr, were the early fruits of this highly successful approach. The year 1904 also witnessed the publication of a children's tale, *William Tell Told Again*. From 1906, Plum spent a period at London's Aldwych and Gaiety theatres as their resident lyricist, briefly collaborating with future songwriting partner Jerome Kern. A semi-autobiographical account of a struggling writer, *Not George*

Washington, was followed in 1909 by *The Swoop*, a topical satire on the Edwardian obsession that Germany was poised to invade the British Isles. An out-and-out romance forcibly conjoined with a sort-of thriller (*The Prince and Betty*) was published in the US in 1912. A Voltairean fable, *A Man of Means*, was serialized in 1914, and in that same year he co-authored a West End stage revue, *Nuts & Wine*, having unleashed Ukridge and Psmith on his readers and prepared the ground for Bertie Wooster's arrival in the character of Reggie Pepper. As we'll see, there's more – much more – but you get the idea for now. Plum was firing off ideas in all directions, pretty much randomly. Or throwing stuff at a notional wall and hoping that at least some of it would stick. Which, fortunately, it did.

To the refined literary sensibility, and probably to himself, Plum was little more than a hack during this period. A 'real' artist would set out his stall, then refuse to deviate from his chosen path until literary taste caught up with him or he died in penury, whichever was sooner. Not so with our hero: Plum wanted success and he wanted it yesterday. Cracking the market – or multiple markets – and parting readers from their cash was his number one priority, and he could hone his skills on the job. Being a true pro, he was clearly visited by every freelancer's hidden fear that every commission might be his last, so he chose to make hay whenever and wherever the sun shone. Even post-fame, his career always seems to have had built-in fallback positions, certainly until the 1960s. If one area of the market went cool, he could focus on one of the others while the public's tastes, the literary fashion, or the entertainment industry's finances sorted themselves out. When the theatres or movie studios were having a quiet time, he would concentrate on his novels and stories; if the magazines weren't paying enough for serializations, there were always the royalties from his book publishers; when Britain was down on him, there was always America; and if Bertie and Jeeves weren't coming up with the goods, there was always Blandings or one of the other regular strands. Not only would this strategy help to smooth out his cash flow, it would minimize the time lost to the inevitable intrusions of writer's block – which, as we'll see, he was afficted with during the period immediately following World War 2.

Moreover, Wodehouse was never precious about his talent; what was important above all else was that his stories 'clicked'. In 1902, he wrote to his publishers:

> I am doing a good deal of work for *Punch* now, and the editor sends back two out of every three of my MSS to be altered, and he always takes them when I return them in their corrected form.

He had always been a dab hand at writing to order, and to just the required length, elongating and telescoping his plots as required – a discipline he honed while satisfying the particular requirements of magazine publication. He could 'write short' or 'write long': he would happily convert a magazine 'novelette' like *Laughing Gas* into a full-length novel, or condense a full-length work such as *Ring For Jeeves* or *Cocktail Time* for pre-publication as a single episode 'one-shotter' for a magazine. As a global success, he would always listen to criticism, even if it meant admitting he had got it wrong and his mistake involved a partial or even complete rewrite of a piece he had already sweated over. When the *Saturday Evening Post* turned down *The Luck of the Bodkins* in early 1935 (the first time anything of Plum's had been rejected in America for 21 years), he didn't throw his toys out of the pram. Rather, he "re-read the book as critically as if it were someone else's", found the problem, and straight away cut 15,000 words. After further reworking, he sold it to *Red Book* magazine in Chicago, and by the following year, the *Post* was back on board, judging the story 'All's Well with Bingo' to be "the best I have ever done" and paying him top whack of $4,000 for it.

And so, unlike the Drones, those lilies of the field who toiled not, Plum committed himself to a life of unremitting toil, but toil that was remarkably congenial. These days, a lazy journalist might claim he was "born to write", only in this case, the statement would be 100% accurate. But *what* to write, when the world's your oyster? As the 20th century dawned, Plum adopted Rule 1 from Writing 101 and started with what, as a 20-year-old, he had already experienced: "I first started writing public school stories because it was the only atmosphere I knew at all", he remembered, elsewhere remarking that "it is far more difficult to write a good school-story than any other story". But Plum managed to – first time out of the traps.

1902–1911

Chapter 2
The School Stories

What hellhounds the young of the English leisured classes are.
Money in the Bank

It is in the dialogue that most school-stories fail.
Even the best of them are behind the times.
Public School Magazine, January 1902

I have made a sort of corner in public school stories.
Letter to J. B. Pinker, January 1906

Wodehouse was quite the controversialist in his early days, particularly on subjects he felt strongly about. One of these was the quality of public school stories, which, in the early years of the 20th century, were proving a guaranteed money-spinner both in book form and as serials in weekly magazines. Writing in 1901, Plum stridently insisted that these stories should be peopled with actual boys and not plaster saints or convenient mouthpieces for adult opinion:

> If...you wish to read a really bad school-story, try and get hold of 'Gerald Eversley's Friendship'. At the risk of courting an action for libel, I really must say a word or two about that book, though I cannot do much more than repeat, with variations, the sound remarks of Mr. E. F. Benson, in 'The Babe B.A.' Gerald is, to quote Mr. Benson, "a little beast aged about thirteen". He spends most of his leisure time forming theories of life and wrestling with spiritual doubts—all this at the age of thirteen.

In Wodehouse's wonderfully dismissive view, the precocious young Gerald was simply too good to be true and, being thus "unfit to live", should have been carried off with "a good, galloping consumption" by way of reparation. If there was one thing Plum consistently hated throughout his life, it was humbug, and the book's author – the Reverend James E. C. Welldon, whose blushes Plum spares by not naming him – was laying it on with a trowel. A school, Plum writes, is not a seminary where boys wander the cloisters lost in contemplation searching their souls; rather, it's a chaotic blacksmith's forge filled with noise and smells in which their *characters* are hammered out. Real schoolboys are too busy getting into scrapes and skinning their knees to have time for a rich, inner life.

So when he came to write his own public school stories, Plum – for the most part – refused to fall into the same trap. He did not major in sanctimony, but rather in describing what it felt like to actually live inside one of these hothouse communities, evoking what he calls their "atmosphere". It's a word that crops up a lot in what follows; as Bertie Wooster tells us in *Jeeves and the Feudal Spirit* from 1954, "if you're a novelist, apparently, you have to get your atmosphere correct". Having left Dulwich only months prior to starting work on his first school novel, *The Pothunters*, in 1902, that atmosphere was still fresh in his memory, those shared cultural references still current with his intended audience. Even in the early 1970s in the halls and studies of my own public school, it was possible to catch the whiff of that ambience he creates so convincingly, with the worthies, bullies, rotters, slackers, and swots all present and correct, as was the chronic over-insistence on competitive sport, lines, random beatings, and Latin prep.

Take this sketch of a deserted, untidy form room very early on a chilly morning in his story 'The Politeness of Princes': "The fire was not lit", we are told, and there "was a vague smell of apples…a tin labelled mixed biscuits…was empty". And that's all it takes. Suddenly, it's 1969, and I'm back at school standing by the lockers in 2A's dayroom. But those highly selective yet utterly telling details don't simply awaken a flash of nostalgic recognition; they also passively anticipate the bustle that will return when the bell rings and the room's usual residents return, with the attendant noise, warmth, animation, and smells of schoolboy occupation. The "very, very grey" atmosphere is soon to be dispelled as the school day gets under way, and "brightness" will quickly be restored by the addition of human life, a lit fire, and a fresh supply of mixed biscuits. It's a synecdoche of what Peter Burns experiences as a teacher in *The Little Nugget*, in a passage that conflates all the images that have impacted on his brain during his tenure into "a confused welter like a Futurist picture":

> [B]oys working, boys eating, boys playing football, boys whispering, shouting, asking questions, banging doors, jumping on beds, and clattering upstairs and along

passages, the whole picture faintly scented with a composite aroma consisting of roast beef, ink, chalk, and that curious classroom smell which is like nothing else on earth.

If you haven't experienced it for yourself, you really haven't missed much; but if you have, you'll recognize, perhaps with a tinge of wistful affection, that Plum's atmosphere is absolutely – brilliantly – spot-on. To his first Edwardian readers, Plum was clearly batting for their team, telling things as they were without trying to smuggle in propagandist agendas from the adult world outside. As a result, he quickly became known as a purveyor of no-nonsense tales that injected this much-needed "note of realism" (as David Jasen refers to it) into the English school story – ironic, given the prevailing assumption about the artificiality of his later created worlds. One contemporary critic noted:

> Mr Wodehouse's school stories are hard to surpass. Both boys and masters in these stories show themselves refreshingly human without affectation or priggishness.

In a series of three articles written for *Public School Magazine* in 1901 ('School Stories', 'The Improbabilities of Fiction', and 'The Tom Brown Question'), Plum dissects his chosen genre in considerable detail, revealing the breadth and depth of his reading – and a very opinionated sensibility. He sets out his stall by sharing his idiosyncratic tastes with Psmith-like brio: "I am not one who can be judged by ordinary standards", he proudly declares, "[w]here I rush in, angels might very well fear to tread". He declares himself particularly partial to the work of Barry Pain, from whom he would purloin the title *Nothing Serious* in 1950, and whom he was still reading in 1955, aged 74. In his private library, there are 20 assorted Pain titles, the 1893 novel *Graeme and Cyril* being a particular favourite: "The atmosphere is just the right atmosphere", he wrote, and "the various characters are life like". The book's "crowning praise", however, is the absence of a bully. In addition to humbug, Plum could not abide cliché both in speech and plot, and for some reason in this and other articles, bullies stuck in his craw. In an unsigned paragraph for *Punch* written in 1913, he parodied one such hackneyed plot trajectory: "'Fetch me my red-hot poker', roared the Bully, with a hideous imprecation, seizing the Little-Delicate-One by the heels and dashing his head with frightful violence against the study wall". Only then does The Hero, "a lithe young form, with blue eyes and curly yellow hair", enter and administer the thrashing the Bully's been asking for. This, Plum claims, is just the sort of "healthy, manly literature" boys can profit from reading – not, of course, meaning a word of it.

Among Plum's other favourite writers were Talbot Baines Reed, of whom it has been written by an anonymous reviewer: "Reed's affinity with boys, his instinctive understanding of their standpoint in life and his gift for creating believable characters, ensured that his popularity survived through several generations"; and Andrew Home, about whom I have discovered very little – but, then, even Plum confesses to forgetting the title of his favourite story by this author. In later articles, he would admit to admiring Max Pemberton's 1893 swashbuckler *Iron Pirate*. But the story that seems to have particularly caught his imagination – and, he claimed, inspired him to write stories of his own – was *Acton's Feud* by Frederick Swainson, published the same year as the article, but which clearly arrived too late for him to include. Supplanting even *Graeme and Cyril* as "the best story of Public School life that has ever appeared", this was "something entirely new in school stories – the real thing". In January 1902, Wodehouse got to review it, once more in the pages of *Public School Magazine*. The book was nothing less than "a classic". Indeed, he writes, "[n]o home will be complete without it. An excellent antidote to the monotony of evening preparation". Always on the side of his readers, he also offers a practical aside: "Its handy size enables it to be hidden with ease and rapidity on the approach of a master".

Of its type, Swainson's is an excellent tale, briskly told, concerning the social rehabilitation of the "beastly cad" of the title, who commits "an abominable foul" during a school soccer match, but who later saves a fellow pupil's life when the pair get lost in a deadly snowstorm. So far, so conventional; but I reckon Plum was attracted more than anything else by the smooth flow and unforced nature of the dialogue, which must have been something of a novelty – boys speaking their own language, and in a timbre Plum recognized. His own schoolboy dialogue is not dissimilar, and in 'School Stories' he expresses this fond hope:

> A time may come when a writer shall arise bold enough
> and independent enough to retail the speech of school as
> it really is, but that time is not yet. The cold grey eye of the
> public-who-holds-the-purse is upon us, and we are dumb.

The issue of authenticity was clearly a problem in schoolboy fiction of the era. Back in 1894, *The Spectator*, reviewing *Graeme and Cyril*, had noted that "[t]he dialogue is spirited and easy, and no one knows till he has tried, how difficult a thing it is to make boys talk on paper as they talk in life". Perhaps as far as Plum was concerned *Acton's Feud* was the very novel that fulfilled those fond hopes and loosened his own tongue in the process; for when reading Swainson, it quickly became apparent that he had found – and would soon start perfectly imitating – what he had been searching for in his reading. Here is a snatch of his model:

> "Gus, my boy, instead of frowsing up here all the afternoon with your books, you should have been on the touch-line watching those Biffenites at their new tricks. Your opinion then would have a little avoirdupois. As it is, you Perry Exhibit, it is worth exactly nothing."

> "You're deucedly classical to-night, Jim."

> "Oh, I'm sick of this forsaken match and all the compliments we've had over it. I'm going now to have a tub, and then we'll get that Latin paper through, and, thirdly, I'll have the chessmen out."

> "Sorry, I can't, Jim," said Todd, discontentedly. "There is that beastly Perry Scholarship – I must really do something for that!"

> "Thomas Rot, Esq.!" said Cotton. "Haven't you been a-cramming and a-guzzling for that all this afternoon? You've a duty towards your chums, Toddy, so I tell you."

And so on. To a modern ear, it's all dreadfully stilted and artificial, but in its time it appears to have been revelatory. More important than authenticity, however, was the feeling that by giving them a voice of their own, Swainson was putting the schoolboys in the driving seat, making them the focus of attention in their own small world. Plum's dialogue of the period clearly owes him a huge debt, although he did prune it of some of its more showy, occasionally cringeworthy features. His sense of rhythm is better, too, but both men are open and alive to the energy, the verbal sparring, and the displays of shared cultural references that make teenage conversations so vital. While they're trying their best to appear nonchalant, breezy, and matter-of-fact, they're at the same time painfully self-conscious, desperately trying to fit in and hold their own. Lobotomize these young blades, and 20 years on you have a working model for the Eggs, Beans, Crumpets, and Pie-Faces of the Drones Club – and *Acton's Feud* does feature characters called Biffen and Worcester…

But this attempt at authenticity was just one piece in a much bigger jigsaw, albeit a hugely significant one. From the very start, Plum sets out his understanding of the genre's rules, which, though limiting, were not, as Swainson had proved, completely inflexible. For a start, Plum continues in 'School Stories', there could be no

> love and adventure…[t]he worst of school life, from the point of view of the writer, is that nothing happens. There is no light and shade. The atmosphere of school is all of one colour.

Note that 'atmosphere' word again. But the rest of the quote requires further explanation. It's true that love would be a problem in a gated community of pubescent boys, although in *A Prefect's Uncle* (1903), Lorimer's 15-year-old sister, Mabel, causes some hearts to flutter, and Plum did write a suite of five stories convincingly told from the perspective of Joan Romney, a school-age heroine on the brink of womanhood. But surely there could be adventure? Getting lost in a snowstorm and saving your delirious chum from certain death – the climax of *Acton's Feud* – was pretty exciting, wasn't it? That's as may be, but there's nothing remotely like it in a Plum school story. And nor would there be, as he explains:

> Of course, if you are brazen enough to make your hero fall in love with the Doctor's daughter or experience adventures like unto those of the mediæval swashbuckler, you may do so, and you may call the result 'A Tale of Public School Life' or words to that effect. But can you look me in the face and tell me that you really think you have portrayed school life as it is? No, you shrink abashed, as I knew you would.

Clearly, he felt, a public school story should mirror life in the school and not transplant the boys into situations that were totally alien to their everyday experience. He could sanction a schoolboy adventure that grew out of school life, but not an adventure that had schoolboys transplanted into it. One might think that Plum was tying one hand behind his back when adopting such a policy, but as things turned out, he was perfectly correct, and for the next ten years, beginning with *The Pothunters*, Plum was to prove one of the best sellers in the genre by keeping things as 'real' as he could. Later that same year, he was still banging on about his rivals' reliance on 'improbabilities' to oil their plots:

> Some time ago I was passing a shop, and my eye was attracted by a halfpenny paper with a school story on the front page. I read it eagerly till a policeman advised me to move on. One of the incidents was a fight with pistols in a form-room. When I got to this I took the constable's advice, thanked him for it, and told him I wished he had spoken sooner. The whole affair filled me with a vague, sad wonder as to what the author's idea of a Public School really was.

There are no guns at St Austin's, Wrykyn, Sedleigh, Eckleton, or any other of Plum's fictional schools, but he did once come unstuck when, in 1908, he was asked by *Chums* magazine to write a schoolboy serial with what he called "a rather lurid plot". The resulting fast-paced adventure, *The Luck Stone*, was turned down by his regular book publisher on the grounds that "the general atmosphere is hardly up to the standard of [Wodehouse's novel] *Mike*", so a magazine serial it stayed until 1997. Atmosphere was what Wodehouse was good at, and was evidently known for, and the experience of how to achieve it in print would stand him in good stead when crafting the lightness that was to prove the keystone of his later, better-known work.

Unfortunately, *The Luck Stone*, although a perfectly serviceable adventure, was to prove an experiment too far. Indeed, it was so untypical of its author, Plum wisely took the precaution of adopting the pseudonym 'Basil Windham' for its serial publication. The inclusion of broad, international vistas, complete with real villains shooting actual guns that draw real blood, would stretch the formula of a Wodehouse-written yarn beyond breaking point, tumbling over into a style of writing he (and clearly his book publisher) didn't favour: melodrama. That said, guns were to be a regular feature of his future plots – most notably in *Psmith, Journalist* – but they would never again be in any real danger of killing anyone. It was a lesson learned, although we're far from done with melodrama, which was to prove a source of continuing fascination for the rest of Plum's life, but one he kept at arm's length in his own writing, more often than not as a target for ridicule.

Back in those 1901 essays, Wodehouse was already having thoughts about how he would achieve the precise tone he needed to achieve the effects he desired, opining that "the excellence of the story lies more in the telling thereof than its plot". This meant atmosphere was in, incident-packed melodrama was out. But it's important to stress that the realism he favoured didn't imply in-the-raw naturalism: a story had to *ring* true, not *be* true. Just as he wasn't going to take his readers on a rollercoaster ride of thrills and suspense, neither was he planning to go in for lurid, warts-and-all reportage as the only way of addressing the less savoury realities of school life. He would be altogether subtler: as the narrator of the 1903 story 'A Shocking Affair' comments, "I dislike sensational writing" – and it appears his creator did, too. Death, for example, was right out: it was "too big a thing to happen in a school-story. The worst thing that ought to happen to your hero is the loss of the form-prize or his being run out against M.C.C". ('School Stories') It's all a question of context: school should be a place brimming with youth, energy, high spirits, and future hopes, however scaly its students may be. Death didn't belong there (with the glorious exception of Gerald Eversley), nor would it occupy a significant place in any of Wodehouse's future work. "If you must kill off one of your characters", the young sage recommended, "do it behind the scenes and let someone else tell a friend all about it". In other words, cushion the blow by having it take place offstage with the narrative delivered in reported speech. A small but telling recommendation from the future master of lightness.

This reticent, self-regulating approach doesn't mean that nothing ever happens in a Wodehouse school story, and that it's one long round of brews, banter, lines, and ragging. While not involving a death, the brutal fight that occurs at the climax of 1904's *The Gold Bat* between O'Hara and the all-round rotten egg Rand-Brown is a good example of Plum following his own advice. He doesn't present it as a live commentary, favouring instead a post factum account delivered in the utterly incongruous accents of Renford – whose voice has not yet broken. "It was just like one of those duels you read about, you know", he pipes – and of course we *are* reading about it, but the fact that it is second-hand news doesn't make it any the less engaging. It's an early example of a 'one step removed' commentary Wodehouse would frequently introduce into the sporting passages in his school stories, and later put to good use in his mature novels when characters have to bring others up to speed on the plot. Renford's narrative is breathless, and he's clearly still living off the adrenalin generated by the event, but instead of simply describing what he's seen, he's telling it in the form of a narrative. So not only are the sensitive spared an up-close-and-personal (and frankly rather ugly) description of two teenage boys beating seven bells out of each other *au naturel,* the event is filtered through Renford's excitable but still-refined sensibility as he tries to convince his one listener that the fight really was as "frightfully exciting" and "ripping" as he claims. This not only allows more "light and shade" into the narrative, it avoids the blood and bruises of what was clearly a bitter encounter between two grudge-laden combatants. And "you can't help smiling" when, in your mind's ear, you hear the grisly events improbably delivered in Renford's "melodious treble" voice. Sometimes telling and not showing pays dividends.

The discipline inherent in writing school stories was already teaching Plum how to assemble a convincing world without many of the building blocks available to other writers, and painting with a restricted palette was a skill at which, of course, he would continue to excel. But even though he was writing within an acknowledged genre, he quickly grew impatient with its conventions and sought to bend and discredit the ones he didn't like – an impatience reflected in his headmaster's comment on Plum's 1899 Dulwich report that he had "the most distorted ideas about wit and humour".

Sometimes these idiosyncratic ideas – scurrilous to a moralistic Victorian patriarch but sound literary lore to us now – crept into his fictions. Plot clichés were a particular bugbear, and Wodehouse's irritation briefly surfaces in *Mike* when Psmith demands of his new friend at their first meeting: "Are you the Bully, the Pride of the School, or the Boy who is Led Astray and takes to Drink in Chapter Sixteen?" Plum often wriggles around inside the genre, sometimes in scarcely perceptible asides, at others in great bludgeoning uppercuts, as we'll see in a moment. First, though, a word about Wodehouse's choice of narrative voice and its early development, through which we can trace the roots of this dissatisfaction.

In that first encounter between Mike and Psmith, the monocled one immediately casts himself as the amused outsider, through whose eyes the reader is provided with fresh, often sideways commentary and perspectives on the plot. On his presence at Sedleigh, the ex-Etonian asks, "Do I look as if I belonged here?" – a question, as they used to say in

Latin classes, "expecting the answer 'no'". But in the years before *Mike*, which first appeared in novel form in 1909, Wodehouse had created other outsider figures who stand apart, though seldom alone, thanks to their facility with words. Psmith is undoubtedly the king of them all, but what of the less-celebrated Charteris in *The Pothunters*, Jimmy Silver of *The Head of Kay's*, Wyatt in *Mike*, Marriott and even Farnie in *A Prefect's Uncle*, who each represent stepping stones to Wodehouse's mature narrative style, which would ultimately attain perfection in the language of Bertie Wooster? All of them are, perhaps inevitably, variations of Wodehouse's own schoolboy voice that he employed in correspondence with his friends, being a mix of accents, idiolect, banter, and slang that can best be summed up in the single word "persiflage". Early in *The Head of Kay's*, the narrator comments of Silver: "It was one of his amusements to express himself from time to time in melodramatic fashion, sometimes accompanying his words with suitable gestures". In each of these characters there is undoubtedly an air of theatricality, of self-dramatization, that seeks to elevate the more mundane aspects of reality into something more entertaining for both the performer and his audience.

It was a style of writing that found its apogee, at least in England, in the writings of Alexander Pope (1688–1744), with whose work Wodehouse was familiar at a young age, particularly his translations of Homer, which the infant student had precociously devoured by the age of six. In fact, Wodehouse's schoolboy persiflage is closely related to the linguistic inflations of epic, and mock epic in particular: Pope's most celebrated poem, 'The Rape of the Lock', when all's said and done, concerns itself with a tiny, split-second haircut grandiloquently expanded to 794 lines of verse. Closer to home, and with a dollop of Wildean insouciance thrown in, you have the persiflage of Barry Pain's "clever but whimsical" schoolboy character "The Celestial" (real name Cyprian Langsdyke) – another of Plum's firm favourites in his schoolboy pantheon, who memorably comments: "All Livy is divided into two parts. One you can translate whether you prepare it or not, the other you can't translate whatever you do". "That", Plum comments, "is only one example of the way in which Mr. Pain holds the mirror up to nature". Here's another less aphoristic example Pain wrote in 1894:

> "Cocoanuts are cheap to-day," observed The Celestial. "Liggers can't eat them; they're too rich for his poor stomach. So he bade me bestow them on the bilious Banks

and the debilitated Douglas. Give me to drink of the gravy of the cocoanut." He seemed to be in particularly high and whimsical spirits, and drained the tooth-mug proffered to him with a fine melodramatic air. "Now, then," he said, "I've got three blessed shillings. Let us go to Hunley's and drink and eat cranberry tarts, for the day after to-morrow we die—at least I do."

Once again, we find ourselves in the company of a born performer with the gift of the gab, and somewhat over-prone to verbal diablerie: The Celestial actually does come close to dying from a serious dose of scarlet fever – but he lives to jabber another day.

I imagine most of us have imitated our heroes when young, and Plum was no exception, as we can see in this extract from a letter he wrote to his friend Eric George in September 1899:

Jeames, friend of me boyhood, and companion of me youthful years, list, I prithee. Your letter was very welcome and prompt. I have not answered it before because I have been <u>wurking</u>! [*sic*] That scholarship at Horiul [Oriel College, Oxford], Jeames me lad, is a certainty. I am a genius. I always knew it.

I haven't read Faust but I have read Palamon and Arcite right through, 3000 lines if it's an inch! It is a rather good poem full of blood and luv! [*sic*]

And so on. It quickly grows wearing in this undiluted form, but by the time it has been alchemized into published fiction three years later, it comes over as fresh and lively, tinged with an (as yet unearned) worldly irony and self-conscious affectation. The literary allusions that were to pepper Bertie's narratives are already present and correct – *Palamon and Arcite* by the 17th-century poet John Dryden is a sort of epic fable that re-told Chaucer's *The Knight's Tale* and was pretty niche reading for an 18-year-old – although, as we'll see, Plum adored tales of chivalry, so it would have been no great hardship to wade through. The nickname he gave his friend ("Jeames") originated with the mighty William Makepeace Thackeray, founding editor of the humorous magazine *Punch*, novelist, satirist, and another of Plum's abiding favourites.

Clearly, much of his youth had been taken up with reading, and a faulty memory for quotations, that mighty cornerstone of Bertie's writing style, makes an early appearance in Plum's debut novel a mere 13 pages in, with reference to having one's legs massaged in between the rounds of a boxing match: "Like somebody's something it is both 'grateful and comforting'". On this occasion, Plum's victim wasn't a lofty literary allusion but an advertising slogan for Epps's Powdered Cocoa first coined in 1855. And 28 pages later comes the first of many subsequent recapitulations of the phrase "patience on a monument", an image that clearly – and perennially – struck Wodehouse as amusing, taken from Shakespeare's *Twelfth Night*. He was already casting his literary net far and wide, on the lookout for quotes his characters could misremember and mangle, perhaps because the self-conscious Wodehouse didn't want to risk accusations of being too clever by half.

The slightly-to-one-side creature of words in Plum's debut novel is "Alderman" Charteris (so nicknamed because, like the stereotypical English official, he "inclined to stoutness"). Having "the journalistic taint very badly", he had made himself quite the literary entrepreneur, writing, editing and publishing the school's "strictly unofficial" monthly paper, *The Glow Worm*. Although it operates under the school radar, Charteris makes sure the editorial line doesn't pursue any overtly subversive agendas or spook those in authority; rather, he gets his thrill from the act of illicit publication, offering a quality alternative to the authorized school magazine, and showing the Establishment how things should be done. The paper is also something of a money-spinner: after expenses (which he tellingly details), Charteris trousers the not-inconsiderable profit of about ten shillings per issue. And why is it so popular?

> ...principally because of the personal nature of its contents.
> If the average mortal is told there is something about him
> in a paper, he will buy that paper at your own price.

For Plum, this commercial principle held good on either side of the school gate, and he offers us the benefit of his short experience free of charge, while letting us know that *he* knows the secret of pulling the paying punters in.

Plum further bolsters his insider credentials while describing one of Charteris's monthly teas, held "in honour of the new number". It is, the narrator tells us, "like a *Punch* dinner, only more so", by which he means the sort of editorial brainstorming sessions the staff and contributors of magazines were periodically wont to arrange, to the accompaniment of much intemperate browsing and sluicing. Plum would have more than 200 articles published in *Punch* over the course of his career, the first coinciding with the appearance of *The Pothunters* in September 1902, and it's tempting to think that his debut (and continual re-hiring) by that publication might even have been the result of attending one such junket around this time. The whole of Chapter 6 is devoted to an account of the tea, and what was discussed. It's a masterly vignette which begins with Charteris extending a bustling, mock-heroic welcome to his fellow journalists:

> Now we're complete…Gentlemen, your seats. There are only four chairs, and we, as Wordsworth might have said, but didn't, are five. All right, I'll sit on the table. Welch, you worm, away with melancholy. Take away his book, somebody. That's right. Who says what? Tea already made. Coffee published shortly. If anybody wants cocoa, I've got some, only you'll have to boil more water. I regret the absence of menu-cards, but as the entire feast is visible to the naked eye, our loss is immaterial. The offertory will be for the Church expenses fund. Biscuits, please.

Once again, quotes and allusions abound: Wordsworth is the most obvious big hitter mentioned by name, but Mozart is also referenced ("away with melancholy"), and some official accountancy-ese Plum might have picked up at the bank is also included ("immaterial loss"). Later, Barry Pain puts in an appearance, as does Psalm 49, *The Tempest*, and the lyrics to a music hall song, 'Private Tommy Atkins'. It's quite a brew, but what we should really take away from this scene after we've completed our cultural trophy-hunting is, once again, the atmosphere of a small overcrowded study, filled with activity, banter, and the smell of boiling coffee – that and, most important of all, Wodehouse's brilliance at describing small, intimate communities of his characters that we, as readers, can imaginatively join in with. When we are allowed privileged access to Beach's pantry in the Blandings books, or Bertie describes us as "my public", he's doing exactly the same thing: making us trusted participants in his worlds, flattering us the while that we have earned our place there – that we *belong*. More of which later, but this scene is pretty much where Wodehouse's clubability started, with a merry schoolboy cabal brought together, significantly, by the power of words.

A second pointer to the future lies in the deft delineation of

Charteris's edgy but mercurial personality, which places him simultaneously in with, yet somehow apart from, the rest of the student body. As elsewhere in Wodehouse, writing can simply be a public expression of the outsider's need for attention, and here *The Glow Worm*'s editor demands an audience not just for his journalism but for himself, being "seldom silent". The role of awed (or numbed) listener is usually fulfilled by J. George Welch, a worthy sportsman who is normally taciturn, and occasionally tells his friend "Do shut up" once he has reached "section five, sub-section three, of his discourse". As such, the pair are direct ancestors of Psmith and Mike, respectively the jabberer and the stone, the literatus and the sportsman. Somewhat inevitably, it's the talkers who hog the spotlight; indeed, by the close of 1915's *Psmith, Journalist*, Mike's contributions to the conversation are so minimal that his friend might just as well be talking to himself. Throwing even further forward, we are perhaps reminded of Bertie's first-person narrations with the occasional Jeevesian punctuation, or even Plum the tireless writer and Plum the reluctant social small talker. We are also told that Charteris "might have been brilliant if he had chosen", but his energies were mainly taken up with his writing. Sound familiar?

Plum clearly had plans for Charteris, perhaps hoping that he would become a significant narrative presence who could be revisited in future material; he later re-appears in the short stories 'The Odd Trick', 'The Babe and the Dragon', 'The Manoeuvres of Charteris', and 'Playing the Game', and much later in *A Gentleman of Leisure*, having gone to Cambridge and joined the Footlights Club, where, like his creator, he reveals his taste for stage musicals. Throughout his run, he continues to delight in rule breaking: his most frequent misdemeanour is to violate school bounds in order to visit the nearby town of Stapleton, which gives him "an awfully jolly feeling. Like warm treacle running down your back", while romantically picturing himself as "a cross between Dick Turpin and Machiavelli". In 'The Manoeuvres of Charteris', which was published in *The Captain* in 1903, the trigger for this habitual disobedience is revealed: the Headmaster's use of the word 'buffoon' to describe Charteris's character and behaviour. Significantly, it is a word that "rankled in Charteris's mind, and which had continued to rankle ever since":

> Everybody who has the gift of humour and (very naturally) enjoys exercising it, hates to be called a buffoon. It was Charteris's one weak spot. Every other abusive epithet in

language slid off him without penetrating or causing him the least discomfort. The word 'buffoon' went home, right up to the hilt... He had, in fact, started a perfect bout of breaking rules, simply because they were rules.

Never underestimate the slighted humourist: it's as if to Charteris, humour is too serious a business to be relegated to mere buffoonery. I remember at my own school, the very worst crime you could commit in my Headmaster's catalogue of venality was that of being what he called "flippant" – usually directed at those in the more academic stream who refused to take anything seriously but should, it was felt, set an example. Wodehouse uses the word with reference to Charteris, who, beneath that surface flippancy, "thought the more". We must remember that Charteris considers himself not just Dick Turpin, the dashing perpetrator of crimes, but Machiavelli, history's ultimate backroom planner and plotter, bad behaviour's ultimate intellectual. Not so much the buffoon, then – at least in his own estimation. But Charteris's anger doesn't necessarily wish harm on the school or its Headmaster. Rather, its aim is to carve a niche *within* the rules where he can be himself and do what he wants. Not everyone sees that, however:

> "You know," said Welch seriously, stooping to unlace his boots, "rotting apart, you really are a most awful ass. I wish I could get you to see it."

> "Never you mind, ducky," said Charteris, "I'm all right. I'll look after myself."

And so he does. Yet his self-containedness doesn't make Charteris a loner. He's saved by his journalism, which represents a way out of himself, being a social vehicle that brings boys together in its production, dissemination, and clandestine readership. At the close of *The Pothunters*, Charteris even organizes a special fundraising edition of *The Glow Worm* to help fellow pupil Jim Thomson pay an urgent debt, and Wodehouse treats us to a schoolboy version of the newsroom scene in the Jack Lemmon/Walter Matthau movie *The Front Page*, lacking only the green eyeshades and serial cigarette smoking. The team of intrepid journos, with Charteris at the helm, sits up until 2.15 a.m. putting the paper to bed, writing and duplicating it on their primitive 'jellygraph', working right up to their self-imposed deadline. Once again,

PELHAM GRENVILLE WODEHOUSE

Wodehouse distils an atmosphere – that of purposeful, illicit toil – beautifully. Working on *The Alleynian* would, of course, have helped, as would his visits to the offices of *The Globe* newspaper, to which he was to contribute over 1,300 humorous paragraphs and poems, jokes, puns, and retellings of the days' news events, starting at exactly this time.

There seems to be a lot of the young Wodehouse lurking within Charteris, but all I'm going to commit to – in keeping with my earlier caveat against identifying the writer too closely with his work – is to state that the character embodies several of his preoccupations, some of which we'll be returning to as this book progresses. Perhaps the one I'd like to take with us from this encounter is that of single-mindedness: Charteris is going to do what *he* wants to do, taking only the most calculated of risks along the way, ducking and weaving his way through the rules and regulations of the society he exists inside. Literary rebellions can be very discreet, and Charteris realizes that his can only continue as long as he draws the minimum attention to himself.

Nine years on from *The Pothunters* in 1911, Plum was still writing about this sort of amateur journalism: in 'Pillingshot's Paper', one of the last school stories he published, *The Glow Worm* continues to be "snappy", "bright, not militant", and "a readable version of the dull *Austinian*" circulated among the school's cognoscenti. But the journalistic landscape at the school seismically changes with the launch of *The Rapier*, a scandal sheet backed by the supercilious and overbearing J. G. Scott, which specializes in the character assassination of fellow pupils in a rival house its editor doesn't care for. The young, gifted, and impressionable Pillingshot is somehow persuaded to do all the donkey work, and what follows is an object lesson in what can happen when a writer betrays his calling. When the first edition is published, it not only causes a sensation: it leads to fights between members of the rival houses, persuading Pillingshot that "it was no small thing to be associated with such an epoch-making event, whatever the risks" – or whatever the consequences.

Tellingly, the venture proves short-lived, folding as its third edition goes to press. Although *The Rapier* is perceived to have filled a gap in the market, and is even accounted quite amusing, Plum lets us know that this sort of thing is not the *done* thing, and that Scott is something of a cad who "seemed to look on the rest of the community more as a collection of entertainers than anything else" – as indeed Psmith was to do, but with an altogether more benign attitude. The venture was conceived in a mean spirit, dividing the schoolboy corpus rather than bringing it together, and although this message is addressed with the lightest of touches, there can be little doubt that a point is being made. The middle ground, to be found somewhere between the orthodox and the outrageous, is where Plum's fictionalized brand of literary rebellion is situated, and would be for the rest of his life.

But on one intriguing occasion, Wodehouse – like the misguided Pillingshot – *did* toy with the dark side of journalism. While he was working on *The Pothunters*, he was also, as we've seen, publishing a variety of nonfiction articles under his own name. One of these, innocently titled 'Notes' – from February 1901's *Public School Magazine* – contains a number of parallels with his debut novel's themes. Writing in the voice of a Dutch uncle (though he was barely out of school uniform), Plum suggests a worthwhile pastime that could be enjoyed during those tedious periods given over to the dreaded 'dictation', when the teacher reads a passage out loud to his pupils who must transcribe it accurately complete with the correct spelling and punctuation. Boring? Absolutely! But here's how to make those lessons just that little bit more interesting:

> A good plan is to occupy yourself with the composition of a journal, an unofficial magazine not intended for the eyes of the profane, but confined rigidly to your own circle of acquaintances. The chief advantage of such a work is that you will continue to write while the notes are being dictated. To throw your pen down with an air of finality and begin reading some congenial work of fiction would be a gallant action, but impolitic. No, writing of some sort is essential, and as it is out of the question to take down the notes, what better substitute than an unofficial journal could be found? To one whose contributions to the School magazine are constantly being cut down to mere skeletons of their former brilliant selves by the hands of censors, there is a rapture otherwise unattainable in a page of really scurrilous items about those in authority. Try it yourselves, my lads. Think of something really bad about somebody. Write it down and gloat over it. Sometimes, indeed, it is of the utmost use in determining your future career.

It's an intriguing prospect to think of Plum the young scholar, bored and seething with self-righteous resentment, straying into the territory of "really scurrilous" writing. Perhaps some of his "contributions" to the *Alleynian* had been spiked or injudiciously filleted "by the hands of censors", and he felt it appropriate to sublimate his revenge into the written word – not, of course, for general consumption but for the amusement of a few close friends. Not only does writing prove a useful pressure valve ("a rapture") for the angry student with a grouch against the powers that be, it may also help him "in determining his future career". Quite how is not made clear: perhaps by sharpening the would-be writer's awareness of what he can and can't get away with, since the censorious teachers of the present would inevitably morph into the copy editors and literary agents of tomorrow. An interesting example comes in 'A Tithe for Charity': Plum was no great respecter of his fellow novelists, but it took him until 1955 to invent one with the single-entendre name of Horace Wanklyn – although the story did mark his debut in the recently founded *Playboy* magazine. Back in 1901, however, he could never have dreamed of such licence: "We can never be like him". Plum says of his imaginary miscreant, "but let, oh! let us be as like him as we're able to be". Note to self, perhaps? Well, yes, up to a point. There will be a whole chapter devoted to Plum the armchair rebel and lifelong satirist in the third volume of these musings – and it will be a longer chapter than you might perhaps expect.

In its directness, the 'Notes' article was to prove untypical of Plum's subsequent output – even though he considered it worthy of reprinting in the collection *Tales of St Austin's* two years later with only minor alterations. Even at this protozoan stage in his career, Plum appears to have decided that only in the most general sense would he use his writing as a form of therapy, for, unlike many of his peers in the writing field, he had no particular axe to grind on the world – or even on editors who were, after all, sometimes in the right. Rather, it was the *craft* of writing that fascinated and energized him: the words on the page, and not the psychology that lay behind them. As that otherwise damning 1899 report has it: "He has a genuine interest in literature and can often talk with enthusiasm and good sense about it".

Getting back to 'Notes', the article homes in on two further targets as it proceeds, this time with somewhat broader issues linked to the craft of writing that would exercise Plum long into his career: fancy literature that doesn't directly say what it means and those who set themselves up as its interpreters – the literary critics. Work by this latter group of miscreants seems to have been the texts chosen by the masters for those dreaded Dulwich dictations: "Why", Plum demands, still mounted on his high horse, "are our ears so constantly assailed with unnecessary explanations of and opinions on, English literature?... How often have we been forced to take down the miserable maunderings of some commentator on the subject of 'Maud'?" Reading, he opines, should be a simple matter: after all, a "person reads 'Maud' and either likes it or dislikes it". End of. And moreover:

> [H]is opinion is not likely to be influenced by...the opinions
> of somebody else concerning the methods or objectivity
> and subjectivity of the author when he produced the work.

Plum was a lifelong fan of Alfred, Lord Tennyson, and he was destined to work in a quote or several from that hugely popular Victorian poet "from his second book to his last", according to Norman Murphy. So we can perhaps understand why he gets a tad peeved when someone tries to tell him what to think about it. The relationship between writer and reader, he felt, should be direct, one-to-one, and transparent. If a text *needed* interpreting by a third party in order to be understood, the writer wasn't doing his job properly and his work probably wasn't worth the bother. This is the problem with some of the obscurer passages from Shakespeare, as Plum later jokes in *Joy in the Morning*: occasionally the mighty Bard "sounds well, but doesn't mean anything", offering an open invitation to the critic to muscle in on the scene with *his* thoughts, interposing himself between writer and reader and generally getting in the way.

In the broader context, Plum viewed literature as a living thing which existed for the purposes of entertainment and possibly even edification, not a dead artefact mounted in a display case to be poked, prodded and analysed. It faced outward, towards its audience; it didn't look down towards its navel or in towards the writer's or reader's psyche. And in selecting Tennyson's best-known poem for his theme, he was holding it up as a model of how words should clarify and communicate the writer's thoughts, not complicate and obfuscate them. Although he was never averse to reading complete rubbish, Plum's gold standard appears to have been popular literature that was also good – like Tennyson's, written not just with skill but with integrity. One of the cardinal sins for authors of any stripe was to write down to their audience, beneath their capabilities, or in a genre with which they were not sympathetic. Not only was it patronizing, it represented a betrayal of the individual writer's own talent, since he knew he wasn't producing the best stuff he was capable of. Once again, the middle ground appears to be the place to be: clever but not too intellectual; populist but not overly demotic.

Moreover, Plum especially hated stories that tried to tell its readers what to do or how to behave – or even who to be. In the genre of school fiction, there was no better example of the latter tendency than that copper-bottomed Victorian classic *Tom Brown's Schooldays*, written by Thomas Hughes and published in 1857, which Wodehouse ably and amusingly took down in an article published in *Public School Magazine* in December 1901 entitled 'The Tom Brown Question'. Clearly, he was no great believer in the rights and privileges accorded to sacred cows, and in going up against this particular title, he was taking on the biggest beast in his own small field. Some commentators have argued that school stories would have died out long before Plum arrived on the scene had it not been for this seminal work, citing its influence on everything from Billy Bunter to Harry Potter. But that wouldn't have stopped Plum accusing its author of indulging in the most monstrous humbug.

In the article, Wodehouse imagines he's on a train journey, sharing a compartment with an unnamed, shadowy figure who insists on discussing his choice of reading matter – *TB's S* – and the theory that it is the work of not one, but two authors. Wodehouse, who has read the book three times already, admits he had not noticed but is quickly brought round to his fellow traveller's opinion. It turns out Hughes has been nobbled, while on holiday in Wales, by the S.S.F.P.W.L.W.T.R.O.E.B.A. S.T.H.G.I. (the Secret Society for Putting Wholesome Literature Within The Reach Of Every Boy, And Seeing That He Gets It) whose president threatens him with dire consequences if he does not allow them to write the second half of his book for him. They've noticed that in the first half, the story "contains no moral. There are scenes of violence, and your hero is far from perfect". To which Hughes indignantly replies, "Tom is a boy, not a patent medicine. In other words, he is not supposed to be perfect". At which point the Society's president announces his intention of launching the writer over a nearby cliff if he does not comply with their wishes. And so it is the revised, propagandized version of the story that has been handed down to posterity – much to Wodehouse's evident annoyance.

And he has a point. At the start of the book, Tom is described as "a robust and combative urchin", who, "at the age of four began to struggle against the yoke and authority of his nurse". Headstrong but good-hearted, a sportsman with an innate sense of social justice, he's just the sort of character young schoolboys would identify with. He is forever "getting into all sorts of scrapes" and refusing to "make regular school work [his] first object". In short, he's too busy being a boy to think about his future role as a patent medicine. Once again, at my own public school I was forever being told to "act your age" – which I actually *was* doing, and getting into trouble for it. What my teachers *meant* was: "act like a miniature adult" – which, at the age of nine, I'll confess was somewhat beyond me.

And so it is with Tom. Despairing of his waywardness, the God-like figure of Dr Thomas Arnold, the real-life Headmaster of Rugby School from 1828 to 1841, takes Tom in hand in Part 2 of the book, giving him new boy George Arthur to look after – who is as unlike Tom as it's possible to be. I hardly ever quote Wikipedia, but the compiler of the relevant page has Arthur down to a tee: he is a "frail, pious, academically brilliant, gauche, and sensitive new boy" whose company has the desired effect on Tom, who gradually evolves into a model pupil with all those attractive (and convincing) rough edges knocked off him. Although Doctor Arnold's patented brand of what came to be known as "muscular Christianity" is here presented as an ideal, it clearly wasn't anything of the kind for Wodehouse, and he loathes the way a perfectly good school story has been hijacked midway through by a moral homily. It was a fault noted by commentators at the time of the book's publication, but in his introduction to the sixth edition Hughes was unrepentant:

> Why, my whole object in writing at all was to get the chance of preaching! When a man comes to my time of life and has his bread to make, and very little time to spare, is it likely that he will spend almost the whole of his yearly vacation in writing a story just to amuse people? I think not. At any rate, I wouldn't do so myself.

Wodehouse would, though, although he is guilty of the very occasional lapse into piety. In *The Pothunters* the narrator comments "how wrong it is to bet", but this is an isolated example. Three years later, in *The Gold Bat*, there is this tonally ambiguous passage on the evils of smoking:

> To smoke at school is to insult the divine weed. When you are obliged to smoke in odd corners, fearing every moment that you will be discovered, the whole meaning, poetry, romance of a pipe vanishes, and you become like those lost beings who smoke when they are running to catch trains.

> The boy who smokes at school is likely to come to a bad end. He will degenerate gradually into a person that plays dominoes in the smoking-rooms of A.B.C. shops with friends who wear bowler hats and frock coats.

Well, maybe not *that* tonally ambiguous. Wodehouse, who was of course a lifelong smoker, is simply stating that a good smoke should be enjoyed to the full, which is difficult in a policed environment. Either delay your smoking until you've left school, he seems to be advising, or wait until there's no chance of being caught. Only then can the joys of smoking be truly appreciated. Although Mike Jackson's Uncle John warns his nephew off it for fear it will compromise his sporting fitness, it's pretty much the last we hear of the evils of smoking until it pops up as a symbol of schoolboy Ogden Ford's all-round ghastliness in *The Little Nugget* (1913).

By and large, though, morals were clearly not Plum's style, and when a lesson is too obviously learned in his fiction, the result is usually disappointing. In the 1906 story 'A Division of Spoil', Merrett is caught 'cribbing', not by the invigilator but by his fellow students, who rather priggishly remind him that while it's OK to cheat in term-time course-work, "we don't do it during exams" – an odd piece of casuistry, to be sure. Even less subtle is 'Educating Aubrey' from 1911, in which the oik of the title learns, after Jack Pearse has comprehensively trashed the study of a posh fellow student because (a) he's posh and (b) he plays boule for money, that "antecedents, however aristocratic, are as nothing beside present performance… [M]uscles were more than coronets, and a simple swagger-stick than Norman blood". Having replaced one form of tyranny (privilege) with another (strength), Pearse takes the spoilt Aubrey in hand and makes a sportsman out of him, on pain of regular thrashings with said swagger stick. Unfortunately, no one, including its author, emerges from this muddle-headed story with much to boast about.

Most of the time, though, Plum refuses to mount on his high horse. At the close of 1903's 'A Shocking Affair', in which two schoolmasters are electrocuted by a 'faulty' doorknob, the narrator, having debated the moral of the story and arrived at no firm conclusion, proposes that it "shall be withdrawn and submitted to a committee of experts. Perhaps they will be able to say what it is". Back in *The Pothunters*, Welch remarks to Charteris that it isn't the winning that counts, but the taking part: "One doesn't always run for the sake of the pot", he says, much as a parent would to a disappointed child who has come fourth in the sack race. "Oh, well", comes the student journalist's reply, "if you're going to take the high moral standpoint and descend to brazen platitudes like that, I give you up".

Yet that's not to say that Wodehouse's school stories are devoid of any moral or ethical challenges. While his protagonists don't often confront the biblical commandments, they do brush up against the school rules and the (largely) unwritten code that governed behaviour within the gated educational communities of Edwardian England. Plum sometimes encourages his readers to think outside these rigidly-constructed boxes. In 'The Manoeuvres of Charteris', for example, our eponymous hero is given some real depth in a brilliant conclusion that sees him emerge as something more than a hormonal, misunderstood rulebreaker. When he rescues the headmaster's 12-year-old niece, Dorothy, from a pair of ruffians in the nearby village of Rutton, it is revealed that in order to have been at the right place at the right time, he was breaking bounds – a serious offence in most boarding schools, who, being *in loco parentis*, quite understandably wanted to keep tabs on their charges. But the Old Man (a.k.a. The Headmaster) proves himself more than a match for this ethically ambiguous situation by punishing Charteris with writing out a token ten lines of Virgil instead of the usual 200. While having to retain a semblance of authority *and* feeling genuinely grateful, he also requests that Charteris give thought to sinning less often, "simply as a matter of principle" – which, we're told, the schoolboy does. His has been a classic teenage rebellion, but one from which good has unexpectedly emerged. Speaking of the Headmaster, Charteris confesses that "I'd be his sweetheart, if he'd be mine. But he makes no advances". So it's down to Wodehouse to provide the means for that advance, and the story ends with both characters symbolically shaking hands, bringing Charteris's adventure to a close.

The problems Wodehouse engineers for his schoolboys don't always involve members of the Common Room. In 1905's *The Head of Kay's*, Kennedy only realizes quite how much his perspective on life had been governed by the "simple creed" of his house, when he is transferred across to another, Kay's, which is in danger of failing and needs sorting out. Suddenly he is jolted out of his habitual patterns of thinking and told to confront a bunch of unruly fellow students who don't share his values. How can he persuade them of the need to reform and shape them into a cohesive unit that is capable of winning school trophies? In Wodehouse's ladder of schoolboy priorities, unlike Hughes's, religious observance comes a distant second to sportsmanship in character formation, and so it proves here. An unwonted regime of physical activity proves redemptive, and Kennedy's reign at Kay's is crowned by his adopted house winning the school sports day for the first time ever. Ordinarily, the masters would put things right, but here Kennedy is placed in the near-impossible position of having to deal with the problem without the help of those in authority. In fact, it's *because* of Mr Kay's complete ineptness that Kennedy is given the job of sorting out the mess.

The White Feather (1907) also demands that some awkward questions are answered as R. D. Sheen achieves personal redemption for a school-shaming act of cowardice (running away from a fight with the local toughs) for which he is sent to Coventry. Seizing the initiative, he secretly takes boxing lessons from ex-pro Joe Bevan and goes on to win the silver medal for Wrykyn at the Aldershot all-schools tournament. The story's central issue isn't one parachuted in direct from the pulpit, but one arising out of a situation in which every *actual* boy would have found himself at some point or other during his passage through school. After all, fight or flight is a pretty fundamental human reality, and once again Wodehouse thickens the story's problematic undercurrents by having Sheen sneak out of bounds to get to his lessons in the upstairs room of a riverside pub. As with Charteris's earlier transgression in the name of sport, the greater good is only gained by rule breaking – at which point it becomes a problem for the authorities. Do you punish someone even though they have brought honour to the school? Or does the end justify the means? On this occasion, the Headmaster has to perform some pretty spectacular logic-chopping to achieve the desired result, but all's well that ends well, and the story shapes itself into a pleasing low-key parable, but one that somehow manages to avoid being preachy.

If we were tempted to lend the subtitle of *The White Feather* some Psmithian capitals (The Coward Who Came Through, perhaps), Wodehouse gets there first and does it himself. When Drummond learns of Sheen's secret ambition,

> It seemed to him that Sheen was trying to 'do the boy hero'. In the school library which had been stocked in the dark ages, when that type of story was popular, there were numerous school stories in which the hero retrieved a rocky reputation by thrashing the bully.

Wodehouse invents just such a 'piffling' story, which he titles *The Lads of St Ethelberta's*, presumably so as not to give offence, but only a few pages later references his writer colleague F. Anstey, in whose stories "the hero is never long without the chance of retrieving his reputation". Does Anstey's type of story belong in those "dark ages"? Seemingly, yes, and Plum suggests one such plot that is way beyond its sell-by date:

> ...there is a fire, and whose is that pale and gesticulating form at the upper window? The bully's, of course. And who is that climbing up the Virginia creeper? Why, the hero. Who else? Three hearty cheers for the plucky hero.

And none, of course, for the bully. Wodehouse clearly doesn't think that kind of storyline deserves particularly rousing cheers since, he informs us, "in real life opportunities of distinguishing oneself are less frequent" than in novels with agendas.

But is Sheen "intoxicated by his imagination"? Has he been taken in by the romance of Anstey-like stories and bitten off way more than he can chew? In short, will he get beaten to a bloody pulp at the boxing championships in Aldershot? Wodehouse is putting himself in a difficult position here because if Sheen triumphs, he's guilty of aping the anti-quated trope at which he's just been poking fun. If, however, Sheen loses, his paying audience who have parted with their hard-earned pocket money to buy the book will be disappointed. There's really no question of what will happen, but having proved his point, Sheen doesn't end up "thrashing the bully" who was responsible for broadcasting his initial shaming. Rather, he shames him back in front of his peers, revealing him for the sneak, liar and shammer that he is. It's revenge enough − except it's not really revenge but cleansing schoolboy society of one of its wrongdoers. Wodehouse's bullies and cads rarely get the thrashing they so clearly deserve; instead, they fail to return to school after their misdemeanours are discovered, either being withdrawn by their guard-ians or expelled. And that goes for the teachers, too: the ineffectual and fussy Mr Kay is banished to the headmastership of "a small school in the north" for his sins; one of his charges − the loathsome Walton, who has thrived during Kay's tenure − suffers the ultimate punishment of being "snapped up...by a bank", where, for a wage of under £40 a year, he has to perform very similar tasks to those Wodehouse had endured only four years before. Rubbing salt into the wound, Plum allows Walton only half the £80 salary he himself received (although by the end of the decade, Mike Jackson is getting £114 for his entry-level bank job, which perhaps reflects the esteem in which he was held by his creator).

But was Wodehouse really in a position to challenge the likes of Anstey or even Thomas Hughes in the pantheon of schoolboy fiction? With his inbuilt self-confidence, he probably thought there was no reason why he shouldn't, and ten years of repeated commissions is eloquent testimony that he was pushing all the right buttons. And yet, in *Boys Will Be Boys* (1948), E. S. Turner's seminal history of literature aimed at young males, Wodehouse is only granted two glancing mentions where one would have thought there should be considerably more. Of course, his work pre-1915 has been considerably eclipsed by the global success of what came afterwards, but for the reader there remains much to enjoy and celebrate, even if he or she did not attend the singularly strange establishment that is an English Public School.

The trouble was that "Boy's Own" literature was such a limiting and conservative genre that a truly gifted author could not stick it for long. It's often been remarked (at least once by Wodehouse himself) that he never grew up, and that his sensibility remained rooted at Dulwich in 1900, but this, it seems to me, is yet another of the myths we have to explode or at least considerably refine if we're going to further our understanding of his literary achievements. Some writers of school stories never moved on, but Wodehouse most emphatically did – personally and professionally – even while he was writing them. True, he may have embarked on a career in school fiction because that was all he knew in 1902, but by 1904 he had already earned enough from his labours in London to start branching out and trying new things. Moreover, it was not simply a case of Plum's horizons expanding: the times themselves were a-changing.

In 1906, Plum produced his first 'adult' novel, *Love Among the Chickens*, and, just as he averred that Anstey had started to appear old and creaky, so in 1907's *The White Feather* Wrykyn's wrinkly Headmaster is portrayed as being left behind by the tide of progress. One of his charges, Jack Bruce, has a rich father who regularly lends him his "motor-car". "You see", Bruce explains, "I am going to take up motors when I leave school, so it's all education". To which Plum adds this:

> The headmaster was silent. To him the word 'Education' meant Classics. There was a modern side at Wrykyn, and an Engineering side, and also a Science side; but in his heart he recognised but one Education – the Classics. Nothing

that he had heard, nothing that he had read in the papers and the monthly reviews had brought home to him the spirit of the age and the fact that Things were not as they used to be so clearly as this one remark of Jack Bruce's. For here was Bruce admitting that in his spare time he drove motors. And, stranger still, that he did it not as a wild frolic but seriously, with a view to his future career.

"The old order changeth," thought the headmaster a little sadly.

Making jokes about prepping "Thicksides" Thucydides would only go so far with pupils like Bruce, and in any case Wodehouse was getting restless and even bored, which really isn't surprising for a thoroughbred writer stuck in a literary classroom. While his next full-length school venture, *Mike*, is never less than competent, I for once get the sense that Plum is phoning it in. The genre has few challenges left to offer him, the plots are becoming over-familiar, and after 550 members of Wrykyn's student body collectively play truant on their Great Picnic, his seven-year catalogue of genteel schoolboy rebellion really hasn't anywhere left to go – although a similar walkout did actually take place at Haileybury school in 1900, boasting future Prime Minister Clement Attlee among its ringleaders. Plum knew about it and even jotted the incident down in his first-ever notebook for future reference.

So maybe this is why the wholly exotic figure of Psmith, a sort of über-Charteris, has to bludgeon his way into Mike's increasingly formulaic world halfway through the book to stir things up a bit. And doesn't he!

1909–1915

Chapter 3
School's Out

*Boyhood, like measles, is one of those complaints which a man should
catch young and have done with, for when it comes in
middle life it is apt to be serious.*

Uneasy Money

*It gave him something of a shock to find how persistently his thoughts refused
to remain in England. Try as he might to keep them there,
they kept flitting back to Alcala.*

'In Alcala'

*At last I have Scope. And without Scope, where are we?
Wedged tightly in among the ribstons.*

Psmith, Journalist

*If a fellow has lots of money and lots of time and lots of curiosity about
other fellows' business, it is astonishing, don't you know,
what a lot of strange affairs he can get mixed up in.*

'Concealed Art'

By the time he entered his fourth decade, the American novelist F. Scott
Fitzgerald (for a time, Wodehouse's near neighbour on Long Island)
reckoned he was all washed up. "Thirty", he wrote, "the promise of a
decade of loneliness, a thinning list of single men to know, a thinning
brief-case of enthusiasm, thinning hair". Not the kind of sentiments
you expect to find in a Wodehouse novel, although in *The Little Nugget*,
Peter Burns has this to say:

> At twenty-one, life being all future, it may be examined
> with impunity. But at thirty, having become an uncomfort-
> able mixture of future and past, it is a thing to be looked
> at only when the sun is high and the world full of warmth
> and optimism.

Plum was 31 when he penned those lines in 1913, and, like most of
us when we approach or pass a birthday with a zero in it, a bit of

self-appraisal may well have taken place – not that I'm at all comparing Wodehouse with Pete, who has rather more reason to be self-deprecating than his creator, having by his own estimation "the soul of a pig". But if Plum *had* conducted an inventory on his literary career thus far, he would have had every reason for satisfaction and even guarded optimism (although literary freelancers, no matter how successful, are never *completely* free of the fear that everything's about to go A over T). As he boasted to his agent in January 1909 (misquoting Macbeth), "I have had golden opinions from all sorts of men".

The only thing that might have been bugging him is the suspicion that in servicing his schoolboy market, he was leaving it later and later to establish himself as the literary all-rounder he knew himself to be. Indeed, he wanted his latest production, 'The Lost Lambs', published "as a 6/- [shilling] novel and not as a boy's story" – even though the latter is exactly what it was. But the three 'adult' novels Plum had published thus far (and by that I mean novels with no actual or recently demobbed schoolboys in them) were a complete mixed bag, which, while never less than competent, gave only the most general indications as to where he would eventually hang his literary hat. While all of them contain elements that would later find their way into his mature style, it's only possible to view in retrospect that the comedy of *Love Among the Chickens* (1906) would offer any significant pointers as to what the market might expect from him in the future. And I think Plum was all too aware of this. In fact, the entire plot of 1907's *Not George Washington* hinges on the irony that writer Jimmy Cloyster is "so confoundedly versatile" he doesn't have an easily identifiable literary persona – then, as now, not good for a writer's 'brand' (dread word).

By his second visit to New York in 1909, Plum clearly wanted to correct the perception the market had of him. In fact, he had long been impatient with his lot, writing as early as spring 1907 that he had gone "as far in that direction now as I am ever likely to get". Two years on, nothing much had happened to address the situation, and there's not just impatience but even a touch of resentment in a letter he wrote to his friend Leslie Havergal Bradshaw from his lodgings on the edge of Greenwich Village:

> So far from wanting to get my boys' books published this side, I look on them as a guilty past which I must hush up. I want to start here with a clean sheet as a writer of grown-up stories. The Captain books are all right in their

way, but their point of view is too immature. They would
kill my chances of doing anything big. I don't want people
here to know me as a writer of school-stories. I want to
butt into the big league... The school stories have served
their time.

Which is about as clear a line in the sand as he could have drawn. His
reasons for wanting to do so are crisply rehearsed. First, school stories
were painting him into an artistic corner: as a mature adult, he was still
writing about boys who were by now half his age in a type of institution
he had last attended nine years previously. What he called the "iron-
bound conservatism" of the school-story genre was never likely to allow
his talent to soar or even develop beyond what he had already managed,
and would force him to keep repeating himself until the public grew
tired of him.

Second, he had a new career in a new town: he was eight weeks into
that second transatlantic sojourn when he wrote these words, and he
now had the opportunity to wipe the slate clean and start over.

Finally, his earning potential was being restricted: the antics of
English public schoolboys were way too niche for the mainstream
American market Wodehouse wanted to seriously "butt into". After all,
as he tells us in *Psmith, Journalist*:

In New York one may find every class of paper which the
imagination can conceive. Every grade of society is catered
for. If an Esquimau came to New York, the first thing he
would find on the book-stalls in all probability would be
the *Blubber Magazine*, or some similar production written by
Esquimaux for Esquimaux. Everybody reads in New York,
and reads all the time.

This was a place he could do business in, and what follows in this chapter
is how Plum reacted to this sudden broadening of his horizons.

Of his first five-week transatlantic visit Stateside in spring 1904,
Wodehouse commented: "Being there was like being in heaven without
going to all the bother and expense of dying". From this point on, he
was torn in two directions – and not just geographically. England and
America respectively embodied different ways of thinking born of
massive intellectual contrasts, including the small and the large, the old
and the new, the past and the future, the familiar and the unknown, the

personal and the corporate, the closed and the open, old money and self-made, aristocracy and meritocracy – all of which are reflected to a greater or lesser extent in a fascinating minor story he wrote almost as soon as he returned. 'An International Affair', published in England in 1905, is an eccentric, almost allegorical piece with which Plum opened his post-America account, and it gives us a few enticing clues about the transatlantic to-and-fro that was only just beginning within his own sensibility.

In the unlikely setting of the small English settlement of Wrykyn, home to the school of the same name, Mr Oliver Ring of New York decides to open a pilot branch of 'Ring's Come-One Come-All Up-to-Date Stores'. "Within a month", he estimates, he can "take to himself the entire trade" of the market town, which has been conducting its business in the same way for centuries in an atmosphere of "primeval calm". The evil invader promptly demolishes "a trio of decrepit houses in the High Street", replacing them with a "striking" building, "finished with incredible speed", and the battle for the town's retail soul commences. Plum's story focuses on the afternoon tea trade: Ring's offers a "public-school tea at one shilling", undercutting the local family-run Cook's tea room, which is described thus:

> Cook's is the one school institution which nobody forgets who has been to Wrykyn. It is a little confectioner's shop in the High Street. Its exterior is somewhat forbidding, and the uninitiated would probably shudder and pass on, wondering how on earth such a place could find a public daring enough to support it by eating its wares. But the school went there in flocks.

So – it's a cranky, traditional joint run by a giant ex-soldier with one leg and his wife. It's clearly not that good, but out of loyalty – and the lack of any available competition – it has attracted the school's custom for as long as anyone can remember. All that tradition – with its good and bad points – is threatened by the arrival of the brash newcomer. Significantly, the new store is a honey pot for the school's cads and bounders, including Merrett and Rand-Brown, whereas the good guys stay loyal to the old firm ("We shall stick to Cook's. I don't want any of your beastly Yankee invaders. Support home industries. Be a patriot. The band then played God Save the King", jokes the loyal Dunstable). But who will win?

Things immediately start looking bad for Cook's, and Dunstable leads a one-pupil deputation to ask the American store's manager – who most un-Englishly spits on the pavement – to have a heart. Nothing doing of course, and the beastly Yankee offers him the following life lesson:

> Let me remind you of a little rule which will be useful to you when you butt into the big, cold world. That is, never let sentiment interfere with business.

And so Dunstable has no other option but to play the game low down and dirty: he laces Ring's tea with sal ammoniac, and blames the resulting bilious attacks suffered by the cads and bounders on transatlantic abominations such as buckwheat cakes and maple syrup. Wrykyn's headmaster places Ring's out of bounds on health grounds, and Cook's is once again flooded with business. England 1, America 0. Old-school guile and quick-wittedness subverts new world money and brawn.

It was a battle between two ways of life and two ways of thinking that was to prove a useful engine for generating comic situations, and one Wodehouse frequently returned to over the following seven decades. In fact, very few of Wodehouse's subsequent stories *don't* have a transatlantic angle in them somewhere. As he aged, however, Plum's published loyalties were not so clearly defined as in this early piece, not just for fear of offending his American readers, but also because of the ambivalence he himself experienced. Cook's had won the opening skirmish for England, but would the home nation eventually triumph in the war? Note how both the store manager and Plum, when speaking in his own voice, use the phrase "butt into". Well, it's clear that Plum wanted to clean up Stateside in much the same way as Ring's had started off doing in Olde Englande. If anywhere was going to give scope to his commercial ambitions, it would be America: no Great British modesty or bashfulness in his stated ambition – Plum was, temperamentally at least, an American already. From 1909 onwards, he practically commuted across the Atlantic until the outbreak of the Second World War, one of the few writers who needed to do so before Hollywood's demand for English scriptwriters led many others to make the same journey. Then came his wartime incarceration and its fallout, following which, in April 1947, he bade farewell to Europe for ever. And that final break, though not necessarily his choice, is foreshadowed incredibly early in his writing – although, of course, he could not possibly have known it was destined to happen – in the smallest of hints. Blink, and you'll miss it.

For his short story debut in the U.K. *Pearson's* magazine in September 1904, Plum decided to create a new school, which turned out to be an amalgam of all his previous ones, calling it "Locksley" and inaugurating a mini-series that would last for a further three outings. His choice of name is intriguing and perhaps significant, although I offer the following observation only as a possibility.

As we've already seen, Plum was a massive fan of Tennyson, whose poem 'Locksley Hall' is among his best known, particularly in America, for reasons that will become apparent in a moment. Read the poem, as April Carroway does in the 1935 story 'Trouble Down at Tudsleigh', and the parallels with Wodehouse's early biography, though completely coincidental, are uncanny – and mostly irrelevant, aside from its narrator's ambivalent vision of past and future in old and new worlds. Locksley Hall represents the narrator's past and a deep, abiding but forever lost love. The future in a distant foreign land offers, by contrast, "scope and breathing space" where he can thrive and fulfil "the promise of my spirit". Torn between the two, he debates the 'stick with what you know' and 'try something new' arguments, eventually settling on the latter and wishing destruction on his past. These are the poem's closing lines:

> O, I see the crescent promise of my spirit hath not set.
> Ancient founts of inspiration well thro' all my fancy yet.

> Howsoever these things be, a long farewell to Locksley Hall!
> Now for me the woods may wither, now for me the roof-tree fall.

> Comes a vapour from the margin, blackening over heath and holt,
> Cramming all the blast before it, in its breast a thunderbolt.

> Let it fall on Locksley Hall, with rain or hail, or fire or snow;
> For the mighty wind arises, roaring seaward, and I go.

While the imagery of the wished-for break is cataclysmic, Locksley hasn't actually been destroyed by the poem's end, allowing it to survive in the writer's memory as a focus for regret, sentimentality, and nostalgia in the future – which, anticipating a clean break with the past, is not quite what he wants. But then (particularly if you're a character in a

Tennyson poem), you can't have everything.

So if Wodehouse's Locksley School is St Austin's and/or Wrykyn, and these establishments stand in for aspects of Plum's own Dulwich College, it doesn't take a great deal of imagination to transpose his *biographia literaria* with that of Tennyson's protagonist. Plum would eventually be forced to throw in his lot with the New World, finally moving there for good in 1947, but he never completely went native – except perhaps once, and then only metaphorically, when late in life he confessed that he had grown to prefer baseball to cricket. For the rest of the time he created a useful and fruitful symbiosis between the land of his birth and his adopted country, fashioning varying combinations of his Old and New Worlds, the former often symbolized by large (and very often decaying) country homes like Locksley. Many of his characters also make that journey: a whole host of English girls marry American men; English men marry American girls; and several characters – including Jimmy Pitt of *A Gentleman of Leisure*, Jimmy Crocker of *Piccadilly Jim*, Freddie Threepwood and, of course, Bertie Wooster – seem equally at home, no matter on which side of the Atlantic they happen to find themselves. And no experience is necessary if you're making the Atlantic crossing east to west: as Bill Dawlish (otherwise known as William Fitzwilliam Delamere Chalmers) of *Uneasy Money* finds out, even if your knowledge of the States is limited to the two revolutionary wars of 1775–83 and 1812, cocktails, and ragtime, you can still make a go of things if only you have an open mind. To Plum, America *was* the land of opportunity, where he experienced a freedom, freshness and 'can-do' spirit that offered such a contrast to the history, tradition and ingrained attitudes that weighed so heavily on his fellow countrymen.

Anyhow – back in 1909, Plum was faced with the problem of extricating himself from those pesky school stories, which, as the price of his success in this new territory, would have to go. Of course, in the person of Bertie and in the troupe of mentally-arrested schoolboys that peopled his fiction to the very end, the side effects of school never completely left Plum's writing. But what he needed in order to move forward was someone rather more eloquent and versatile to tell his stories and convey his humour than a typical English public schoolboy. The need to crack on was made all the more urgent by an unforeseen setback: although his second visit to America in 1909 had started well (Plum sold two short stories for big money almost as soon as his feet hit dry land), that lightning bolt of good luck proved reluctant to strike a second time, and he was back at the London offices of *The Globe*, from which he had resigned to pursue his American dream, by early 1910. None of the alternative literary avenues he had pursued had generated sufficient sales to allow him to definitively alter his writing habits, therefore he couldn't immediately surrender his school-story meal ticket, even though his imagination and ambition were both tugging at the leash. So it was back to the grindstone, at least temporarily. But there was one light on the horizon: Plum *had* already solved the problem of straddling school and post-school sensibilities, perhaps without being fully aware of what he had done, for in April 1908 Psmith had made his print debut in that proto-adult serial *The Lost Lambs*. And it was this monocled mutineer who would allow Wodehouse to hoof it over the school wall and charge off into the outside world.

Before we meet Psmith in person, we need to back up slightly and take a brief look at how Plum's talents were developing in some of his non-school writing at this time. He makes this particularly easy for us, as he created umpteen artist figures during this period, each reflecting and acting out aspects of the creative life that he had probably experienced in his own. In fact, in a 1909 story tellingly entitled 'Out of School', Wodehouse hints that far too many writers were writing about writers writing and that the market was growing saturated: "Read on. Read on. This is no story about the young beginner's struggles in London. We do not get within fifty miles of Fleet Street". That said, he regales us with the adventures of James Datchett, a would-be literatus who is threatened with deportation to Western Australia to look after his uncle's sheep, but who takes a job teaching at a private school by way of compromise with his non-comprehending relative. Writing in his spare time, he is finally freed from the threat of an ovine-filled future when he receives a letter "from the editor [of a magazine] accepting the story if he would reconstruct certain passages indicated in the margin". Another editor, another pesky rewrite, but with each returned MS, Plum – like Datchett – would refine the balance between his artistic instinct and commercial nous, polish his style, and find characters that could credibly deliver what he wanted to write.

Sometimes he used creative types from other disciplines to voice his preoccupations: 1911's 'Pots O'Money' has Owen Bentley desperately trying to establish himself as a dramatist (while working, somewhat inevitably, in a bank), but his work ends up being plagiarized. Painters populate both 'The Man Upstairs' and 'The Good Angel', and 'Archibald's Benefit' has a good deal to say about poetry (especially his old favourite Tennyson). Now and again, Plum breaks rank and addresses his readers in what must be his own voice, keeping us up to date on specific problems he was facing. In the 1912 short story 'The Goal-Keeper and the Plutocrat', another over-fussy editor must have recently upbraided him for writing too much, for the text is regularly punctuated by a chorus-like blue pencil:

> London was in a ferment. I could have wished to go into details, to describe in crisp, burning sentences the panic that swept like a tornado through a million homes. A little encouragement, the slightest softening of the editorial austerity and the thing would have been done. But no. Brevity. That was the cry. Brevity. Let us on.

"Brevity, brevity – that is the cry" he reminds us a few lines later, as if we hadn't already got the message. It's annoyingly self-indulgent, and we soon discover that the narrator is prey to a kind of self-pitying monomania when he informs us that "[h]onestly, it is but a dog's life, that of the short-story writer", before regaling us with the 'B' word yet again.

In the 1910 school story 'Stone and the Weed', the narrator wants to stretch himself but feels there's not much point:

> I could haul up my slacks with considerable vim on the subject of Stone's thoughts; I could work the whole thing up into a fine psychological study, rather in the Henry James style; but it would only be cut out by the editor, so what's the use?

What we have here is a writer champing at the bit and bridling at the conservatism of editors who think they know his work better than he does. Similarly, in 'Playing the Game' from 1906, the narrator remarks that "[i]t is a pity that the Problem Story has ceased to be fashionable" because it would be more artistically adventurous to leave his plot hanging in the air than tying it up with a neat little bow. Plum might have cringed if he'd read that later in his career – or else pointed out that it was a fictional character talking and not him. He felt he could 'do' serious if he wanted to, but it seems – thankfully – no one would let him. I say "thankfully" because when he does venture outside his school or light comedy comfort zone during this early period, the results are, shall we say, mixed.

This is most clearly demonstrated in the 1907 novel *Not George*

Washington, a collaboration with his friend Herbert Westbrook, the "King of Slackers", who is viewed by several reputable Wodehouseans as providing the template for that semi-loveable rogue, Stanley Featherstonehaugh Ukridge. This being the case, it's more than likely Plum put in the lion's share of the writing chores – doubly obvious when we realize that he scarcely even bothers to disguise aspects of his own writing career. One of the first themes he presents us with is the nexus between commercial art and "art for art's sake", a distinction efficiently rehearsed by Margaret Goodwin's mother, who says of her daughter's play *The Girl Who Waited*:

> "I had expected to listen to a natural, ordinary, unactable episode arranged more or less in steichomuthics. There is no work so scholarly and engaging as the amateur's. But in your play I am amazed to find the touch of the professional and experienced playwright. Yes, my dear, you have proved that you happen to possess the quality – one that is most difficult to acquire – of surrounding a situation which is improbable enough to be convincing with that absurdly mechanical conversation which the theatre-going public demands. As your mother, I am disappointed. I had hoped for originality. As your literary well-wisher, I stifle my maternal feelings and congratulate you unreservedly."

I *think* that's a compliment…

Once we've recovered from the shock of Plum pulling out all the stops to create – and no doubt satirize – a 'sophisticated' character, it's possible to appreciate the distinction he's trying to make, which recurs throughout the book and is lifted straight from *New Grub Street*: the central character James Orlebar Cloyster is torn between being a writer who entertains a romantic notion of what art is (the 'amateur' and 'original' writer who is guided by his own artistic conscience) and one who simply gives the public what it wants (the 'professional and experienced'). Either way, prior to any public recognition he or she may receive, the writer is working in isolation, hence the dreadful pun in Cloyster's surname. Writing is a solitary activity, a shot in the dark, an experiment conducted away from the sight of the world. And while that situation pertains, the artist can either blame his inevitable lack of success on "malice or stupidity on the part of the public", as the artist Reginald Sellers does in 'The Man Upstairs', turning his regular bouts of bitter frustration into "the basis of a monologue act"; or doggedly hope for a breakthrough, like Annette Brougham in the same story, preserving an outwardly "bright and cheerful" countenance by day, while "gnaw[ing] her pillow in the watches of the night". Clearly, a writer's lot is not a happy one if all he has is his Art for company. What he actually needs is an audience – but how to get it?

Like Plum, Cloyster is trying to get himself noticed. But unlike his creator, whose only strategy at the time was to become successful and solvent, he still yearns after artistic respectability. He soon discovers that the terms and conditions he's placing on his acceptance are somewhat wide of the mark:

> I had read nearly every journalistic novel and "Hints on Writing for the Papers" book that had ever been published. In theory, I knew all that there was to be known about writing. Now, all my authorities were very strong on one point. "Write," they said, very loud and clear, "not what you like, but what editors like."

And in those early years, Plum was unabashedly doing just that – writing for others in order to keep the cash rolling in. Cloyster continues:

> I knew just enough to hamper me, and not enough to do me any good. If I had simply blundered straight at my work and written just what occurred to me in my own style, I should have done much better. I have a sense of humour. I deliberately stifled it...[y]et I toiled on.

Once again, this sounds familiar. While Plum's school stories are light-hearted in tone, they are hardly comic. But they were the biggest profile-generating strand in his portfolio, albeit within a small corner of the wider literary market – so his "sense of humour" would still be held back were he to stick to his guns.

Ironically, for all Cloyster's plotting, planning, research, versatility and ambition, he is trumped by someone – his fiancée – who hasn't got a clue what she's doing. Margaret Goodwin neither whinges about a writer's lot nor chews the bed linen: she gets things right first time out of the traps simply by sitting down and writing what she knows. She sends Cloyster the manuscript of *The Girl Who Waited* (a title that exactly reflects her own romantic predicament), and he instantly recognizes it for what it is: a smash hit, despite his opinion that it is variously "stupid stuff", "nonsense", "rot" and "the exact shade of drivel which the London stage required". Mrs Goodwin's cynicism is vindicated, the show is produced – under Cloyster's name – and it is a whirlwind success, relaunching a literary career that had hit the rocks.

Although a dismal effort by Plum's later standards, *Not George Washington* offers the reader an intriguing possibility of how Wodehouse might have turned out had he not enjoyed the steady income stream afforded by the school stories. Like his creator, Cloyster starts out with high hopes, and even writes in "a bright and optimistic style". But he then grows horribly confused, torn between the conflicting demands of magazine editors, his creative ambitions and his own versatility. He ends up falling between all three of these stools and, ironically, only achieves success writing under three separate pseudonyms and developing his own embittered 'monologue act':

> The early struggles of the writer to keep his head above water form an experience which does not bear repetition. The hopeless feeling of chipping a little niche for oneself out of the solid rock with a nib is a nightmare even in times of prosperity.

This is so overwritten – and Cloyster such a narcissist – that it must have a satirical intent. But that doesn't stop the sentiment being genuine: post-fame, "[t]he grey days of my literary apprenticeship" are a period Cloyster has no wish to revisit – and I suspect Plum didn't, either, even though his own proved mercifully short. But Wodehouse was lucky compared to several of his writer figures, for his early successes allowed him to mature his writing style in public, getting useful, practical feedback on his efforts in the form of sales figures and repeat commissions. Not so some of the struggling writers he created, who live in a kind of existential vacuum, not knowing what to try next. The final ironies of Cloyster's success are that (a) he didn't actually write his breakthrough work, which in any case he despises; and (b) Margaret – who *did* write it – spent no time whatsoever perfecting her craft or worrying about who would read her work.

Another interesting test case – and a pointer to what happens next in this book – is Rutherford Maxwell, from 1911's 'In Alcala', who carries over all kinds of bits and pieces from Cloyster and Wodehouse himself. He's an Englishman in New York – a younger son – who subsidizes his writing habit by working at – can you guess? – the New Asiatic Bank. So far, so familiar as we follow Rutherford on what the narrator calls "the uphill road of literature". He works hard, with "dogged persistence", and mainly in isolation ("He was not used to visitors"). And then everything changes when he meets Peggy Norton, an actress who has an 'in' with the successful actor/impresario Winfield Knight. She suggests that Rutherford's half-written story 'Willie in the Wilderness' would be a perfect theatrical vehicle for the famous thesp, and contributes her insider knowledge to help Rutherford tailor what he writes to suit the star performer. Suddenly, he's writing with a fixed goal in mind, and it transforms not only his art but his self-confidence and personal happiness.

Now, this would appear to be a classic case of a "professional" writer writing to order, willingly surrendering his amateur status in order to put food on the table. But Plum employs a very different argument from that put forward by the snobby Mrs Goodwin: the demands of the commercial ethos can serve to sharpen up your act; and you won't necessarily end up despising yourself for betraying your art, because your writing will actually improve.

Having a well-known mouth ready and available to put words into, Rutherford finds that writing with Winfield Knight in mind unlocks his creativity rather than restricting it as we might expect. Yes, it's a commercial project, but it engages his imagination, with Peggy helping him envisage what will work and what won't:

> And so, little by little, the character of Willie grew, till it ceased to be the Willie of the magazine story, and became Winfield Knight himself, with improvements. The task began to fascinate Rutherford. It was like planning a pleasant surprise for a child. "He'll like that," he would say to himself, as he wrote in some speech enabling Willie to display one of the accomplishments, real or imagined, of the absent actor.

In time, "Rutherford was amazed at the completeness of the character he had built. It lived". Being a writer is like acting out Frankenstein, but without the dire consequences: "You're alive, my son", Rutherford says of Willie, "But you don't belong to me". And that's a good thing – the character has "real individuality" that will help the audience "recognize him in the street". And he's most definitely not a caricature, since "[a]ll the contradictions in the character ran true: the humour, the pathos, the surface vanity covering a real diffidence, the strength and weakness fighting one another". Willie has grown independent of his creator, which, as many actual writers have stated before and since, is the point at which they know they've done a good job.

Although Rutherford goes on to become a highly successful play-wright, he never recaptures the creative rush, that "utter absence of labour which made the writing of 'Willie in the Wilderness' a joy". Would Margaret Goodwin's mother have liked it? Probably not, but as with her daughter's play, Wodehouse seems at pains to point out that although it's a flawed piece of work, it pushes the audience's buttons. Here's his post mortem:

> Critics forgave the blunders of the piece for the sake of its principal character. The play was a curiously amateur thing. It was only later that Rutherford learned craft and caution. When he wrote Willie he was a colt, rambling un-checked through the field of play-writing, ignorant of its pitfalls. But, with all its faults, *Willie in the Wilderness* was a success. It might, as one critic pointed out, be more of a monologue act for Winfield Knight than a play, but that did not affect Rutherford.

Interestingly, almost exactly the same thing happens in *Not George Washington*. When Cloyster receives Margaret's manuscript, he imme-diately thinks of the actor Stanley Briggs as being perfect for the hero of the piece. In fact, "[t]he part might have been written round him". Once more, we have a 'monologue act', but in the theatre, that's seem-ingly all that was needed – what we now call a "star vehicle" – to enjoy the fruits of a commercial success. Plum doesn't tell us anything further about Cloyster's career, probably because he doesn't like him much. Rutherford, however, is a different matter; he does learn the necessary "craft and caution" from this early success – as no doubt his creator was doing.

The only thing was, Plum was still at the stage where he was running fast to effectively stand still. He remained in search of his own 'monologue act' that would both anchor his writing and set his already successful career truly alight – and in Psmith, he had very nearly found him.

It is well known by now that Psmith was based on an actual person, which possibly makes him Plum's equivalent of Cloyster's Briggs or Rutherford's Knight. Here's Wodehouse's own account of his inspiration, from the introduction to the 1969 edition of *Something Fresh*:

> People are always asking me...well, someone did the other day...if I draw my characters from living originals. I don't. I never have, except in the case of Psmith. He was based more or less faithfully on Rupert D'Oyly Carte, the son of the Savoy Theatre man. He was at school with a cousin of mine, and my cousin happened to tell me about his monocle, his immaculate clothes, and his habit, when asked by a master how he was, of replying, 'Sir, I grow thinnah and thinnah.' I instantly recognized that I had been handed a piece of cake and I bunged him down on paper.

Psmith even repeats the 'thinner and thinner' motif in *Mike and Psmith* in case there was any doubt in the matter, although some scholars claim Wodehouse somehow managed to confuse Rupert with his brother Lucas. Benny Green also plausibly suggests that Plum stirred in a touch of Henry Mayers Hindman, the only Communist dandy on record, who had only adopted Socialism because he'd been left out of the Cambridge University cricket team. Whatever.

But before we delve further into the development of Plum's first truly great character creation, we need to ask why he needed to be invented. I've already indicated the strategic reasons why: the requirement for a fresh, more adult-oriented voice that would be of use outside the school grounds. Tactically, however, the answer ultimately lies with Mike Jackson, the focus of attention in, er, *Mike*.

Although he is the cricketing hero of Wrykyn and later Sedleigh, and therefore a shoo-in for any writer's school yarn, Mike is, unfortunately, a man of few words – so not very useful for a writer like Wodehouse, who needed jabberers like Charteris to say what his heroes couldn't say in the light, airy, literary style favoured by their creator. Likewise, his transatlantic counterpart, Kid Brady, who talks mainly with his fists, has to have someone else present in the story 'How Kid Brady Joined the Press' who can string a reasonable sentence together. For this task, Wodehouse transports Tom Garth from Oxford University over to Manhattan, and Garth immediately assumes the lion's share of the talking. Stir the narrator's voice into the story, and the Kid, despite his star billing, is like a sort of 'missing middle', confined to nodding his agreement and offering four-word comments on what's being discussed around him. While Garth quotes from William Wordsworth and even the minor Elizabethan playwright Thomas Otway, the Kid is limited to the odd interjection and in effect becomes a spectator – which is amusing for a short while, but becomes something of an embarrassment thereafter. Mike Jackson, of course, has Psmith to help him out, but not before we're treated to an entire serial (or novel, depending on which version you read) in which Mike is forced to fly solo. (Through the years, the story was variously called 'Jackson Junior' or 'Mike at Wrykyn', or it formed the first part of the much longer novel *Mike*.)

Throughout *Mike*, Wodehouse is continually straining to make space within the novel for interesting and arresting things to happen until Psmith happens by and rescues him halfway through. Here are the options open to him up to this point:

It's summer, and Wrykynians aren't confined to barracks in dark winter weather; in fact, we're told that there are "few better things in life than a public school summer term... The freedom of it...is intoxicating". So the lads can move out and about and get up to stuff. Then there's Mike's impulsive disobedience: we're informed that he "always found a difficulty in obeying Authority and its rules". So he's free to get into scrapes. There's also the town-versus-gown flashpoint, the former specializing "in a mild, brainless, rural type of hooliganism" – so we can catch glimpses, however small, of life outside the school walls. And, for the first-ever time, Plum allows us privileged access behind the (I imagine) green baize door into the Masters' Common Room, where his favoured urbane, sophisticated conversation appears to thrive, especially in the figure of Messrs Seymour and Spence.

And that – apart from the technical freedom of employing a third-person narrator – is about all the narrative space Plum has at his disposal. He had become the victim of his earlier observation that nothing much can really happen in a school story without making it unbelievable – and the character of Mike himself was clearly beginning to bore his creator. Although he scores the winning runs against Ripton School at the climax of *Mike*'s first section, he's unaccountably absent for the 30-odd pages it takes to describe the Great Picnic, when all Wrykyn's boarders take the unprecedented step of playing truant for a day.

The truth is, as Plum confesses, that in everything but cricket, Mike is simply "just ordinary...resembl[ing] ninety percent of other members of English public schools". In 1956 he went even further, telling Richard Usborne that "I never cared very much for [Mike]. He is too straight a character to be really interesting" – in other words, a nice chap and a good egg, but not much use to a novelist. In 1924, during his fleeting appearances in *Leave It to Psmith*, Mike still talks as if he were at school (he tells Psmith, "You *are* an ass"), and remains "a young man of complete ordinariness". His psychological development is minimal: being of an impulsive nature, he is possessed of a quick temper, usually roused by an instinctive sense of right and wrong. Self-analysis is not his strong point, so learning anything proves a slow process; his early education is entrusted to his study-mate Wyatt, another Charteris-esque jabberer, who, three-quarters of the way through *Mike at Wrykyn*, finally manages to instil in his friend "a clear idea of what the public school spirit, of which so much is talked and written, really meant". Which, for the record, is that *"[t]here are some things you simply can't do"* (perhaps like publishing scurrilous magazines). It's one of those rare occasions when Mike gives houseroom to thought, and although "[h]is feelings were curiously mixed", things fall into place and he's psychologically all set to stop sulking in his tent and start severely punishing Ripton's bowlers.

Then, at the start of *Mike and Psmith* (or 'The Lost Lambs' *or* the second half of *Mike* – take your pick), he finally fulfils his destiny: to be the almost Trappist foil for a world-class talker. The spotlight is immediately taken off our tongue-tied lead and trained on the true star of the show. Some writers have identified Psmith's arrival as the moment Wodehouse found his adult voice, but I'm afraid I must demur. It's true that, voice-wise, Psmith is absolutely sui generis and a glorious creation, but he's only really a stepping stone on the way to Bertie, and a natural, though highly mannered, development from Charteris et al. His primary use in the one school story he appears in is to direct our vision beyond the tropes of schoolboy fiction, like some sort of legal alien, before waltzing out of academe and heading off on fresh adventures – more of which in a moment.

Psmith was, essentially, an early ancestor of Wodehouse's many "knuts" (or "cnuts") – Edwardian slang for an upper-class man about town who, like the lilies of the field, usually toiled not. Bertie and the entire cast of the Drones Club are his sons and heirs, all overgrown boys, "genial and good-tempered, friends of all the world...lovable figure[s], warming the hearts of stone" (except, of course, for the club millionaire, Oofy Prosser). Whatever you thought of their social status, wealth, upbringing – or even their congenital immaturity – "you could not help being fond of [them]". Those epithets are Plum's, written much later in his career, by which time the knut had become extinct outside the pages of his books. Psmith, however, is a markedly different creation: he has a quick brain and can run several rings round the Catsmeats and Gussies of this world before they realize he's set off. His best friend Mike never truly understands him, and with his sombre, still face it is often impossible to tell if he is being serious or joking. Add to this a devil-may-care attitude to life, his sense of the ridiculous, and the energy and inventiveness of his voice (a garish knitted waistcoat becomes "a sort of woollen sunset"), and Plum finally had an utterly infectious character he could have fun with. (I know Ukridge, who first showed up in 1906, has his champions; but unfortunately I'm not one of them, as you'll discover if you make it to Volume 2).

I'm going to ration myself to two examples of the ways Psmith sticks out like a sore thumb, or we'll be here all day basking in his verbal brilliance since, with the exception of Mr Wooster, he's just about Plum's most quotable character. Asked why he hasn't admitted to being a decent cricketer, he remembers that "the last time I played in a village cricket match I was caught at point by a man in braces. It would have been madness to risk another such shock to my system". This is not a schoolboy talking, nor is the following definition of socialism, in whose name "you work for the equal distribution of property, and start by collaring all you can and sitting on it". Tellingly, as Mike and cricket captain Adair square up to one another in a classic discharge of teenage testosterone, Psmith doesn't just refuse to join in, he's engaged in a monologue about his deteriorating physical state, and the danger a fight might pose to the precious bibelots on open display in his study.

To Plum, Psmith's arrival must have felt like unlacing a pair of particularly unyielding leather shoes: "At last", Psmith comments to an uncomprehending Mike, "I have Scope. And without Scope, where are we? Wedged tightly in among the ribstons" – a reference to a bulging apple barrel that was an apt metaphor for Plum's career up to this point. But before he could take advantage of all this new Scope, Plum had to extract Psmith from Sedleigh. From being a big fish in a small pond – or, as his creator describes him, a "whimsical monarch condescending for a freak to revel with his humble subjects" – he goes out into the wide world of gainful employment…and behaves in exactly the same way to everyone of whatever type and rank he encounters. Psmith is always unapologetically Psmith, waltzing through reality to his own tune, and making it join the dance. *His* dance.

Truth to tell, he doesn't truly *belong* anywhere. The victim of his father's many caprices and untimely death (Wodehouse creating some more elbow room in his plotting), Psmith, like Mike, inevitably begins post-school life in that Wodehousean graveyard of boyish hopes and dreams, The Bank. The resulting *Psmith in the City* from 1910 (previously serialized as *The New Fold* between October 1908 and March 1909), is one of Wodehouse's finest novels, just a year or so on from the water treading of 'Jackson Junior'. I reckon, for what it's worth, that it's his first true Classic, yet on the surface little seems to have changed from what had gone before: Mike and Psmith, reunited, are incarcerated in a rulebound institution with a rigid hierarchy that contains a substantial proportion of ex-public schoolboys from "Tonbridge, Dulwich, Bedford, St Paul's, and a dozen other schools". Change, when it comes in Wodehouse, is usually of the evolutionary rather than revolutionary order.

But although the Bank is another of Plum's closed eco-systems, it does benefit from being situated in the heart of London, that Wodehousean symbol of all that is alive and interesting. And now that Wodehouse had got his double act right at the centre of things, with a constantly rotating cast of supporting players, he had sufficient scope to prise himself out from between the ribstons without leaving his core schoolboy audience behind – because many of them would end up sharing a similar fate. Indeed, "Mike found two old Wrykinians in the first week" at the Bank who quickly become his "companions in misfortune". This is just as well, since Mike clearly misses the security of his schooldays, and his choice of lodgings in Dulwich is influenced solely by their proximity to a public school "where he might get a game of fives...and, in the summer, occasional cricket". This is before he discovers that the New Asiatic Bank, being stuffed full of ex-public school chaps, is "keen on sport" and has a viable cricket team. This helpfully cushions the transition between school and work, between the former's atmosphere of "good-fellowship "and the latter's "cold impersonality".

Psmith, by contrast, couldn't care less about his schooldays and doesn't look back. He is the supreme adapter, a breath of fresh air in the City's fusty wood-panelled corridors, being out to amuse himself rather than actually do any work like the rest of the inmates. At this point in his life, his daddy is rich, unlike Mike's, and whether he gets fired or not is of little consequence. At least partly because of this, "he had a way of treating unpleasant situations as if he were merely playing at them for his own amusement...his attitude towards the slings and arrows of outrageous Fortune was to regard them with a bland smile, as if they were part of an entertainment got up for his express benefit". A bit like J. G. Scott, then, only without the caddishness; and there's more than a touch of Oscar Wilde's studied foppishness thrown in with his bons mots.

So it's immediately clear that Psmith doesn't play by anyone's rules except his own: he isn't bound by reality, but rather creates his own wherever he goes, or else masters what already exists to suit himself. Most people are at the very least apprehensive of their boss when they first enter the world of work. Not so Psmith, who immediately decides to play Henry Higgins to Mr Bickersdyke's Eliza and mould his superior into a respectable citizen who will not shame the human race. Writing to Mike, Psmith expresses the hope that "I shall make a man of him yet – some day", despite the fact that his eyes betray "no animated sparkle of intelligence", the cut of his clothes "jars my sensitive soul to its foundations", and, worst of the lot, he wears "a made-up tie at dinner". (Incidentally, Plum loosely based Bickersdyke on British ex-Prime Minister David Cameron's great-grandfather, Sir Ewan Cameron, who was his superior at the HSB.)

More seriously, Psmith is a lifesaver to Mike. Having plucked him from his "scaly" lodgings out in Dulwich and established him in his own "snug little flat" in Clement's Inn – a real-life location conveniently located between London's financial district and theatreland – the old firm is back together and living under the same roof.

They really are the oddest of odd couples. Mike quickly grows into his new role of semi-professional sounding board, and although he is almost Psmith's plaything, he does perform the useful role of keeping his friend more or less grounded on those occasions when his flights of fancy threaten to spin off into an entirely different universe. To Mike, as to us, Psmith must appear exciting, unpredictable and *fun* to be around, if something of a liability: without him, Mike's life would resolve itself into a tedious round of work and sleep leavened by the odd bit of sport and good fellowship.

Wodehouse isn't usually one for psychological analysis or direct authorial comment, wisely allowing action, dialogue and characterization to do this job for him. But he does include a telling passage about halfway through *Psmith in the City*, in which he allows himself to differentiate between his two lead characters:

One of the many things Mike could never understand in

Psmith was his fondness for getting into atmospheres that were not his own. He would go out of his way to do this. Mike, like most boys of his age, was never really happy and at his ease except in the presence of those of his own years and class. Psmith, on the contrary, seemed to be bored by them, and infinitely preferred talking to somebody who lived in quite another world.

Which is precisely what I've just been saying about 'Scope' – and note that word 'atmosphere' again. But here's the interesting bit of authorial intervention that immediately follows:

Mike was not a snob. He simply had not the ability to be at his ease with people in another class from his own. He did not know what to talk to them about, unless they were cricket professionals… But Psmith was different. He could get on with anyone. He seemed to have the gift of entering into their minds and seeing things from their point of view.

Psmith is free to roam anywhere and bring lightness wherever he goes – and in anyone's company – which is a boon to his creator. Mike, by contrast, does not only remain umbilically attached to the old days back in school, but to the sensibilities that underpinned the rigid social hierarchies of Edwardian England. He may not be a snob, but he's still effectively cut off from people only a couple of rungs down the social ladder from where he himself is situated.

This awkwardness is reflected in some of the humour in *Psmith in the City*. Take, for example, the pair's Sunday visit to the home of fellow clerk Mr Waller, a considerably older time-server at the bank who lives in a humble semidetached villa on the north side of Clapham Common. These days, such a property would command a seven-figure sum and be home to a high-flying media type; back in the Edwardian era, it would have been regarded as about as lower middle class as you could go without actually joining the ranks of the working class. Hanging around such a neighbourhood was distinctly infra dig to anyone with social aspirations. Indeed, 'The Man on the Clapham Omnibus' was popular shorthand for Mr Average, someone who had received an education of sorts and was capable of reasoning, but who was in all other respects utterly nondescript. Both Mike and Psmith's families are somewhat higher in the social pecking order than Mr Waller, and would have otherwise had no cause to venture South of the River – then, as now, terra incognita to some of the more timid North Londoners. Indeed, Psmith claims never to have heard of Clapham: "The first thing to do", he declares, "is to ascertain whether [it] really exists. Having accomplished that, we must then try to find out how to get to it. I should say at a venture that it would necessitate a sea voyage".

Having safely arrived, Mike is distinctly uncomfortable in these Pooter-esque surroundings, whereas Psmith manages to navigate the swirling social undercurrents with practised ease, despite his unfamiliarity with the prevailing mores. One perhaps might have expected things to happen the other way round: socially, Mike has 'ordinariness' on his side in Clapham, yet he sits through the ordeal of Sunday tea ("the most depressing meal in existence") at Mr Waller's house in a state of profound discomfort which is made even worse when he upsets the water jug into an open jam tart. He never truly recovers from this setback ("he was a broken man"), but Psmith remains – as ever – in his element, a still point of geniality amid the general chaos that reigns as seven ill-assorted people try to establish some kind – any kind – of social rapport.

But Psmith's cordiality with all and sundry has no wider corollary. It doesn't for one moment make him the political, financial or ideological Socialist he sometimes affects to be. Notice, for example, how he insists on travelling wherever possible by 'taximeter' rather than public transport, and only 'supports' Man Utd to get Rossiter, the head of the bank's post room, to deal more leniently with his various misdemeanours. But he does give everyone, from whatever station in life, an equal opportunity to enter *his* world and be talked at without prejudging them. So for a toff he is remarkably emancipated, open-minded and, of course, supremely adaptable.

Which is just as well, because for his next adventure, Plum transplants him to the slum tenements of New York. In 1915's *Psmith, Journalist* he just about manages to pull off the unlikely literary coup of juxtaposing a man who wears a fresh white rose in the buttonhole of his silk pyjamas with the gun-toting gangs of the Bowery district. Mike and Psmith, who by now have escaped the life of Mammon to end up at Cambridge University, are on a cricket tour of the United States' eastern seaboard, and Psmith in particular is seeking additional scope in the Big Apple, of which he has heard much. Perhaps the last scenario he would have expected was to end up as a crusading journalist – and one, moreover, who becomes emotionally attached to the story he's investigating. By way of explaining why he engineered this unexpected scenario, Plum allows us a rare glimpse of the heart that beats behind the immaculately tailored waistcoat:

> It was not Psmith's habit, when he felt deeply on any subject, to exhibit his feelings; and this matter of the tenements had hit him harder than any one who did not know him intimately would have imagined... Psmith was one of those people who are content to accept most of the happenings of life in an airy spirit of tolerance. Life had been more or less of a game with him up till now. In his previous encounters with those with whom fate brought him in contact there had been little at stake. The prize of victory had been merely a comfortable feeling of having had the best of a battle of wits; the penalty of defeat nothing worse than the discomfort of having failed to score. But this tenement business was different. Here he had touched the realities.

But those harsh and even violent 'realities' are destined to bow to Psmith's airy tolerance rather than the other way round. Ultimately, Psmith triumphs in New York against almost impossible odds (and some of the most incompetent and unthreatening hoodlums in literature). But, although his heart may have entered the equation as never before, Psmith remains essentially unchanged. He has simply brought his genius to bear on a serious subject, and he emerges just about intact with the requisite happy ending. This juxtaposition is not the happiest, at least to this reader, and while I absolutely adored *Psmith, Journalist* as a teenager, my adult readings have found it annoyingly contrived. As in *The Luck Stone*, perhaps Wodehouse too realized that American thugs with shooters was just a bit *too* much Scope, and by the end of the novel, it's as if time has travelled backwards to an altogether cosier and familiar milieu, and the earth has returned to its accustomed axis:

> It was a drizzly November evening. The streets of Cambridge were a compound of mud, mist, and melancholy. But in Psmith's rooms the fire burned brightly, the kettle droned, and all, as the proprietor had just observed, was joy, jollity, and song. Psmith, in pyjamas and a college blazer, was lying on the sofa. Mike, who had been playing football, was reclining in a comatose state in an arm-chair by the fire.

Essentially, we're back safe and sound where we started at school. Mike only manages to contribute the odd monosyllable to the conversation before falling asleep, leaving Psmith, once more, alone with his words. "I try not to show it", he says to no one in particular, "but I seem to myself to be looking down on the world from some lofty peak". His brush with the realities and his temporarily awakened sensibilities seem not to have baptized him into some radical new relationship with the world outside his head, and one fails to see how it ever could have done. If Psmith wasn't so funny, his intense loneliness might even be deemed tragic.

Much more convincing is his next and final outing, 1923's *Leave It to Psmith*. During the eight-year hiatus between the novels, Wodehouse had been working on what the relationship between his writing and the world outside *his* head was going to be. And as he approached mid-season form, so the importation of Psmith into Blandings Castle is much more tonally certain than his sojourn in New York, even though his role as both fixer and stirrer remains substantially intact.

Ultimately, it is Psmith who retrieves Lady Constance's 'lost' necklace, thus allowing the plot's many threads to be happily tied together, but while he is doing it (and falling in love with Eve Halliday), he creates all kinds of verbal havoc. The normally quiescent Freddie Threepwood finally cracks when confronted with Psmith's incessant yakking and yells in frustration: "Don't *talk* so much! I never met a fellow like you for talking". And nor has anyone else: the imperturbable matriarch and former teacher Clarkie experiences "a slipping grip of affairs" when he's in full flight, demanding of her "any reasonably salaried position that has nothing to do with fish". Lord Emsworth is made to feel "a trifle dizzy" in his presence, as if "a pin had worked loose in the machinery of the conversation". After Psmith walks out of a three-handed exchange with Eve Halliday and the Efficient Baxter, "it began to seem a little difficult to carry on an ordinary conversation". For by this stage in his development, Wodehouse delights in letting Psmith act as a lord of high chaos, and what better disguise for him to wear than that of Ralston McTodd, a modernist Art poet whose work doesn't make any kind of sense? Psmith's "guiding rule in life", we are told, is "always to avoid explanations". He is "essentially a young man who took life as it came, and the more inconsequentially it came the better he liked it". His currency is the "entertaining possibilities" life presents him with as he skilfully extemporizes his way through it. Being Master of the Revels is a far better job than that of the crusading journalist – or perhaps I should say it's a more *suitable* role for a man of Psmith's unique talents, disposition and broad vocabulary.

But that, unfortunately, was that. Apart from a 1934 stage adaptation of *Leave It to Psmith*, we are destined to hear no more of him (although in 1935 Plum did refer in a letter to the character of Uncle Fred as "really a sort of elderly Psmith" in his desire to spread sweetness and light). Wodehouse later explained that he left the character behind because he couldn't think of anything else for him to do. As he wrote to Townend in 1929, "what a vital thing it is to have plenty of things for a major character to *do*. That is the test. If they aren't in situations, characters can't be major characters". And Psmith is at a loose end because, being able to talk the hind legs off a drove of donkeys, he ends up being isolated by his words, having no one who is his equal in eloquence. Even Ukridge has something to do in every plot that features him, even though he fails at whatever he tries. But all Psmith can do is steer the narrative away from the action by talking so damn much. In those rare moments when Psmith's mouth isn't operational, the reader feels an eerie quietness has descended. The cry rings forth, "Where is Psmith?" – and Psmith usually obliges us by quickly making good this vacancy. Quite how his marriage to Eve will square up is anyone's guess, but one hopes he will at least learn to allow his bride to get a word in edgeways now and then, or, once again, he will have talked himself into insularity.

Plum's next contender for a steady narrative voice and returning character was Bertie Wooster's direct antecedent, Reggie Pepper, who first appeared in the story 'Absent Treatment' in 1911 and lasted for six further outings until he quietly morphed into Bertie around 1915; indeed, two of the Reggie stories were later rewritten to feature Bertie after Jeeves's arrival. Plum hit on the obvious solution to an inveterate talker: make him the narrator. And so Reggie sets out to tell us of his adventures.

Like his successor, Reggie is a thoroughly likeable chap: four of the seven titles allude to the fact that he is doing someone "a bit of good", as Bertie would later put himself at the disposal of his friends or family (usually as a result of blackmail), and he has plenty of the necessary "time, money and curiosity" in order to pursue this calling. But Reggie isn't Bertie – not by a long chalk – and he almost talks himself out of the job of the narrator in his third-ever sentence:

I want to tell you all about dear old Bobbie Cardew. It's a

most interesting story. I can't put it in any literary style and all that; but I don't have to, don't you know, because it goes on its moral lesson.

To which (if you haven't shouted it already) one could counter: "But *Bertie* can, and there isn't a moral lesson either!" Then, at the start of 'Helping Freddie' (also from 1911), he is once again apologizing for his storytelling inadequacies:

I don't want to bore you, don't you know, and all that sort of rot, but I must tell you about dear old Freddie Meadows. I'm not a flier at literary style, and all that, but I'll get some writer chappie to give the thing a wash and brush up when I've finished, so that'll be all right.

No it won't, old chap. In about as lame and clumsy a pair of sentences as Wodehouse ever wrote, our man condemns himself out of his own mouth before embarking on a plot involving rescuing from drowning that Plum had already used at least twice before in *Love Among the Chickens* and the short story 'Deep Waters'. Maybe Plum knew that Reggie couldn't last long in his current incarnation, as he disconsolately signs off his penultimate appearance, 'Concealed Art', with this telling comment:

It seemed to me that this was a scene in which I was not on. I sidled over to the door, and slid forth. They didn't notice me. My experience is that nobody ever does – much.

Not something Psmith would ever say about himself. And at the close of the final story, 'The Test Case', Reggie similarly "slid silently into the night", never to return.

On the positive side, however, Reggie is certainly breezy, innocent and good-hearted, and once Plum has purged him of most of the "don't you knows" and "and all that" tics that are already proving to be annoying by the end of the first paragraph of the first story, he's a perfectly efficient, if somewhat uninspiring, narrative voice. But therein lies the problem: most of us already know from our reading that Plum's default narrative style is anything *but* uninspiring. Reggie's limited vocabulary and syntax represent Plum deliberately hobbling his own considerable literary skills because the character he's invented is a slightly tongue-tied, self-confessed 'chump'. Which makes his attempts to 'write down' to Reggie's level resemble a Frazer Nash sports car stuck in first gear.

Then there's a second, more general problem, once again to do with narrative space. As Plum later remarked to Bill Townend, the chumminess, colloquiality and characterization gained by having a first-person narrator come at the high price of omniscience. Third-person narrators can potentially know everything about the story they're telling. First-person narrators for the most part operate within a limited perspective for the simple reason that they can't be everywhere at the same time. "It's not all jam", Plum writes. "[T]he reader can know nothing except what Bertie tells him, and Bertie can know only a limited amount himself". So once again the narrative space is constricted, and with Reggie not having a Jeeves or a trusted accomplice at his disposal, Plum left himself with a pre-circumscribed number of options for increasing the necessary flow of information that oils the wheels of the plot.

This brings us, third and last, to the narrator's role as ringmaster – where Reggie once again falls down. In trying to help his mates, he usually manages to mess things up before leaving chance, fate or someone else to sort out the muddle in which he's involved himself, having no reliable trump card up his sleeve that will restore order to the narrative and draw its strings together in the consummate manner of Jeeves. This is why Reggie sometimes ends up on the margins of the resolution, as though his non-involvement and/or bewilderment at how things have panned out make him an intruder – like Kid Brady before him – in his own tale. This in its turn lends a distinctly downbeat tone to the story's conclusion, sometimes even bordering on bitterness and resentment. For example, the finale of 'Absent Treatment' sees him limping wounded from the fray "to piece myself together again" and mentally composing the text to be inscribed on his tombstone, which will read: "He was a man who acted from the best motives. There is one born every minute". And at the close of 'Rallying Round Old George' he is simply ordered to "pop off". Which he does. Alone. His isolation, albeit in a very different way, mirrors that of Psmith: both characters are somehow outside the stories they star in. Bertie, on the other hand, having had everything neatly arranged for him, is usually celebrating a lucky escape or a job well done – albeit sometimes with a bruised ego.

But as Reggie slinks off wounded, Bertie makes his debut, and even by the end of the first paragraph of 1915's 'Extricating Young Gussie' – the Pepper-esque title and odd verbal tic notwithstanding – one senses that Plum has hit on a more assured, versatile and far funnier narrative style than he had ever managed before. With this new character, he had no qualms about letting the "mentally negligible" Bertie, possessed of "a brain like a peahen", speak with an inventiveness and elegance that belies his lowly IQ rather than apologizing for his own inadequacy, except with the odd "if that's the word I'm looking for". Where does this eloquence come from? Plum doesn't explain, except in a stray line from 1930's *Very Good, Jeeves* when Bertie acknowledges that "I have picked up a vocabulary of sorts from Jeeves". But by adopting this simple expedient, he allows the Frazer Nash to roar off in top gear. For now, here are a couple of early Bertie zingers that Reggie could never have managed:

> My experience is that when Aunt Agatha wants you to do a thing you do it, or else you find yourself wondering why those fellows in the olden days made such a fuss when they had trouble with the Spanish Inquisition.

And, having just been dragged out of bed (at 11.30am) by said aunt after a night on the tiles:

> I was feeling like a badly-wrapped brown-paper parcel.

Still not quite mid-season form, but a massive leap towards it. And in this first story, Jeeves's later godlike status is scarcely even hinted at in his two vocal interventions ("Mrs Gregson to see you, sir" and "Very good, sir...which suit will you wear?") for the simple reason, as Plum later admitted, that he hadn't even begun to fathom Jeeves's future potential.

But we should perhaps be thankful for what we do have, for it was at exactly this time that Plum hit on the idea of a series of short stories narrated by a dog. We can only speculate what he thought he was doing, but he quickly saw sense and 'The Mixer' ran off with his tail between his legs after only two outings ('He Moves in Society' and 'He Meets a Shy Gentleman', both from 1915), leaving the field free for Bertie to flourish.

Notwithstanding the canine flirtation, 1915 and the years that immediately preceded and succeeded it would define what Plum would do – and how he would do it – for the rest of his career. He was still some way off literary greatness, but his writing was to take a massive leap forward when he upped sticks and moved to New York for the duration of the First World War. For it was there he was to start perfecting the writing style that was to flourish so gloriously in the 1920s and beyond

– and finally get reality out of his system so he could create a world he could fully own.

A thought to leave you with until we rejoin these themes in Chapters 5 and 7, courtesy of journalist Claud Cockburn, who hits the nail squarely on the head in his essay 'Wodehouse All The Way' (published in the collection *Homage to P.G. Wodehouse*):

> Wodehouse's first serious writing – I do not use the word ironically or facetiously – was done in the United States. An English writer exposed to, immersed in and inspired by the American writing-style and life-style, and writing for a mass circulation periodical such as the old *Saturday Evening Post* must be jolted, or boosted, into an awareness of the English language which a man who had never experienced the creative schizophrenia of the partially expatriated might never acquire.

What a great phrase "the creative schizophrenia of the partially expatriated" is – and how utterly appropriate when discussing Wodehouse. Separated from his homeland by 3,000 miles of ocean and a common language, Plum was about to show his mother tongue just what he could accomplish with it.

1904–1920

Chapter 4
Problems with Reality

What is the art of writing? Simply, when you boil it down,
being able to put plain statements in an uncommon way.
'The Literature of the Future'

It's the treatment that matters, isn't it?
Letter to Bill Townend, 1935

[T]he snag I always come up against when I'm telling a story
is this dashed difficult problem of where to begin it.
Right Ho, Jeeves

Throw a half-brick at random in just about any Wodehouse story and
you stand an even chance of hitting a writer of some sort hammer-
ing away at a typewriter or balling up sheets of foolscap. There are
dozens and dozens of them, of which the following is but a small selection: the Imagist poet Ralston McTodd in *Leave It to Psmith* ("across the
pale parabola of joy"); modish Bloomsbury novelist Stultitia Baldwin
(author of *Offal*); that prolific purveyor of thrillers, Cyril Mulliner (*Gore
by the Gallon, Severed Throats, Blood on the Banisters, Strychnine in the Soup,
The Missing Toe*); the queens of romance, Leila J. Pinckney (*Heather o'
the Hills, Scent o' the Blossom*) and Rosie M. Banks (*Only a Factory Girl,
The Courtship of Lord Strathmorlick; Mervyn Keene, Clubman*); and even Gally
Threepwood, busy compiling his scurrilous reminiscences. There are
Hollywood screenwriters, writers of musical comedy, and even real-life
authors make regular cameos, from T. S. Eliot to Dorothy L. Sayers,
Agatha Christie to Zane Grey.

Thousands of literary allusions and quotations pepper every single
one of Plum's novels. To pick a title at random – *Stiff Upper Lip, Jeeves*
– there are the inevitable Shakespeare and Tennyson (from one of his
lesser-known poems 'The Princess'), but also references to Bertie's (and
Plum's) favourite Erle Stanley Gardner (author of the Perry Mason detective novels), the pre-Raphaelite poet Dante Gabriel Rossetti, Robert
Browning, Percy Bysshe Shelley, the incredibly obscure 19th–century
versifier Thomas Hayne Bayly (supplied by Jeeves), the hymn writer
Reginald Heber, and the American poet James T. Fields – and that is

by no means an exhaustive list. Further evidence arrives courtesy of the hundreds of literary comments that form the spine of Wodehouse's correspondence, often referring to the book (or more likely books) he has on the go at the time of writing. One of my favourites comes from a 1929 letter to Bill Townend:

> How are you on the Elizabethan dramatists? My opinion, now that I have read them all, is that they are a shade better than Restoration dramatists, but as you rightly remark, that is not saying much.

"Now that I have read them all" is evidence that even as he approached 50, Plum was still boning up on his literary heritage – probably on the lookout for plots – yet he refused to be awed by its antiquity or the veneration in which it was held. The similarities between elements of farce in Restoration Comedy and Wodehouse's novels would be a fruitful subject for someone to get their teeth into one day. But in any such analysis of Plum's work, it would never do to lose sight of his populist leanings: the last time his grandson Edward Cazalet saw him alive, he was busy devouring *Smokescreen*, a 1972 thriller by Dick Francis.

The quality of his own writing is prima facie evidence that Plum's mind was steeped in literature of all kinds. He knew how it worked not just on the page, but also in the imaginations of his readers. His tastes were catholic: in his private library, there were shelves and shelves of crime, mystery, and thrillers, but also a liberal sprinkling of classics, 'serious' fiction, poetry, drama, and even a sizeable section on spiritualism. Yet, in common with just about every other comic writer, Plum is only given grudging credit for any awareness of literary theory despite the obvious fact that his winning style simply couldn't have materialized out of thin air: it came from *somewhere*. And although he is not commonly thought of as a writer who made a special discipline for himself out of literary technique, his intimacy with different styles and approaches to writing is clearly evident – though worn lightly – throughout his work.

A great writer's style is the end product of many conscious and informed choices: of ethos, genre, tone, vocabulary and so on, as Plum himself acknowledges in his 1914 article 'The Literature of the Future'. Taking the five-word nano-story "Jones crossed Thirty-third Street" as proposed by "[t]he ordinary man, who is not an artist", he speculates what fellow fiction writers Arnold Bennett, Sir Arthur Conan Doyle, Robert W. Chambers and E. Phillips Oppenheim would make out of it.

Respectively, he suggests, they would turn that seemingly innocent and uneventful road crossing into a biography, a mystery, a romance and a thriller. "Different, you see, in every case. That is the secret". Indeed. And Wodehouse, we would be tempted to say, would naturally turn it into a light comedy.

But how would he *do* that?

"By altering the reality to suit his vision" would be the simple answer.

But how would he do *that*?

As the Oldest Member might say to one of his victims, "It is curious that you should have asked that question", and "you will, no doubt, wish to hear the story from the beginning". And so you will over the next few chapters. In this one, I'm going to examine how Plum, after the odd guilty hiccup here and there, finally purged his stories of all unmediated reality prior to entering his 'golden period' in or around the early 1920s: for only then could his writing attain the maximum lightness that characterizes Wodehouse at his best.

Back in the earliest days of his career, he was something of a realist, drawn to what he called the "journalistic novel" – perhaps not unnaturally, as he was employed by the *Globe* newspaper at the time, albeit writing humorous pieces and not, as far as we know, doing actual reporting. To this end, he would prowl the streets of Edwardian London for likely material, talking to a wide variety of people and jotting down conversations in the notebooks that he kept from around 1902 to 1905, probably because he believed this is what serious journalists on the lookout for stories spent most of their time doing. He observed "the sorrows of a busman's life", "[s]tanding up all day. Getting wet clothes drying on one. The monotony of it ('The same old tuppences')". Another encounter took place in West Kensington on 28 December 1904, when he met a City worker who had fallen on hard times, buried his wife in Kensal Green cemetery, and "spent...Xmas Day sitting on Barnes Common like a fool and crying like a baby". That kind of heartbreaking story would never prove any use to Plum, but what caught his attention was the fact that his interviewee "interlard[ed]" the conversation with Latin phrases" and still "retained a pipe in his poverty". Or take this small slice of life from his encounter with a waitress, 'Miss Congreve': "if people put her back up, she doesn't give them sugar or forks or napkins the next time".

Plum's early work shows some evidence of these expeditions, and at least flirts with the depiction of real life; indeed, some of the stories are almost Gissing-esque in their studied ordinariness. A quick glance through *The Man Upstairs* (which gathers material published between 1910 and 1913) reveals that in plot, setting, and the odd telling everyday detail, Plum's reality did at least retain a tenuous connection with that experienced by some of his readership. One of the best of these, 'When Doctors Disagree', is for the most part set at the hugely popular 1910 Japan/British exhibition at White City in London (or, if you read the American rewrite, Coney Island), where the excited crowds would queue to ride the 'Flick Flack' and the 'Wiggle-Woggle' at the funfair or gawp in wonder at 'the Hairy Ainus' – a tribe of hirsute Japanese gentlemen – in their replica village. The featured characters, Arthur Welsh (a barber) and Maud Peters (a manicurist), are resolutely working class, use the Tube to get around, and conduct the type of hands-off relationship that hangs on in quiet desperation, not expressing their inner feelings to anyone, least of all one another. When they need advice on personal matters, they write to *Fireside Chat* magazine, which dispenses choice nuggets of populist wisdom for a penny a week (a role Plum had briefly attempted at *Tit-bits* magazine in 1908, but from which he was summarily fired for the twin crimes of flippancy and plugging his own books). And so life trundles along in its not altogether unpleasant rut, until Arthur and Maude's relationship (such as it is) is threatened by the well-off, yellow-gloved American Lothario, Clarence Shute, who very nearly turns Maude's head. But Clarence is sent away with a flea in his ear, after which, one assumes, the love story of our anti-hero and heroine will continue to develop at its former glacial pace and with its very English reserve.

Plum seems to feel considerable warmth towards these ordinary working people – albeit, perhaps, a sentimental one. But life down among the wines and spirits was no great attraction, and he quickly stopped writing this kind of story using these kinds of characters. That said, he did occasionally return ordinary people to centre stage, rather than treating them as rude mechanicals, most notably in what Rudyard Kipling was to call "one of the most perfect short stories ever written", 1926's 'Lord Emsworth and the Girl Friend'. Gladys and Ern, two London 'fresh air' children from a poor home sent to the countryside for the sake of their lungs, form an unlikely alliance with Lord Emsworth against the powers that be – in this case, Angus McAllister. Two worlds temporarily unite and draw sustenance from one another as Gladys slips her "small, hot hand" into the belted earl's, and together they face down the wrath of the tyrannous Scottish gardener who's not too happy about Gladys picking his flowers. It's a rare moment in every sense of that word, and Kipling might well have been right.

Leafing through Plum's notebooks, we can see that, 20 years earlier, his attention was darting all over the place. Just about everything seemed to be catching his eye, yet very few of these quotidian observations (except the odd one that concerned schools and schoolboys) were making it into his published writing. One such entry might offer us a clue why that was:

> The average schoolgirl or shopgirl when telling a story
> begins every other sentence with "And so - -" eg "And so
> I went in [illeg.] and she said & I said. And so I went out
> again etc" etc.

Accurate, perhaps: useful, no. Indeed, the year after he stopped compiling his commonplace book, he had his narrator Jeremy Garnet complain in *Love Among the Chickens*:

> A search through his commonplace book brought no balm.
> A commonplace book is an author's rag bag. In it he places
> all the insane ideas that come to him, in the groundless
> hope that some day he will be able to convert them with
> magic touch into marketable plots.

Garnet is trying "to hammer out something which, though it might not be literature, would at least be capable of being printed". But to no avail: he might just as profitably have spent the time banging his head against a brick wall – or simply making stuff up. Half a century later, in 1961's *Ice in the Bedroom*, the romantic novelist Leila Yorke is having similar problems with inspiration: when she impulsively announces her intention to ditch the rose-tinted spectacles, roll up her sleeves and write "a novel of squalor" – she finds she can't.

> I thought I'd be able to wing it by going the round of the
> local pubs and having the peasantry bare their souls to me.
> Thomas Hardy stuff. Not a hope. At the end of the week
> all I had discovered about these sons of toil was that they
> were counting the days to the football season.

While it may have worked for Thomas Hardy with his sagas of Wessex country folk, Leila isn't seeing what's right in front of her nose *because it doesn't strike a single imaginative chord*. And so, much to her publisher's relief, she beats a hasty retreat back to her wildly successful made-up world of "tripe". And so it was with Plum, who once claimed that "it takes a steam drill to extract anything of any interest from anyone". Writing to Bill Townend in the 1940s, he described how he had recently met a woman who asked him:

"Why don't you write about real things?"

"Such as?" I asked.

"Well, my life, for instance."

"Tell me all about your life," I said.

And then she thought for a while and came up with the hot news that when in Singapore during the war she had gone about with a tin helmet on her head. I explained to her that would be terrific for – say – the first 20,000 words, but that after that one would be stuck.

For "20,000" we of course need to read "20", because Plum was being drily ironic to the point of almost total evaporation. To a writer of his disposition, day-to-day reality was a total bore, and back in 1912 the narrator of 'The Tuppenny Millionaire' is similarly dismissive of such humdrum, unimaginative yet undeniably 'real' existences. The "army" of clerks and pen pushers that teems into London every weekday morning is crammed with:

...respectable, neatly-dressed, mechanical, unenterprising young men, employed at modest salaries by various banks, corporations, stores, shops, and business firms. They are put to work when young, and they stay put. They are mussels. Each has his special place on the rock, and remains glued to it all his life.

This was, of course, a fate Plum had been threatened with at HSB, so he knew whereof he wrote. In this story, George Albert Balmer is

116

another such wage slave (working for an insurance company this time), but one who decides he's going to give up being a rock dweller and branch out a little, particularly after the chirpy Cockney office boy Harold Flower informs him that he's "a vegetable – I seen turnips with more spirit in 'em than what you've got". Fortunately, he's been left a modest legacy in order to effect this change, and George's first step from root vegetable to butterfly involves taking a holiday to the South of France and sporting a light-coloured flannel suit complete with natty homburg in place of the lower middle-class camouflage he's accustomed to wearing. Almost immediately, he realizes that his past outlook has been "a little limited" and that his guardian, having raised him with this lack of ambition, was in actuality "a narrow-minded chump". Literally, for the first time, George "was seeing colour", and Plum vividly contrasts his character's erstwhile black-and-white existence with a new technicolour version that "intoxicates" him:

> The silky blueness of the sea was startling. The pure white of the great hotels along the promenade and the Casino Municipale fascinated him. He was dazzled. At the Casino the pillars were crimson and cream, the tables sky-blue and pink. Seated on a green-and-white striped chair he watched a revue, of which from start to finish he understood but one word – "oui", to wit – absorbed in the doings of a red-moustached gentleman in blue who wrangled in rapid French with a black-moustached gentleman in yellow, while a snow-white commère and a compère in a mauve flannel suit looked on at the brawl.

Meeting a young lady whose name we never discover, but who is in a similar rut working as a lady's companion, the couple impulsively decide to "cut the painter" that ties them to their past lives and emigrate to Canada. There's something improbable about the speed with which this decision to "jerk" themselves "out of the groove" is taken, but there's something a little heroic about it, too – after all, until the story's close, they don't even know one another's names. Plum is also attracted to this couple, and it's clear in this case that fortune will favour the brave. George may not have vast wealth, but what he has got will open doors for both of them, allowing them to reach an escape velocity which will propel them from drabness into a new, more exciting future, albeit one that will involve hard work.

Suddenly, Arthur and Maude's barber's saloon, though homely and familiar, is made to seem a little, well, *dull*, and Plum returned to the everyday world less and less as time went on. By the time *If I Were You* appeared in 1931, the hairdresser's shop at its centre was a place to run from, rather than retreat into. In a plot that resembles *Pygmalion* in reverse, Tony (actually the 5th Earl of Droitwich) may enjoy briefly slumming it as a hairdresser, but when a means of escape is offered him, he ends up back at the ancestral home where he so clearly belongs. When push came to shove, Plum preferred his fictional world to be tuppence coloured rather than penny plain. And that included the characters in it.

As he opened his literary account in the 1900s, Plum resembled journalist Tom Garth, from 1906's 'How Kid Brady Joined the Press', who confesses that "My passion for the dramatic's quite a disease". Garth isn't particularly wedded to telling his readers how things actually are. He plays fast and loose with the truth to keep himself amused. And so it was with Plum: he had no abiding ambition (or aptitude) to be a social chronicler, and writing from direct, first-hand experience would not prove to his taste. Real life might offer some amusing snippets or diverting detail, but ultimately, as with the episode of his West Kensington widower, recorded in his notebooks, gloom would most likely result. Two entries on from that sad encounter, he recorded how he was hobnobbing with the aristocratic Bowes-Lyon family – still maybe not much use but decidedly more congenial.

Almost 50 years later, Plum was still marvelling at his inability to extract useful material from his real-life experiences, even the harrowing period he spent in internment:

> I was cooped up for a year with 1300 men of all trades and professions and nothing to do all day but talk to them and find out their jobs, and I didn't bring a thing away with me.

By comparison, he asserts, Bill Townend would have collected "material enough for twenty novels" if he'd been placed in a similar predicament. Indeed, Plum had a history of borrowing from his friend's global adventures by land and sea to help fuel the back stories of some of his own more risk-taking characters, notably Gally Threepwood (passim), Bill Hardy in *Company for Henry*, Sam Shotter in *Sam the Sudden*, and *Big Money*'s Berry Conway. When Plum restarted a regular journal during his internment, he tended to accentuate the larkier side of camp routine, steadfastly refusing to turn it into a historical record or misery memoir. He gave it the working title of *Wodehouse in Wonderland*, and if you've read the hilarious anecdote about the art of spitting (reprinted near the end of *Performing Flea*), you might contest Plum's claim that he brought away nothing with him, particularly the passage about how hard it is to score a direct hit on an albatross in a force nine gale. But then, if you fed Plum on an exclusive diet of harsh reality, he would manage to extract *something* funny and uplifting from it. This habit did, of course, lead to all the hoo-ha which surrounded, and continues to surround, the 1941 Berlin Broadcasts Business (BBB), during which, in the course of five talks over German Shortwave Radio, he gave a humorous and in places deeply touching account of his eleven-month confinement in various Nazi detention facilities.

This sad interlude in Wodehouse's life has been raked over so many times, there's no pressing need to stoke the fire again. Therefore, this is one of very few times I propose to mention this tediously obstinate elephant in the room at any length, and only then because it impacts on the theme of this chapter, which has rather more to do with Plum's imagination than his biography. If you'd care to read a factual and balanced account, visit the P.G. Wodehouse Society (U.K.) website, where Tony Ring's brief yet comprehensive account is the first and last place to find one.

Even among those who give Plum the benefit of the doubt, his self-acknowledged misdemeanour has been used by several critics (including at the time by George Orwell) as proof that Plum not only created a fantasy world, but somehow contrived to live in one for the whole of his life. Quite simply, they assert, Plum could have had no idea of the consequences of what he was doing on the grounds that he was clinically naïf. This might have been a useful argument at the time to help offset the charges of collusion and treasonous intent that were levelled at him in England, but taken out of its immediate wartime context, it simply doesn't stack up, acting as a roadblock to any sophisticated understanding of his work (and I'll be looking at this topic in greater detail at the close of Volume 3). No one with a functioning consciousness can fully divorce themselves from what's going on around them, even if they would like to. And Plum *didn't* want to. Ever. And even if he did, you don't hear writers such as J. R. R. Tolkien, C. S. Lewis and J. K. Rowling disparaged for living inside their own brilliantly realized fantasy worlds, even though they clearly must have done for the many years they spent creating them. So why Wodehouse tends to get singled out for this honour is, I'm afraid, beyond me, although it probably has something to do with the assumptions made about the humourist we examined in Chapter 1: if you manage to find the world funny, the thinking goes, you can't be terribly well connected *to* it. That said, Plum's *analysis* of cataclysmic events taking place around the world was often way off the mark, but that's a completely different argument: besides, so were many other people's – including a number of those in high office at the time.

No – the argument I'm going to start developing in a few paragraphs will need to be more nuanced than, say, the following one, which was published recently and whose writer's name I am withholding in order to spare his blushes:

> [T]he painful absence of parental – particularly maternal – affection drove the young man into an imaginary world, where he created his own comforts and generated his own laughs, in the process discovering himself as a storyteller. But in a sense, he never emerged from it.

This is just lazy thinking – and desperately old hat. In the fields of both psychology and literary criticism, we should have moved on from Vienna in the early 1900s; yet, as I've already noted, some studies of Wodehouse seem reluctant to do so. And in so doing, they violate Rule 1 on the Literary Criticism 101 course: that The Writer is Not Necessarily What He Writes. Or, put another way, Do Not Confuse the Created with Its Creator. For Plum, writing was not an escape from anything, but a job he loved to the exclusion of just about everything else. It was not the sublimated cry of his damaged inner child or a man who wished the world would go away.

And one last word on using the BBB as evidence to support the argument that Wodehouse couldn't recognize reality if it was presented to him on a tray garnished with watercress: if we're talking about 'reality', surely war represents the ultimate *suspension* of reality and not its ultimate expression? Total war is not the 'realest' condition there can be, but surely it is the *least* real, in which everything we take for granted is turned on its head. Suffering, grief, mass murder, the slaughter of innocent civilians, and the triumph of cruelty over every single one of mankind's civilized values can hardly be thought of as business as usual, unless, of course, you're a psychopath. And there was Plum, in the eye of that storm in Berlin, 60 years old, separated from his family and friends, in a country whose language he didn't speak, with only the sketchiest information about what was happening outside his immediate surroundings, having been driven from pillar to post across eastern Europe, and with no idea of what his own future held. Where, what or who could he look to for orientation? Where could *anyone?* A kind, decent man who found it difficult "to hate in the plural", Plum had only his innate good grace as his compass during that utterly bewildering and frightening period in his life. Perhaps it is more appropriate to bear *that* slant on the argument in mind before looking into his fictional works to supply ourselves with answers to real-life issues – and mistakenly using our answers to pass judgement on both the man and his work.

Here's what Plum had to say about being totally cut off from the world and how debilitating and mentally disorienting it proved, taken from the closing paragraphs of his fifth and final broadcast:

> It is a curious experience being completely shut off from the outer world, as one is in an internment camp. One lives principally on potatoes and rumours. One of my friends used to keep a notebook, in which he would jot down all the rumours that spread through the corridors, and they made amusing reading after the lapse of a few weeks. To military prisoners, I believe, camp rumours are known for some reason as "Blue Pigeons". We used to call them bedtime stories, and most dormitories would keep a corridor hound, whose duty it was to go through the corridors before lights-out, collecting the latest hot news.
>
> These bedtime stories never turned out to be true, but a rumour a day kept depression away, so they served their purpose. Certainly, whether owing to bedtime stories or simply to the feeling, which I myself had, that, if one was in, one was in and it was no use making heavy weather about it, the morale of the men at Tost was wonderful. I never met a more cheerful crowd, and I loved them like brothers.

The inmates had to build what reality they could: but note how their instinctual drive is *towards* reality and not away from it. They may have been making bricks without straw, but that was hardly their fault.

So what sort of world did Plum live in to have created what he did? Even though the physical locations he chose to inhabit for much of his life both pre- and post-war were often small and self-enclosing (the last being the small, sleepy hamlet of Remsenburg, Long Island, where he lived from 1955 until his death 20 years later), they were wholly permeable, and he could have ventured outside them had he wished. But by and large he rarely did, being simply too busy doing what he was driven to do. Writing requires long periods of peace and quiet, so someone with Plum's work ethic was never going to be a rabid socialite, even allowing for his natural shyness. As Stephen Fry notes in his review of Robert McCrum's biography, it's amazing the book is so interesting "considering [his life's] lack of eventfulness".

But that didn't stop Plum turning his gaze outwards. In his novels and stories, there's a steady drip of topical references to the world beyond the borders of his fiction: Hitler, Stalin, Gandhi, Manchester United, the Wall Street Crash, Mickey Mouse, Clark Gable, the splitting of the atom; and latterly student sit-ins, The Twist, Marilyn Monroe, and even the Beatles all make appearances. He in no way resembled that stereotype of the British high court judge who has to ask who the Beatles *are*; Plum never put himself 'above' the world in that way. But although he would regularly walk to the corner store on Montauk Highway to collect his newspaper, one gets the impression (which I'll explore more fully in Chapter 9) that the news it contained was not his main reason for buying it. I suspect, and his private scrapbook confirms this, that he was on the lookout for stories he could turn into plots, once again indicating that his work was always at the front of his mind, taking top priority among his thoughts. As such, while he was most definitely *in* the world, he was only intermittently *of* it. His was not an *inability* to engage but a *disinclination* – there were far more congenial things to do and think about than the antics of governments, or the lifestyles of the rich and famous. Simple, private things.

Thus, while Plum took what he wanted from the world, it was never going to be much, and it would rarely survive unalchemized into his writing. For example, in the middle of one of his playwriting partner Guy Bolton's celebrity-studded parties when Plum was the toast of Broadway, he would excuse himself and go off to do some solitary reading or writing, preferring to curl up with a book or a crossword rather than hobnob with A-listers like Rudolph Valentino, Enrico Caruso, George Gershwin, F. Scott Fitzgerald, Isadora Duncan and dozens of others whose stars have since faded from history. 'The Wodehouse Glide', as it became known among his friends, was a regular feature in the social gatherings he did bother to attend: one minute he was there, the next – gone, usually unannounced. Advancing age did nothing to make him more curious: when he turned 50, he and Ethel were apparently planning a round-the-world trip, but then started to question "if we want to see the ruddy world". The holiday never happened: dismissing the Grand Canyon, Niagara Falls and even the Taj Mahal, Plum claimed to prefer Droitwich, an unassuming spa town in the English Midlands, "which has no real merits". And he wasn't being sarcastic: by that stage, the world could show *his* world almost nothing. Witness Bertie's reluctance to go on Jeeves's much-anticipated 'Round-The-World Cruise' in *The Code of the Woosters*: when the latter points out that travel is educational, his employer merely comments, "I can't do with any more education. I was full up years ago".

Well, that was a long digression – but it needed saying. So let's go back to those early years in Plum's career, when his fictional world was busy establishing itself, and pick things up from there. To sum up what I'm going to argue for the rest of this chapter, Plum's created world – not his understanding or experience of the real world – gradually extricated itself from the constraints of reality in order to attain peak lightness.

Despite his equivocal relationship with the ebb and flow of real life, what Wodehouse called "sombre realism" did pop up on his literary radar on one or two telling occasions and gave him cause to stop and suck a thoughtful tooth during the 1910s (by the way, I'm using that phrase to describe happenings of greater pith and moment than the deeply sad, but essentially personal example of the grieving widower a few pages back). In a June 1916 *Vanity Fair* (US) article, Plum – then the magazine's theatre critic – drew his readers' attention to the plot of a tragedy written by fellow Brit John Galsworthy (he of *The Forsyte Saga*) that seemed to have profoundly affected him:

> Mr. Galsworthy's tragedy is not so much a play as a surgical operation. You come out of the theater with your complacency and self-satisfaction neatly removed, feeling that you were wrong in supposing yourself a pretty good sort of fellow, for if you were a pretty good sort of fellow you would spend a great deal more of your time trying to alleviate some of the suffering in the world. "Justice" is unique. It tears your heart-strings. It takes your soul and plays football with it.

By Plum's standards, this is strong, heartfelt stuff, and his habitual levity is put on hold for at least a few sentences while he confesses his temporary befuddlement. Two years previously, he had written Galsworthy off as a purveyor of "the ghastly Thoughtful Modern Drama (*morbus Galsworthiensis*)". Now, at least temporarily, things had changed: although the play was way outside his personal comfort zone, he was nevertheless full of admiration for Galsworthy's talent for spotting the dramatic potential in what must have begun life as "a paragraph at the bottom of a back page of any morning paper" which might have read: "Central Criminal Court. Before *Mr. Justice Floyd* and a jury, *William Falder* (23) was found guilty of forging a cheque. His lordship found himself unable to admit the plea of extenuating circumstances, and sentenced him to three years penal servitude". But then the playwright "thought of going a little deeper into the matter" and "the first-rate tragedy" *Justice* resulted, which, opined Plum, "ought to run forever".

In selecting this real-life story, Galsworthy had sought to highlight the appalling state of British prisons, which were, in reality, somewhat different from the cosy sanctuaries of Wodehouse's debut song lyric from 1904, 'Put Me in My Little Cell', where they more closely resemble hotels:

Where you didn't have to pay for board and lodging,
Where your meals were always ready on the nail,
When in Bow or Piccadilly Little Mary aches for skilly [a thin gruel-like soup]
Then you miss the quiet comfort of a jail.

By contrast, William Falder's main concern isn't rest, relaxation and regular meals: his treatment at the hands of the justice system eventually drives him to commit suicide. In the normal course of events, Plum would probably have moved on to review more cheerful shows, but something about *Justice* clearly haunted him. Back in England some years later, he actively sought Galsworthy's friendship.

More immediately, Plum's response was to produce a curious article for his next month's column about a "dramatic fixer" – a certain "Mister Whoosis" – brought in to 'doctor' *Justice*'s plot for a Broadway audience, thus converting a tragedy into something resembling a musical comedy and allowing "another happy ending" to win out "over logic and truth". For once in his life, Plum wrote these words as if leaving reality behind was somehow a bad thing – and note how the name "Whoosis" contains just a suggestion of the author's own…

Like Shakespeare with Bacon, here's how Whoosis effects the transformation, pointing out the deficiencies of the original plot to Galsworthy as he goes along in a kind of imagined masterclass:

- "Poor clerk" Falder is changed to "the son of a millionaire" who has lost all his money on Wall Street, but is determined to restore the family fortunes.

- Rather than being in love with a married woman in an abusive relationship, the fixer has Falder fall for the daughter of another millionaire who obstructs his suit on the grounds that he is no longer wealthy.

- Then, instead of Falder forging the cheque, he is framed by the managing clerk, Cokeson and the theft comes to court…

- …at which it is revealed that Falder is in fact the unacknowledged son of the trial judge.

- Sentenced nevertheless to three years in jail, there's a prison revolt, Falder escapes, the true story emerges, Cokeson is unmasked, and Falder, his name and fortunes restored, gets the girl.

Amid the jaw-dropping liberties taken with an original work of art, Whoosis talks of "peppy situation[s]", what the "matinée-girl" demands of a play, and the chance for the heroine "to come on in another dress". His main charge, however, is that Galsworthy has "chucked away all the dramatic possibilities… Why, gee! you don't make *anything* happen". Well, no, he might not have done, because he was trying to remain faithful to the story as it happened in real life. But real life isn't always as dramatic as it might be, and it needs the occasional leg up from the fixer. Or, in this case, a bunk over the wall into a whole different universe.

Amid all the knockabout fun, Plum is sailing quite close to the wind of what was going on within his own creative alchemy. By this stage in his life, he was regularly writing for the theatre, making *him* the fixer, not Whoosis; *he* was the one whose art spoke an entirely different language to that of a serious and sincere writer like Galsworthy, who, in Plum's imagination, "still wakes up screaming in the night after a nightmare in which he is sitting watching the fixed version of his play". On this occasion, Plum's own little set-up has a happy ending: the fixer's crimes against literature are deemed so great that he and his ilk have suddenly and thankfully "passed out of existence". Which they clearly hadn't, since Plum himself was within weeks of joining their ranks – although he was never let loose on anything quite as earnest as Galsworthy's dramatic oeuvre.

What was going on in the back of Wodehouse's mind as he wrote the Whoosis piece is difficult to fathom. It's clearly something that travels some way beneath the surface of the satire, since he was still mentioning *Justice* in his regular theatre column seven months later. He was emphatically on Galsworthy's side, despite the slight queasiness one senses in his original review at the play's 'warts and all' account of a tragedy that actually happened. Does all this depressing reality belong on stage, he seems to be demanding of himself; is this what theatre is *for*, to play "football" with your soul? And, having quickly decided it absolutely is despite the profound discomfort it provokes (how could such a massive fan of Shakespeare think otherwise?), it's as if he's reached the crossroads he proposes in his "two ways of writing novels" comment from 1935. Every writer on Wodehouse quotes it, and I'm no exception:

> [T]here are two ways of writing novels. One is mine, making the thing a sort of musical comedy without the music, and ignoring real life altogether; the other is going right down deep into life and not giving a damn.

Galsworthy had chosen to go "right down deep into life and not giv[e] a damn", where Plum couldn't follow him, and it seems this gave him a slight tremor of self-doubt that he uncharacteristically allowed to leak into print. As we see him poised on the brink of a whole new chapter in his professional life while he wrote his first Broadway lyrics, it's possible to detect some introspection going on, the posing of some fundamental questions. Any scruples about fixing reality would, of course, quickly evaporate, but it's interesting to note this incredibly mild outbreak of cold-ish feet in one so habitually self-assured.

Any vacillations Plum might have experienced in 1916 would, of course, been heavily amplified by the First World War rumbling away – albeit at a distance of three thousand miles – in the background. On the rare occasions he acknowledged its existence in his writing, Plum's usual mastery of tone tended to wobble and even flounder: in our own era of hair-trigger outrage when a solitary ill-advised Tweet can end a high-flying career, his default light-heartedness (he referred to the war in December 1914 as "the scuffle in Central Europe") can appear callous, and would have demanded emergency damage limitation. But then again, what could a comic writer possibly *do* when faced with such terrible and unprecedented human slaughter? By 1953's *Ring For Jeeves*, he could get away with dropping the unlikely bombshell that Jeeves "dabbled in it to a certain extent", but at the time his flippancy reads rather more iffily.

His first instincts were, as usual, to look on the bright side: in an interview for the *New York Times* in November 1915, he predicted that far from the English sense of humour being pounded to pieces by the experience of war, it would actually end up renewing itself. Hitherto, the nation's funny bone had been serviced with half-hearted, closeted, class-ridden and snobbish comedy, unlike its American counterpart, which was bold, brash, classless and fearless. In time, the English humourist would adopt the virtues of his transatlantic cousins – as Plum himself was already in the process of doing – and thus freed of his shackles, he would no longer be "bludgeoned" every time he "raise[d] his head" above the parapet. Soon, he opined, "[p]eople will be so depressed that they will become less critical of the methods used to cheer them up", and a new era in comedy would at last be free to dawn.

This was a somewhat niche and even obtuse take on the outcome of the war, though it did, to a degree, prove prophetic, as we'll see in the chapter on satire in Volume 3. But Plum knew what his American audience needed to read in 1915, and here he had a golden opportunity to set out his stall just as he was starting out as a stage lyricist on Broadway. The war 'over there' in Europe was of little concern to those of the American smart set who would read the article, or, we might speculate, to Plum – although it is virtually impossible at this remove to discover how much he kept up to date with the news from back home, or how remotely accurate anything he did read might have been.

That said, in the gaps between his wartime novels *Something Fresh* (1915), *Uneasy Money* (1917) and *Piccadilly Jim* (1918), Plum ventured a few tonally uncertain attempts to acknowledge the new realities – and they are, not surprisingly, far from his best work. In the story 'A Prisoner of War', published in the U.K. *Strand Magazine* in March 1915, a rich, feckless American, Hailey Bannister, escapes from Paris at the onset of hostilities and washes up penniless at his aunt's house in the English countryside, where she puts him through a regime of hard labour ("the simple-life treatment") to rid him of his arrogance. Her tough love bears fruit, and as George Simmers remarks in his contribution to the excellent *Middlebrow Wodehouse* collection of essays, the story constitutes perhaps the only example in the fiction of the period where the lead character is redeemed by fleeing war rather than heading towards it. The plot opens with the aunt, the redoubtable Lora DeLane Porter, firing her odd-job man for "singing patriotic songs in the garden at midnight", and she would have further angered every British Lion with the following paragraph:

> From the beginning of hostilities Mrs. Porter's attitude towards the European War had been clearly defined. It could continue, provided it did not bother her. If it bothered her it must stop.

Although intended humorously, the story would still have been slightly off-message for a wartime audience. Not only was it swimming against the tide of populist opinion, it was just begging to be misconstrued – and Plum was lucky that nothing appears to have come of it, at least on this occasion. Certainly if we throw forward to the Berlin broadcasts in 1941, we can see the literary parallels all too clearly: Wodehouse, that "born neutral", was sending his humour out into a conflicted world that was anything but neutral, and which didn't take kindly to any kind of writing that muddied its limpid patriotic pools, however light-hearted it was intended to be. Context, as ever, is all.

And so the timing of Plum's update of *The Swoop*, his absurdist fantasy from 1909 which crossed the Atlantic to become *The Military Invasion of America* in July 1915, could not have been more unfortunate, coming a matter of weeks after German U-Boats sank the passenger liner *Lusitania* with the loss of 128 American lives. In Plum's conceit, America has been overrun by Germany and Japan, whose post-victory martial rivalries are played out not in bloody trenches – or on the high seas – but in the vaudeville theatres of New York. In the opening Editor's Note, Plum facetiously remarks that "Realism…can be carried too far", and fears he might have "painted in too lurid colors the horrors of a foreign invasion", before delivering up a half-baked and no doubt hurried reworking of the original, which had grown a fine set of greying whiskers in the six years since it had first appeared. It is perhaps the least convincing piece Wodehouse ever published, and proof – if any were needed – that The War to End All Wars had instantly and irrevocably altered every perspective that preceded it. Once again, no one in America seemed to pay it much attention, and it's perhaps only with hindsight that its absurdist take on militarism sits so uncomfortably with what we now know to have been happening over in Europe. Similarly ill-thought-through was 'Diary of a War-Time Honeymoon' from May 1916, which featured the serial misadventures of a rich American on his postnuptial vacation amid the privations of wartime London, where bars close at 2.30 in the afternoon and the street lighting doesn't work. Actually, it was switched off to hinder bombing raids from Germany's Zeppelin airships – the so-called "baby-killers" – that ended up dispatching over 500 British civilians. Maybe not the kind of material to make jokes from, then.

Of course, Plum was not alone in floundering through these unprecedented historical events, and we'd be rather smug if we thought we could have done any better at such a distant remove. "Keep It Unreal" might have been the best policy – and so things proved. After these brief but telling quivers, it was in the medium of the musical theatre that things began to stabilize. On firmer tonal ground after America belatedly joined the fighting with Germany in 1917, his commercial instinct would have told him where he should follow the money, and the book and lyrics for the patriotic show *The Girl Behind the Gun* quickly resulted. A comic disquisition on love set against a background of mass slaughter, it debuted on Broadway the following year, but was a far bigger box office smash in London where, postwar, it transferred with the unlikely new title of *Kissing Time*. No copies of the libretto are known to survive, but we can get a reasonable idea of the show's overall tenor from Plum's lyrics, which make it a kind of *Oh! What a Lovely War* shorn of its politics, pacifism – and much of its irony. Amid the general air of jokiness, modern sensibilities are likely to blench at the sentiments of 'Back to the Dear Old Trenches' (a variation on the theme of 'Put Me in My Little Cell') in which the three male leads declare themselves happy to face German artillery shells but not their wives' scolding tongues. Awkward tonal shifts once again abound, strikingly so when this grim preamble sung by Colonel Servan gives way to the knockabout love song 'I Like It, I Like It':

> *Over the top through shot and shell,*
> *Thro fire and hell*
> *I'll lead my herd,*
> *The fighting Forty-third,*
> *Smashing our way along*
> *Over the top where bullets soar,*

Where cannons roar,
Where heroes fall,
Yet off in the distance through it all,
I'll hear this wondrous song…

The show's popularity with critics and audiences alike indicates that once again it's we in the 21ˢᵗ century who have to amend any squeamishness we might experience. Moreover, according to Barry Day, the show remained a favourite of Plum's, and when he died there were notes on his bedside table indicating that over 50 years later, he was still revising some of its lyrics. Quite what relevance the show might have had in the 1970s is difficult to say – it may have tanked or have ridden the wave of absurdist treatments of war ushered in by Joseph Heller's *Catch-22*, whose premise is that reality has grown so unreal that nothing surprises anyone. Perhaps *The Girl Behind the Gun* was simply way ahead of its time. And one final thought on this subject: it's instructive to note that the *Wipers Times*, a news-sheet produced under incredible duress by British front-line soldiers in the trenches of Flanders, somehow managed to adopt a humorous tone distinctly reminiscent of Plum's work for the *Globe;* in fact, some of it is so similar, he might as well have written it. Which raises the prospect that he might perhaps have been more on-message than we – at 100-plus years' remove, following long, uninterrupted periods of peace – can possibly grasp.

Anyway, come November 1918 and the Armistice, Wodehouse and the world once again moved into alignment. A little over a year later, normal service was resumed in the short story 'The Man Who Married an Hotel' – the first of a series he would later co-opt into 1921's *Indiscretions of Archie* – which begins thus:

> Peace had come at last. The Great War, with all its horrors—its spy plays, its war novels, its articles by our military expert, and its revues with patriotic first-act finales—had passed away like a dark cloud. The time of Reconstruction had arrived, and all the old problems had sneaked back like unwanted dogs from the background into which war had thrust them. There they all were, clamouring for attention, just as they had been five years ago. England was asking herself: "How about Ireland? How about Labour? And what on earth are we to do with Archie?"

This passage was cut from the later collection, probably because the war could now safely be relegated, at least in Plum's purview, to the status of a bad dream. Despite the fact that its central character, Archie Moffam, has served in France for four years, he seems to have emerged completely unscathed both physically and mentally; in fact, he talks, thinks and acts just like any other Wodehouse knut who didn't get his spats muddy. In the book version, he opens his account by complaining that the Hotel Cosmopolis – the seven-star establishment that provides the book's portmanteau structure – doesn't seem to offer an overnight shoe-cleaning service, and that he has been kept awake by a dripping tap. How different from those dear old trenches – although in a nod to realism, an amnesiac war veteran, known only as "the Sausage Chappie" for much of the book, does help Archie in and out of some scrapes.

War, it seems, had not chastened Archie's creator. Rather, as he had predicted in that 1915 *New York Times* article, it emboldened him to damn the torpedoes and write exactly what he wanted, and, of course, what he thought his readers would like. From this perspective, the odd withdrawal symptom such as those detailed above was perhaps inevitable: the Whoosis in Wodehouse's aesthetics would from now on reign (virtually) unchallenged, and he stuck to what he knew – and knew he did best – for the rest of his career.

As an aside, it's interesting to note that adaptations of Wodehouse's work in various media – particularly film and TV – are almost invariably set in the 1920s and 30s, and not the Edwardian period that is the bedrock of their writer's sensibility. It's as if the years spent working through post-traumatic stress on both sides of the Atlantic – symbolized by Bright Young Things dancing the Charleston and drinking cocktails against an Art Deco backdrop – is better suited to Plum's stories than the epoch of tailcoats and bodices that Wodehouse tells us *actually* inspired them. In other words, his stories sit best within an era that was trying its best to forget, avoid or offset reality by any means possible – not record, confront or dominate it.

It's clear to us now that Plum could never have thrived as a socially engaged writer even if he'd wanted to. His temperament just wasn't right for the job, and by the 1920s he was leaving only the occasional anchoring point in reality to prevent his created world completely slipping its moorings. In the *Ukridge* collection of stories and *Bill the Conqueror* (both from 1924), just about all we're left with is a precise geography of London; the latter even boasts a car chase you can still follow perfectly accurately on a road map. But all the rest is wonderfully implausible and improbable and has no truck whatever with the ugly truth. Certainly by the time the ironically titled 'A Slice of Life' appeared in 1926, Plum's skirmishes with reality were over, the issue dead and buried – and his writing was all the better for it. At the beginning of that story, in the bar parlour of the Angler's Rest, a debate is raging over a "film-serial" entitled *The Vicissitudes of Vera*, in which a young lady is nearly turned into a lobster by a mad professor with a grudge against her. "This seemed plausible", the narrator mischievously comments, before noting how another contributor questions its veracity: "I don't like stories like that", he said. "They aren't true to life". Cue the following intervention from Mr Mulliner:

> "[Y]ou, sir, have opened up a subject on which I happen to hold strong views – to wit, the question of what is and what is not true to life. How can we, with our limited experience, answer that question? For all we know, at this very moment hundreds of young women all over the country may be in the process of being turned into lobsters. Forgive my warmth, but I have suffered a good deal from the sceptical attitude of mind which is so prevalent these days."

At which point, he relates the story of his brother Wilfred's Raven Gipsy Face-Cream, which, although a wildly implausible shaggy dog story (or, as he puts it, "a little outside of the ordinary run of the average man's experience"), he insists is "nothing but the bare truth". This becomes something of a catchphrase for Mr Mulliner, as he delights in taxing his listeners' credulity to its limits.

But to Wodehouse, there was no longer any epistemological issue to confront. Lightness had triumphed, both in his mind and on the page, and he was writing with an ease and fluency his previous work had hinted at but never quite attained. He was now – finally – the sole owner and proprietor of his own created world. The expression of this final divorce from reality was the mimesis – the representation of reality – that he had been busy honing for 20 years, and it's some of the deeper roots of the "Wodehousean" style into all its mid-season glory that I'm going to start looking at now.

1902–1970

Chapter 5
Alternative Realities

The principle I always go on in writing a novel is to think of the characters in terms of actors in a play.

PGW in *The Paris Review*

It was all so exactly as it would have happened in a dream. He had gone to sleep thinking of this girl, and here she was.

A Gentleman of Leisure

[Writing] was like planning a pleasant surprise for a child.

In Alcala

[They catch the train and live happily ever afterwards.]

Love Among the Chickens (1906 version)

In 1921, *Strand Magazine* published a gushing profile of one of its most prolific contributors as a curtain-raiser for a new set of Jeeves and Bertie stories, and tried to put its finger on what made him tick:

> P.G. wanders happily up and down the world, watching humanity at work and at play, rather like a curious and intelligent boy who has just left school and has not yet had time to lose hope and interest. Where most of us see only gloom and despair and ugliness, P.G. sees humour and laughter and beauty.

The 40-year-old married veteran of 25 or so books might have allowed himself a wry grin if he saw himself described as a recent school leaver, since the question of whether he ever truly grew up was one he asked himself into old age: "Mentally", he wrote in 1953, aged 72, "I seem not to have progressed a step since I was eighteen". It's a perspective whose adhesive qualities have proved remarkably long-lasting, since even now it's widely assumed that the taproot of Plum's creativity is a textbook case of arrested development married to a phenomenal literary ability. But really, that's nowhere near good enough, even for a shorthand summary in a publicity blurb. For a start, the *Strand* quote tacitly assumes that with age automatically comes a loss of "hope and interest", and because Plum appeared not to have lost those qualities, but to have maintained the ability to experience "humour and laughter and beauty", he was somehow the Peter Pan of literature. And while it's true that he did manage to keep the forces of "doom and despair and ugliness" at a greater arm's length than most of us are capable of – at least in his writing – it doesn't follow that the guiding principles of his voice, style and choice of subject exclusively originated in his youth and then somehow stopped growing and changing.

Wodehouse's writing career falls into two sections, as I've already noted. His mature period which arrived at around the time of that *Strand* quote, is pretty straightforward to write about, given that once Wodehouse had found his voice, he used it consistently throughout the rest of his career with only minor tweaks here and there. *Finding* that voice was quite another matter: until it reached that point in his early 40s, Plum's literary odyssey was an unholy mess. This chapter is going to be the biggest ragbag of all since, having looked at Plum's gradual retreat from realism, we must now start to investigate exactly what he started to replace it *with*. And comic melodrama, as Plum understood it, is as good a lead-in as any.

The first thing to note is that Plum knew his stuff. Although he's regularly praised for his facility with language, he's rarely credited with any great literary awareness; by which I mean a knowledge of how literature actually works *behind* those elegant phrases and well-turned metaphors. And yet it was there, right from the start, presumably distilled from the prose, poetry and drama he had read as a schoolboy. In 1902, aged 21, he involved himself with a publication called *The Onlooker*, to whose November 1 edition he contributed a column of anonymous reviews entitled 'Stage and Stalls'. À propos of a play called *Captain Kettle*, he wrote:

> The audience at a melodrama does not demand that the probabilities shall be respected or that there should be a great deal of character action. What it looks for is incident.

Obvious, yes, but valuable as an early example of the close attention Plum would always pay to the tastes of his paying public. But a more nuanced understanding of technique is evident in the next paragraph, in which he contrasts melodrama with burlesque, addressing the somewhat niche question of whether it is ever possible to take melodrama with

anything more than a pinch of salt, since it seems to intrinsically burlesque itself. In *Captain Kettle*, "the result is that all through, with the
exception of some serious dialogues, the authors appear to be laughing
at themselves, and this, we think, is a mistake". In this observation, the
child proves the father of the man: comic melodrama – as written for
the stage – was without doubt one of the deepest roots of Plum's mature
style, but filtered through a sophisticated understanding of its impact on
the overall tenor of his writing. Plum wasn't going to fall into the same
trap that *Captain Kettle*'s authors had, in his view, blundered into, even
though he clearly had a facility for writing in that melodramatic style –
as he proved in 1908 when he inserted the note-perfect parody 'Women,
Wine and Song!' into the *Globe By The Way Book* he was editing. This is
the opening of Chapter 4:

> Marjorie recoiled from the door. It was locked! She was
> alone with this man!
>
> "Aha, my pretty one!" said Luke, cynically, lighting a ciga-
> rette. "So we are alone! At last! You shrink from me? You
> spurn me? Why? I love you. Damn you, I love you. Why do
> you spurn me? True, I am a murderer, a forger, a thief, and
> a liar, but otherwise I'm all right. You love this Baldwin
> Berkeley? Pah! I will follow you to the end of the earth."
>
> "You won't," cried Marjorie.
>
> "Why won't I?" enquired Luke, cynically, lighting a
> cigarette.
>
> "Because," said Marjorie, all the woman in her flashing
> from her eyes, "I'm not going there."

Great fun, but not a line of writing Plum would ultimately pursue, at
least in its pure form. Melodrama is, in essence, reality on steroids, even
more pumped up than the mock-epic inflation of Pope's *The Rape of the
Lock* we examined earlier: but do you play it straight, or, as here, with a
massive wink to the audience? Not being alert to this crux can lead, said
the sage young Wodehouse back in 1902, to an unevenness of tone that
undercuts *Captain Kettle*'s undoubted attractions. If you're determined
to write melodrama, have no shame and lay it on with a trowel – or,

as Plum puts it, make it move with "a snap and a rattle" and let it be packed with incident. Give no quarter to reticence: at least *appear* to have 100% confidence in what you're writing. To do otherwise is to effectively apologize for the style you're writing in, unless, of course, you happen to be poking fun at it – which was a temptation Plum couldn't often resist, since his ear for the ridiculous was too highly developed. In *Jill the Reckless*, the narrator informs us that "[t]here was once a melodrama where the child of the persecuted heroine used to dissolve the gallery in tears by saying "Happiness? What *is* happiness, moth-aw?" – which ickiness (or in Plum's view bathos) was not a million miles away from the words Galsworthy had placed in the mouth of the repentant Cokeson following Falder's death in *Justice*, that 'realistic' play we encountered in the previous chapter: "No one'll touch him now! Never again! He's safe with gentle Jesus!" Quite how Plum managed to stifle a giggle from his reviewer's seat when that closing line was delivered – immediately followed by the curtain – is difficult to imagine. His reaction might well have been that of Hamilton Beamish in *The Small Bachelor* when he catches Fanny Welch red-handed with a stolen jewel-case and she feeds him a sob story that he doesn't buy for a moment:

> Fanny: If you was out of work and starvin' and you had to sit and watch your poor old ma bendin' over the washtub…
>
> Hamilton: All wrong!
>
> Fanny: What do you mean, all wrong?
>
> Hamilton: Mere crude Broadway melodrama. That stuff might deceive some people, but not me.
>
> Fanny: Well, I thought it was worth trying.

In 'Sundered Hearts' the young golfer listening to the Oldest Member's tale of love lost and found baulks at his use of "the white mantle that covered the earth" as a substitute for the rather more prosaic "snow". This, he tells the storyteller, might prove the thin end of the melodramatic wedge: next thing you know, your hero will "find [his wife] dead in the snow, covered except for her face, on which still lingered that faint, sweet smile which he remembered so well". If you're going to carry on like that, he says, "I'm going home". Seemingly chastened, the old buster continues his tale in a less florid manner for a few sentences before delivering precisely those lines. "I call that a dirty trick", the young man erupts. And in 'Fair Play for Audiences', Plum suggests that theatregoers should strike, or at least demand a refund, if "any character or characters looks or look at a locket or lockets containing the photograph or photographs of his or their mother or mothers".

By contrast, Plum's own agenda was not to convince, or to tug at heartstrings quite so shamelessly, but simply to entertain. However, that didn't imply that anything went and discipline could be sacrificed; in fact, it was quite the reverse. Like Whoosis, Plum edits and refashions reality into something faster, neater and more compelling than life as we might live it, not simply reporting what's already there with a bit of gentle editing and re-emphasis. So if *Justice*'s power comes from its plausibility (Galsworthy insisting that "it more or less happened like this, and let that be a lesson to us all"), Whoosis's version revels in its self-conscious *unreality* – and this has everything to do with how the writer controls the reality within the play or story itself. By bringing the plot *inside* his created world, the writer frees himself from the straitjackets of history, chronology, precedent and plausibility in order to manufacture his own version that works within the boundaries of his fiction. And so he's not exaggerating reality – as in melodrama – but fashioning it into something quite *other*. And if he's a good writer of this type, this new world will be whole and consistent *on its own terms*. Indeed, Plum's trademark lightness owes its roots to the artistic freedom the creation of this alternative reality grants him. He would never have chosen a story so confining as Galsworthy's, not least because Plum's plots are all ultimately about escape, possibility, and moving onwards and outwards. And you can only achieve these desirable outcomes for your characters if you own and control the reality you create (more of which in Volume 2).

So what Plum ended up with – and what we find in his best books and stories – is not melodrama's augmented reality, but an alternative reality altogether. And crucial to the success of his fantasy worlds was how absolutely straight he was to play his bat. His plots and characters may have been preposterous, and there are many occasions where his narrators draw the reader's attention to this, but we are never left in any doubt as to Plum's ultimate sincerity. He, and we, *must* believe in what we're reading from the get-go, even if – paradoxically – it's not remotely believable. Take the Blandings novels, for example: there's usually a brief description of the weather, and BANG! off they go without further ado, with Plum demanding our unconditional suspension of disbelief in very short order. And before we know it most of us are seduced, not just by the story but also the peculiar reality it sits *inside*. After all, why waste time defining your story's relationship with reality when you can sidestep the issue entirely and jump straight into the story?

This is Wodehouse's theatrical sensibility at work. The minute you set foot in a theatre, you're well aware that what you're watching isn't real. You know you've travelled to a building with a stage, and are set to watch a bunch of people in borrowed clothes speaking someone else's words. Put like that, it sounds like a ridiculous thing to do, but it's the job of everyone involved in the production to convince you otherwise, and to help you put aside your disbelief in the most satisfactory way possible. Which was, to Plum, a most congenial challenge, both onstage and in his fiction. Moreover, with no important messages to convey, no issues with credibility or accuracy, no need to be seen to be clever, this was a scenario that opened up many new possibilities, as Plum occasionally delights in telling us. In *Bill the Conqueror*, the narrator remarks that in real life, were we to seek an appointment with media mogul Sir George Pyke, we would have to jump through a tortuous set of bureaucratic hoops. But in "a story such as this", the artifice of fiction allows us to breeze right in without bothering to knock. As such, the reader is endowed with "all the advantages of a disembodied spirit…[h]e can go anywhere and see everything" while remaining "noiseless and invisible". This lends an extra dimension to the story, allowing the reader to be "uplifted, entertained and instructed" more successfully than if he were bogged down in life's minutiae. Moreover, the writer doesn't have to keep stopping to explaining everything away, accounting for the smallest detail or justifying why something has happened. It simply does. And we accept that. Or rather, we are *made* to accept it.

Plum's mastery of alternative reality is no mean feat; but even his patented brand of lightness didn't arrive fully-formed. Rather, it was the fruit of a great deal of experimentation in those early years, making its root system long, tangled and therefore difficult to explore. For example, although his bread and butter in those early years was his "life as it is" school stories and hack work for *The Globe*, he had intermittently flirted with a completely different style of writing: stories with fast-moving, scene-based, musical-comedy-type progression – not entirely dissimilar to *Captain Kettle* – that served to heighten his readers' sense of unreality, drawing on fables, fairy stories, medieval allegories, and even pantomime to create worlds that are aggressively fantastical, whimsical, and at times even absurd while remaining controlled and true to themselves. So these stories, written between 1903 and the early 1920s, are effectively stepping stones to his mature style as it manifests itself both in his prose works and his writing for the stage. In effect, they're a sort of halfway house to both, casting Plum as a sort of Whoosis-in-training. And while they may all be decidedly minor works, hindsight allows us to judge that collectively they would prove of greater significance than at first seems apparent. They include the story sequence *A Man of Means*, the revised version of his novel *The Prince and Betty*, the political satire *The Swoop!*, and short stories such as 'Sir Agravaine' and 'The Coming of Gowf'. There may even have been further titles in this vein, either planned and not executed or sadly lost to posterity, for in the first volume of his 1902–05 commonplace books, Plum speculates in a note to self that he might one day "collect all my fairy stories under the title *Tales of Aldebaran*". He occasionally jotted down possible scenarios for further "fantastic" tales, one such note reading as follows: "For fairy story: king who was so rich that he slept in sheets made of banknotes stitched together".

Unfortunately, it appears that only one of these mooted projects ever materialized: a short story written in 1903 entitled 'The Idle King', which was Plum's sole contribution to *The Sunday Magazine*, an improving journal aimed mainly at Christian women. The monarch of the title (who is the King of Aldebaran) grows so bored doing nothing all day, he sets off to see the world and learns how having a job can lead to satisfaction and personal fulfilment, even a task as menial as breaking large stones into smaller ones. The tale is punctuated, musical theatre style, with three songs, ending on this grand moralistic flourish which, performed by the King himself, is just aching for a tune:

> *You may do whatever sort of work you please.*
> *You may do whatever task you're most inclined to.*
> *You may do it on the earth or on the seas.*
> *You may do it in the air, if you've a mind to.*
> *You may choose to work at sums or plough your lands.*
> *You may choose an ordin-ary or a rum thing.*
> *You may do it with your head or with your hands.*
> *But every one in future must do something!*

More than anything else, 'The Idle King', complete with its improving message brings to mind (or my mind, anyway) an Aesop's Fable shot through the prism of Walt Disney, only more sophisticated and less gooey: it's short and has a clear, ordered set-up; scene-by-scene exposition; and a nice, neat moral at the end. It was a way of structuring a story that evidently appealed to Plum, as did the ethos that anything, no matter how implausible, is possible to use as a story, provided you keep its telling as tight and disciplined as possible. Let your imagination roam where it will, as long as you are in full control of your material, you will have a viable story.

Interestingly, as a seven-year-old, Plum wrote a short story about a song thrush which, at 99 words, has many of the features of an Aesopian tale, and is possessed of some elegant and sophisticated rhythmical cadences within its prose:

> About five years ago in a wood there was a Thrush who built her nest in a Poplar tree (/), and sang so beautifully that all the worms came up from their holes and the ants laid down their burdens. and the crickets stopped their mirth, and the moths settled all in a row to hear her. she sang a song as if she were in heaven – going up higher and higher as she sang.
>
> at last the song was done and the bird came down panting (/).
>
> Thank you said all the creatures.
>
> Now my story is ended.
> Pelham G. Wodehouse

Which is really rather lovely, both in sentiment and execution. Later I'll be discussing Plum's rigid adherence to the Aristotelian principles of beginnings, middles and ends in stories, but really we need look no further than this (I've inserted forward slashes within the quote to indicate the transitions). The precocious little blighter had it off pat before he hit double figures – and note how the subject of the poem is a hard-working *performer*: the Thrush as leading lady, the lesser creatures her adoring public, stopped in their tracks by the sublimity of her art. The stage and the page already seem to be equal partners in his writing.

A second stylistic feature within this overlooked body of work is the care with which Plum regulates the narrative speed within their boundaries. The golden rule was not to let the reader's attention drift, and Plum occasionally allows his narrators in other works to break the fourth wall so they can let us know what they think they're up to. In this example, from the opening paragraph of *A Damsel in Distress*, we are told why writers should get going from the git-go:

> [I]n these days of rush and hurry, a novelist works at a disadvantage. He must leap into the middle of his tale with as little delay as he would employ boarding a moving tram-car. He must get off the mark with the smooth swiftness of a jack-rabbit surprised while lunching. Otherwise people throw him aside and go out to picture palaces.

Speed is of the essence. But even if you manage to grab the punters straight out of the traps, there can be no let up. This is from *The Girl on the Boat*:

> A story, if it is to grip the reader, should, I am aware, go always forward. It should march. It should leap from crag to crag like the chamois of the Alps.

In this unusual metaphor (one he was to grow inordinately fond of), Plum asserts that boring interstitial stuff should be jumped over or at least given the shortest of shrifts in order to get to the story's high points; so what its plotline needs in addition to speed is economy and selected emphasis. Here's that chamois again, this time from *Summer Lightning*, where Plum justifies "flit[ting] abruptly" from one character's activities to another:

> It is perhaps as well, therefore, that we did not waste valuable time watching Hugo in the process of digesting Percy Pilbeam's sensational announcement, for it would have been like looking at a statue. If the reader will endeavour to picture Rodin's Thinker in a dinner-jacket and trousers, he will have got the general idea.

You can't hang about producing a "faithful record of events" when you've got an audience to entertain, so the flitting was all in a good cause. Over 30 years later, he was saying the same thing in *Ice in the Bedroom*: the writer must "select and abridge, giving merely the gist of [his characters'] remarks and not a full stenographic transcript".

By the 1920s, Plum tirelessly reminds his readers that brevity is now one of his watchwords. Clearly the minatory advice of those editors he had previously despised in 'The Goal-Keeper and the Plutocrat' had been taken on board, as encapsulated in "Corky" Corcoran's observation from 1923's 'The Return of Battling Billson': "the true artist's instinct", he informs us, "[is] that the secret of all successful prose is the knowledge of what to omit". By this stage in Plum's career, "drama" and "prose" are virtually interchangeable, and he ruminates further on this desirable straightforwardness when he allows the narrator of *Something Fresh* to indulge in some *ex cathedra* dramatic theory. In the following extract, he considers the new discipline of writing stories for the screen, helpfully informing us that even the sleepy village of Market Blandings now has a sort-of cinema in a room above the grocer's shop:

> The reason why all we novelists with bulging foreheads and expensive educations are abandoning novels and taking to writing motion-picture scenarii is because the latter are so infinitely the more simple and pleasant.

Once again, clarity achieved through simplicity of expression seems to be the touchstone; in a motion picture script, the scene Plum is about to describe at some length – when J. Preston Peters discovers the loss of his precious Fourth Century BC Cheops Scarab ring which has been innocently purloined by Lord Emsworth – "would be over in an instant". Plum hadn't yet had any prolonged experience of working in the movies, but having clearly attended a few, he appears to envy the scenario writer's limited range of options which would serve to keep his plot simple, pacy and engaging. The talkies hadn't yet arrived, so onto the screen would flash the caption…

MR PETERS DISCOVERS THE LOSS OF THE SCARAB

…immediately followed by a shot of "a little angry man with a sharp face and starting eyes" whose face would first register "**DISCOVERY** and then **DISMAY**". The audience immediately gets the picture and the story can quickly move on. But this economy isn't possible in the pages of a novel: instead, Plum laments, the laws of prose composition "demand a greater elaboration", which seems to irk him. And, of course, in life, neatness is an even rarer commodity – to quote Bertie once again, it does tend to "drool on". So it is the writer's duty to ensure that this drooling is kept to a minimum, and that his prose yields its sense briskly and efficiently.

In an example of how *not* to do it, Plum once again creates an example dreamed up by the "scenario-lizards" of the silent film, who have replaced economy of that first effort with a verbosity born of indiscipline. At the opening of *The Girl on the Boat's* Chapter 4, instead of the overly-purple…

AND SO, CALM AND GOLDEN, THE DAYS WENT BY, EACH FRAUGHT WITH HOPE AND YOUTH AND SWEETNESS, LINKING TWO YOUNG HEARTS IN SILKEN FETTERS FORGED BY THE LAUGHING LOVE GOD

…Plum substitutes the more prosaic but far more efficient, "It was the fourth day of the voyage". "That is my story and I mean to stick to it", he shamelessly informs us, refusing to justify his insistence on bald, stripped back prose any further. This habit of "plain frank statement" is part and parcel of what he later described in *Performing Flea* as "having as little stuff in between as possible", moving from scene to scene with the minimum of verbiage and distraction – and giving his readers the fewest possible chances to drift away.

That said, you can lose your audience another way – by leaping *so* fast and frequently that the reader literally loses the plot. Although Bertie is all for speed (if you don't "grip the customers, they'll walk out on you"), he has this to say in *Thank You, Jeeves* about the writer who is over-eager to move things on:

> I must say, as a general rule, I always bar stories where the chap who's telling them skips lightly from point to point and leaves you to work it out for yourself as best you can just what has happened in the interim. I mean to say, the sort of story where Chapter Ten ends with the hero trapped in the underground den and Chapter Eleven starts with him being the life and soul of a gay party at the Spanish Embassy.

It's a delicate balance between speed and orientation: controlling the flow of the plot is crucial to avoid the twin evils of boredom (too slow) or bewilderment (too fast), with the overall aim of keeping the audience's collective posterior glued to its seat, whether it is in the dress circle or in front of the fire at home.

More than anywhere else in the Wodehouse canon, speed is the principle that drives the narrative progression in *William Tell Told Again*, a glorious anomaly in his work published one year on from 'The Idle King' in 1904. More or less a scene-driven stage play with brief linking passages, it is nevertheless a prose tale squarely aimed at children – not a market Plum regularly targeted but one, significantly, lacking vast reserves of patience. Set in the Alps, both style and imagery helpfully underpin that earlier chamois simile – and it certainly marches and leaps, especially in comparison with Friedrich von Schiller's rambling five-act version from 1804 on which Plum likely based it. Here are the two opening paragraphs in full:

> Once upon a time, more years ago than anybody can remember, before the first hotel had been built or the first Englishman had taken a photograph of Mont Blanc and brought it home to be pasted in an album and shown after tea to his envious friends, Switzerland belonged to the Emperor of Austria, to do what he liked with.

> One of the first things the Emperor did was to send his friend Hermann Gessler to govern the country. Gessler was not a nice man, and it soon became plain that he would never make himself really popular with the Swiss. The point on which they disagreed in particular was the question of taxes. The Swiss, who were a simple and thrifty people, objected to paying taxes of any sort. They said they wanted to spend their money on all kinds of other things. Gessler, on the other hand, wished to put a tax on everything, and, being Governor, he did it. He made everyone who owned a flock of sheep pay a certain sum of money to him; and if the farmer sold his sheep and bought cows, he had to pay rather more money to Gessler for the cows than he had paid for the sheep. Gessler also taxed bread, and biscuits, and jam, and buns, and lemonade, and, in fact, everything he could think of, till the people of Switzerland determined to complain. They appointed Walter Fürst, who had red hair and looked fierce; Werner Stauffacher, who had grey hair and was always wondering how he ought to pronounce his name; and Arnold of

Melchthal, who had light-yellow hair and was supposed to
know a great deal about the law, to make the complaint.

And that's it. Every one of these brisk, business-like sentences has
a job to do in carrying the plot forward so we can get to the funny
dialogue quicker. In fact, Wodehouse uses a mere 287 words to establish the tale's entire opening scenario, complete with its main protagonists, while still managing to sneak in the odd satirical swipe. All
the way through what follows, he never takes his foot off the accel-
erator, powering along right to the end, where the tale's crisp moral
("one great strength we have: we are united. And united we need fear
no foe") comes and goes before we're given the chance to get bored.
Aesop would have been proud of him.

It's perhaps significant that Wodehouse dedicated the book to Biddy
O'Sullivan, the young daughter of his bohemian actor friends Denis
and Elizabeth O'Sullivan, whom we'll meet in the next chapter. While
wheeling his charge around in her pram, he might well have buffed
up some half-remembered stories from his own infancy to help keep
her quiet. And this hadn't been Plum's first stint at keeping young girls
amused: the dedicatees of 1902's *The Pothunters* were the Bowes-Lyons
sisters, Joan, Effie and Ernestine (aged 15, 13 and 10 when he first met
them), in whose company he had spent considerable time, and whose
bons mots and behaviour he had regularly recorded in his notebooks.
Thus mindful of the limited patience of children, and needing to free
himself from the more attention-sapping demands of plausibility and
causation, it's tempting to speculate that this breezy style of storytelling
was first tried out on his female charges, and some years later on his
young stepdaughter Leonora, when he first met her aged 11 in 1915.

One group of fantastical tales Plum regularly referenced was that
of King Arthur and the Knights of the Round Table, whether in the
medieval originals or Alfred, Lord Tennyson's epic reworking, *The
Idylls of the King*. Indeed, the very first example of Plum's writing we
possess is a sort of battlefield epic (or "a bit of poertory I made up",
as he described it) involving dead pets and men which he wrote aged
5. Throughout his career, he used the figures of Sir Tristram and Sir
Galahad as casual metaphors for male gallantry towards women, the
medieval forerunners of Bertie's *preux chevalier* ("one's either *preux* or one
isn't", he tells us in *Much Obliged, Jeeves*). But in his parody 'Sir Agravaine'
from 1912, Plum once again borrowed the fable form for a cautionary
tale of an ugly and incompetent knight who, unlike his better-looking

and more chivalrous colleagues at Camelot, never expects to win a maiden's heart. Significantly, the story begins by deploring his alleged sources' long-windedness and inability to structure a story:

> I have found it necessary to touch the thing up a little here and there, for writers in those days were weak in construction. Their idea of telling a story was to take a long breath and start droning away without any stops or dialogue till the thing was over.

Not so Plum. Even the title of the story doesn't escape, which he has been forced to "condense":

> In the original it ran, "'How it came about that ye good Knight Sir Agravaine ye Dolorous of ye Table Round did fare forth to succor [sic] a damsel in distress and after divers journeyings and perils by flood and by field did win her for his bride and right happily did they twain live ever afterwards,' by Ambrose ye monk."

> It was a pretty snappy title for those times, but we have such a high standard in titles nowadays that I have felt compelled to omit a few yards of it.

Once again, Plum's account bowls along, oiled by hefty chunks of rapid-fire dialogue linked by a minimum of scene-setting. Nestling among these theatrical exchanges is "the first genuine cross-talk that had ever occurred in those dim, pre-music-hall days. In years to come dialogue on these lines was to be popular throughout the length and breadth of Great Britain. But till then it had been unknown". After a series of misadventures, Agravaine finally gets the admittedly "plain" Yvonne, proving the adage that "Love is a thingummybob who what-d'you-call-its", which roughly translates as "beauty is in the eye of the beholder".

Moving on from King Arthur to that other body of stirring tales – the Arabian Nights – another regal winner in love is King Merolchazzar of Oom, in the last of Plum's short fables, 'The Coming of Gowf', from 1921. Once the King has adopted golf as the official religion of his kingdom, it ushers in a Golden Age of happiness, full employment, peace, and prosperity for all his citizens – and bags him a wife. But perhaps more significant for Plum, the quality of song lyrics, particularly those praising the King, also improves, admittedly from a low bench-mark. As the narrator informs us:

> Lyric writers in those days had not reached the supreme pitch of excellence which has been produced by modern musical comedy. The art was in its infancy then, and the best the minstrels could do was this— ...

> *"Oh, tune the string and let us sing*
> *Our godlike, great, and glorious King!*
> *He's a bear! He's a bear! He's a bear!"*

Merolchazzar, who just at that moment in the performance is at the top of his stroke, misses the ball and throws a hissy fit. But as he slowly perfects his game, so the minstrels up theirs, replacing their earlier football chant with this rousing celebration:

> *"Oh, praises let us utter*
> *To our most glorious King!*
> *It fairly makes you stutter*
> *To see him start his swing:*
> *Success attend his putter!*
> *And luck be with his drive!*
> *And may he do each hole in two*
> *Although the bogey's five!"*

Much snappier, I'm sure you'll agree. A comic turn straight out of Harry Lauder's bottom drawer arrives courtesy of the unnamed Scottish gardener who becomes Merolchazzar's golf instructor, and the whole story has the air, like 'Sir Agravaine', of an extended music-hall sketch. Once again, what made for a thoroughly competent short story could have been given far greater pep, vim and *espièglerie* had it been adapted for live performance, with all the necessary ingredients ready and waiting in the prose version.

Of Plum's full-length novels that borrow from the conventions of myth, legend and fairy tale, perhaps the most interesting for our purposes is *The Prince and Betty*, first serialized in America in early 1912, and whose utterly confusing publishing history only serves to emphasize the competing influences of fantasy and reality that were jostling for elbow room in Plum's writing style at the time. For the subsequent American novel version turned out to be a very different animal, with two separate plot lines inappropriately conjoined, one tenuously anchored in reality, the other most decidedly not. So that we don't drive ourselves nuts with the five (I think) different versions of *The Prince and Betty*, let's focus on the recent Everyman/Overlook editions of those two plots, which are now published separately as *Psmith, Journalist* and the 1921 re-issued text of... *The Prince and Betty*. If you haven't read the original conjoined version, you wonder how the two could ever have been such intimate bedfellows. It was a bold, possibly foolhardy move for Plum to have yoked the two stories together in the first place. In effect, we have two worlds that don't really speak the same language finally allowed to breathe, each in its separate universe, once they've been sundered.

The later version of *TPAB* (the fourth of the story's five iterations – I think) is now nothing more or less than a straightforwardly structured fairy tale, set in and around the "musical-comedy island" of Mervo, and featuring an orphaned prince who at first doesn't know he is a prince (John Maude), his courtship of a commoner (Betty Silver) who actually isn't a commoner, and a pantomime villain in the person of Betty's step-father, Benjamin Scobell, who comes good in the end, and everything ends happily. Shorn of the journalistic interludes in New York's slum tenements, the story moves along at quite a clip, and there is little to distract the reader from the emerging destinies of the romantic leads. This tightening of the story's focus and the pruning of extraneous detail further heighten the tone of artifice, and it's something of a miracle given Plum's tendency to recycle his intellectual property that this later version didn't make it to the stage in some form or other.

But it's not just two plots that get divorced in *TPAB*, but two different versions of reality. John is a man of "invincible good humour" who "liked nearly everybody" – in stark contrast to his uncle Andrew, who hates him, nurses grudges, and is thoroughly cold and unpleasant. So what does John do?

> He fitted his uncle into the scheme of things, or, rather, set him outside them as an irreconcilable element, and went on his way enjoying life in his own good-humoured fashion.

It's a significant change of emphasis: rather than trying to accommodate his wicked Uncle Andrew within his "Mervian" world, John views him as an anomaly who can never be part of it. So he effectively shuts him out. But then Andrew turns the tables and boots John out of the family business. Each has now divorced from the other, the separation of their two worlds is complete, and Uncle Andrew obligingly disappears from the novel, never to return. And so the fairy tale can truly begin, as Mervian reality now holds sway over what had earlier passed for what was real.

Once he's been set free, John looks back, catching "a glimpse of something ugly" disappearing over the horizon. We are told that "[h]e felt this was the last scene of some long-drawn-out tragedy" – and that tragedy was now well and truly over. But what was he going to do with his new-found freedom? For many of us, getting fired would be the *start* of our woes rather than their termination, the *opening* of many a traditional tragedy (like Galsworthy's) rather than the close. But to John, who always looks on the bright side of life, it represents liberation. Like Peter Burns in *The Little Nugget*, George Balmer in 'The Tuppenny Millionaire' (both tales written about this time), or Plum's legion of bank employees, John longs to be out in the world doing something significant, getting his hands dirty, and not mouldering away in an office. But he begins his new, unsupported life by checking in to a luxury hotel, watching the Test Match at the Oval for two days, and eating hearty meals. Most of us in his position would be pounding the pavements looking for a regular source of income, not squandering what little we already have in the hope that something is bound to materialize. John, meanwhile, is wondering what job he will eventually choose. That's "choose", not "get". All John has to do is select "the most congenial job" – at least in his own head, anyway. Although Plum is, at least in part, alerting us to John's otherworldliness, this is precisely the way things will turn out in practice. As Sam Shotter finds out when he visits a palmist and her predictions come true in *Sam the Sudden*, the Wodehouse/Whoosis/Mervian universe contains a good many guardian angels and benevolent spirits who make things happen as we like them (more of which in Volume 2). The only person who seems not to realize this is John himself: as the narrator informs us, so obvious is the ultimate plot trajectory that "[i]t seemed incredible that he had not foreseen what must happen". Predestination? Well…yes!

So, at the end, it comes as little surprise that John is offered his dream job of looking after his future father-in-law's considerable financial operations in the States, despite having absolutely no personal experience of the smoke and mirrors of high finance. As if to rub in quite how fantastical this is – not to mention Mr Scobell's conversion from devil to do-gooder – John thanks his benefactor by commenting, "What you've done with your wings and harp, I can't think".

It's all rather lovely or sickly sentimental, uplifting or implausible, depending on the reader's ability to suspend his or her critical faculties. If you 'get' the fairy-tale atmosphere, there's never any doubt that everything will turn out right for our star-cross'd lovers, particularly since we're told early on that "the poet" has decreed: "The man who's square, his chances are always the best". The poet turns out to be Wodehouse himself, and his hero is the squarest of the square, like so many of those single, soon-to-be-married characters who succeed him in Plum's pantheon of young, eligible male leads. John may not always think or act with the greatest intelligence, tact or self-knowledge, but cancelling out any of these minor peccadilloes is our knowledge that he has a good heart – and that is what counts. He also lives almost entirely in the present, and "[h]is views were unvaryingly optimistic".

And that goes for the tone of the whole book: with the odd blip here and there, everything is on the side of renewal and progress – which is not unequivocally better than the old, but certainly more dynamic, life-affirming and forward-looking: in Mervo, the old regime (John) is happily supplanted in favour of a republic ("a model to every country in the world", says its former ruler, relieved to be shot of the job); America is the place to be, not England with its bad plumbing and its decadent and faintly ridiculous class system; money and hard work have overtaken privilege as the means to get on; and, rare in a Wodehouse novel, it's hinted that the happy couple might even procreate once they are married.

Now add a touch of the absurd to this pure Broadway applesauce and you have *A Man of Means*, a serial Plum co-wrote with fellow song lyricist Charles H. Bovill and which began publishing in April 1914. While *The Prince and Betty* had been a tightly plotted update of a Cinderella-type fairy story, *A Man of Means* is the picaresque love child of Voltaire's 1759 cautionary tale *Candide*, Charles Dickens at his most puckish, and George Barr McCutcheon's 1902 novel *Brewster's Millions* (which had been adapted as a Broadway play in 1906). Consisting of six through-plotted episodes (and thus the forerunner of such portmanteau titles as *The Inimitable Jeeves* and *Indiscretions of Archie*), it tells the story of Roland Bleke, "a second clerk in a provincial seed-merchant's office" and a man of "intense ordinariness" who has "a horror of definite appointments" and commitment of any kind. Roland's life is suddenly transformed by the promise of a £500 cheque from an office sweepstake, which quickly rises to £40,000 when his winnings are finally totted up. Various unlikely adventures can now ensue, which, despite Roland's lack of nous in just about every department of life, he gets himself hopelessly wrapped up in: gold mining, a theatre, a weekly magazine, and a revolution (in the country of Paranoya). These result in his capital alternately multiplying exponentially or being squandered by an army of chancers taking advantage of his good nature and naivety. Throughout, Roland is a model of puzzlement and, like Candide himself, a plaything of an interventionist kind of Fate that simply can't leave him alone to enjoy his new-found fortune.

Once again, we are treated to fast and furious plotting, complete with abrupt gear changes when things happen for no good reason, comic book characterization, and slabs of theatrical dialogue. There's also what must be one of the first appearances of an aeroplane in a literary plot, as Roland is conveniently whisked away from the grasping Potter family by a French aviator – a sort of update of the *deus ex machina* from classical Greek drama. A *deus cum machina* perhaps?

Particularly tonally, the tales in *A Man of Means* remind me of the sort of novel Evelyn Waugh would begin writing in more convincing style some years later. The choice of the name 'Bleke' provides us with a clue: Plum's narrative voice is just that little bit more sophisticated, edgier and judgmental than usual – at times it's even mildly sardonic – and it doesn't suit him, with its unwonted offhandedness skirting the fringes of cynicism. This is particularly evident in 'The Theatrical Venture', in which Roland is hornswoggled into buying a decrepit firetrap of a theatre by a sultry but devious actress:

> Being a comparative stranger in the Metropolis, [Roland] was unaware that its nickname in theatrical circles was 'The Mugs' Graveyard' – a title which had been bestowed on it not without reason. Built originally by a slightly insane old gentleman, whose principal delusion was that the public was pining for a constant supply of the higher drama...the Windsor Theatre had passed from hand to hand with the agility of a gold watch in a gathering of racecourse thieves.

And so on. The mordant tone is perhaps Bovill's doing, and the narrator loses few opportunities to ridicule Roland's banality, his lack of drive and general cluelessness. This leads to the problem – as in the *Kid Brady* saga – of the missing middle in the stories, this time caused by the fact that we have been urged to dismiss Roland by these frequent authorial prompts. Unlike any of the classic picaresque heroes (Tom Jones, Nicholas Nickleby, Don Quixote or, of course, Candide himself), Roland keeps fading away in the reader's mind. There's nothing particularly sympathetic, likeable or even interesting about him – which perhaps accounts for why the stories weren't collected in a single volume until 1991.

Roland's odyssey fizzles out in a breach-of-promise case brought against him by another femme fatale, Miss Chilvers, with whom he has involved himself only to escape the clutches of yet another gold-digger, Lady Eva Blyton, whose aristocratic family has fallen on hard times. We are not told of the outcome, only that if successful it would only cost him £10,000 of a fortune that we are told has now reached a cool £250K. And there things abruptly end. Maybe the *Strand* magazine grew tired of the conceit, but while it lasted, it proved an interesting experiment in out-of-the-frying-pan-into-the-fire absurdist literature that Plum would not repeat, but which he quite clearly learned from, particularly in the ways in which his future storylines would move quickly and often improbably. As the narrator of *A Man of Means* tells us, "epic moments are best related swiftly" – and here is a blueprint for that principle. In fact, while neither comes close to being classic Wodehouse, *The Prince and Betty* and *A Man of Means* in their plotting and handling of reality sowed the seeds of some of the key elements of Plum's lightness that would quickly bear fruit and lead to him finding his mature voice, as we'll see later in our own story.

But we're not quite done with this chapter yet, for almost four decades on from the appearance of the last of these works, up pops this fairy-tale sensibility again, as if it had never been away, having lain submerged – or rather sublimated – in Plum's writing style throughout his golden age. In 1961's *Ice in the Bedroom*, it once more sticks out like a sore thumb, rather like those wonderful improbabilities Plum would have known from Shakespeare's later romances like *The Winter's Tale* and *The Tempest*, when the man from Stratford taxes his audience's ability to suspend its disbelief to breaking point...and sometimes beyond, what with his cast of living statues, wizards and sprites. Plum doesn't go quite that far, but he's definitely headed in that direction...

Mr Cornelius, the house agent in Valley Fields – Plum's idealized London suburb based on Dulwich – is described as having "a long white beard which gave him something of the dignity of a Druid priest" – not a fashion accessory you often see among the fraternity of realtors, so it immediately becomes clear from his description on the very first page that Plum is up to something. Moreover, it's one of the few occasions when he doesn't ridicule the facially hirsute, for Mr Cornelius is nothing less than the guardian angel of the district, as well as its historian and chronicler, having been engaged in writing his "labour of love" for "a considerable time". Somewhat needlessly, Freddie Widgeon then asks, "You like Valley Fields?" – to which the old buster replies:

> "I love it, Mr Widgeon. I was born in Valley Fields, I went to school in Valley Fields, I have lived all my life in Valley Fields, and I shall end my days here."

For Mr Cornelius *is* Valley Fields, its *genius loci*, a humble man of the suburbs who loves his cocoa, pink blancmange and kippers for tea, and looking after "my house, my garden, my wife, my flowers, my rabbits". At the story's end, however, Plum ramps up his significance even further as he doubles as the plot's deus ex machina: suddenly revealing himself to be a millionaire, he loans Freddie the £3,000 he needs to invest in a coffee-planting venture in Kenya when everyone else (including two other millionaires) has failed him. Freddie is, of course, hugely grateful, describing his benefactor as "an angel in human shape", and Mr Cornelius exits the novel appropriately singing 'Rock of Ages', single-handedly transforming an otherwise conventional Wodehouse farce into something of a late-flowering fairy tale. Valley Fields is a place for kindness and generosity where dreams *can* come true, musical comedy style; it's Mervo, but within a 20-minute train ride of Central London.

Perhaps an even more fantastical figure is the bank robber-cum-butler Horace Appleby from 1968's *Do Butlers Burgle Banks?*, who, together with his gang of crooks, end up bailing out the bank they had previously intended to rob to the tune of £100,000. Once again, Horace is outed as "an angel in human shape" as he saves not just the bank's bacon but the rural community of Wellingford whose fortunes it underpins. As the plot draws to a close, the timely interventions of a benevolent Fate that characterize Wodehousean endings seem even more coincidental, and certainly more accented, than he usually makes them. As Horace says, there's something "providential" going on: "one has the sense of having been, as one might put it, *protected*" [italics Wodehouse's]. Mike Bond, the bank's manager and local squire who has been spared a jail term by these mysterious machinations, can only comment that "[o]ur guardian angels were certainly on the job there". "With bells on", agrees Horace. And as if to emphasize the unreality of it all, Mike appears to drift off into another dimension:

> The first thing he felt was a thrill such as he had never felt before. It was as if the chair in which he sat had abruptly become electrified. Somewhere out of sight an orchestra was playing soft music and the air was heavy with the scent of roses and violets sprouting through the floor.

Perhaps some of the Hippy Dream of 1968 had rubbed off on Plum, or maybe he was temporarily channelling Rosie M. Banks. Either way, this is pure musical theatre/Hollywood kitsch of the kind that closes yet another novel of the period, 1967's *Company for Henry*. They say the darkest hour is just before day, and on page 180, things are looking black for Bill "Thomas" Hardy, who is about to sail off to America minus the object of his adoration, Jane Martyn. But then...a mere 20 pages later, everything has come right and we await the happy couple's reconciliation. Plum is careful to set the scene, which takes place at the substantial lake of Ashby Hall, whose shores are surrounded by the odd classical statue and marble temple "without which no gentleman's ornamental water was thought complete". To Bill "it seemed like something out of a fairy story book, needing in his opinion only one thing to make it perfect, the presence of the girl he loved". Immediately, "this omission was...rectified" as, bang on cue, Jane approaches him from behind, dressed like some Naiad of Ancient Greece, (albeit in a white bathrobe and not a silken peplos), "her head bare, her feet in sandals" – and you can guess the rest.

Yes, these last three examples are taken from novels – but the sensibility that contrived these endings could just as easily have turned them into stage musicals or romantic movies without too much trouble. In fact, at the close of 1969's *A Pelican at Blandings*, Gally Threepwood supplies this information himself:

> "It makes me feel as if I were sitting in at the end of a play... lightly sentimental, the smile following the tear... The storm is over, there is sunlight in my heart. I have a glass of wine and sit thinking of what has passed. And now we want something to bring down the curtain. A toast is indicated."

This uncharacteristically sentimental speech might just as well have been spoken by Gally's creator, as, in the late evening of his days, he looked back in satisfaction at another plot successfully woven together in a genre of prose drama virtually no one else was writing any more. Like the ageless Mr Cornelius, Plum was one of the few writers left alive who could remember a time when this lightest, airiest type of romantic confection was the norm in theatrical productions the length of Broadway, and all over London's West End. *The Girl in Blue* (1970) even ends with a song, 'Spread a Little Happiness' from the 1929 stage musical *Mr. Cinders* (later murdered by Sting, of all people):

> *Even when the darkest clouds are in the sky*
> *You mustn't sigh and you mustn't cry*
> *Spread a little happiness as you go by*
> *Please try.*

> *What's the use of worrying and feeling blue*
> *When days are long keep on smiling through*
> *Spread a little happiness till dreams come true.*

Even as the Vietnam War rapidly escalated, men walked for the first time on the surface of the moon, and Plum entered his 90s, he was still carrying that torch for romantic love and cheery optimism, perhaps hoping against hope that one day the golden age of musical theatre would return, and he could supply the lyrics for it as he had over 50 years earlier.

So it's high time we start looking at how Plum's theatrical awareness grew and developed in parallel with the earlier works we've been examining in this chapter, for they grew together simultaneously, along with the novel writing, the journalism and the school stories in the period covering 1900 to the early 1920s. Before he would reach what we might call 'peak Wodehouse', there would be yet more learning on the job, more refining of his style and, above all, a lot of creative choices to be made as to his career's overall trajectory. Our errant Tardis will now whisk us back to the beginning again so we can look at facets of his craft that his stint in the theatre helped him perfect.

1915–1924

Chapter 6
Wodehouse and the Language of the Theatre

"You're a novelist, ain't you? I thought so. Well, novelists can't write plays."
'The Dramatic Fixer'

There's a heap of money in plays.
'In Alcala'

On no account introduce him into theatrical circles. Vitally important.
'A Letter of Introduction'

The past season has shown, by the success of 'Under Cover', that audiences do not object to being fooled. One of these days somebody is going to fool them by producing a coherent musical comedy.
Vanity Fair, September 1915

P. G. Wodehouse's career in the theatre began at the age of 7 when he collaborated with "a boy named Henry Cullimore" on a drama reproduced here in toto:

> ACT ONE
> *[Enter Henry]*
>
> HENRY: What's for breakfast? Ham and oatmeal? Very nice.

After which the muse fell silent. "A pity", Plum later wrote, "for I think it would have been a great audience show".

This represented something of a false start: his Damascene moment actually arrived six years later in 1895, courtesy of a comic opera staged at the Crystal Palace, that gigantic cathedral of iron and glass erected on a prominent hill in southeast London, conveniently situated two miles from Dulwich, where he had recently started school. It may not have been his first trip to the theatre, but it certainly proved the most epochal, because over half a century later he still remembered how it had made him "absolutely drunk with ecstasy. I thought it the finest thing that could possibly be done". The hyperbole is all the more powerful for being so uncharacteristically intense.

Specifically, *it* was a production of W. S. Gilbert & Arthur Sullivan's

Patience, the fifth of the partnership's wildly popular Savoy Operas, written in the year of Wodehouse's birth and still occasionally revived in the 21st century. So impressed was Plum that it pops up nearly 40 times in his writings, the final occasion being in *Stiff Upper Lip, Jeeves*, published in 1963, 68 years after he first saw it. Clearly, the production Bertie Wooster attended wasn't quite so memorable:

> "Oh, yes, now I recollect. My Aunt Agatha made me take her son Thos to it once. Not at all a bad little show, I thought, though a little highbrow."

Which, of course, it wasn't in the least, being a brilliant skewering of the kind of arty pretension Wodehouse loathed, complete with a chorus of Madeline Bassett–like "rapturous maidens" singing meaningless phrases like: *"How Botticellian! How Fra Angelican! Perceptively intense and consummately utter"*. But although the theme might have been congenial, something far greater had clicked, or rather *exploded*, in Plum's imagination during the performance. From that moment on, he was a sucker for the smell of the greasepaint, the roar of the crowd and, arguably greater than either of these, the visceral appeal of the popular song. As he staggered out of Crystal Palace Park and re-entered everyday reality, the bedazzled Wodehouse could not have foreseen how, in a little over 20 years, he would become a celebrated theatre lyricist with his name in lights on both sides of the Atlantic.

It was a consummation devoutly to be wished: as he remarked in 1906, "if a song is a success — fame! Imagine the feelings of the man who wrote 'Bill Bailey'!" Within ten years, he wouldn't have to. And even in his 70s, with his Broadway and West End triumphs long since behind him, his enthusiasm remained undimmed: "I would rather have written *Oklahoma!* than *Hamlet*", he observed, meaning every word. And, as if to prove it, he wonders out loud at that musical's success in 1951's *The Old Reliable*; quotes from the show's lyrics in 1961's *Ice in the Bedroom*; and occasionally namechecks its composers, Rodgers and Hammerstein, in the other novels and stories of his later years. Once Wodehouse had been bitten by the showbiz bug, he stayed bit to the very end of his life.

Although well documented, Wodehouse's work for the stage has received scant critical attention, most likely because it represents a second vast body of writing scholars have to get their heads around on top of everything else. Work comparing his plays and lyrics to the novels and stories is scarcer still, and one glance at the statistics will probably tell you why that is, for once again Wodehouse proves he was no slouch:

- Plum had a hand in nearly 40 musical comedies between 1904 and 1934, his 'golden age'.

- He wrote or co-wrote around 300 song lyrics for theatrical productions. The cultural historian Mark Steyn has claimed, with some justification, that had Wodehouse died in 1918, he would be better remembered as "the first great lyricist of the American musical" and not as a British novelist.

- He wrote or contributed to around 40 plays, including 10 'straight' plays or adaptations performed in London's West End and 10 separate titles staged elsewhere. Indeed, from 1926 to 1935 (to quote historian Tony Ring, from whose invaluable work many of these figures are sourced), "plays with which Plum was involved had a run of success which was equal to that of any other comedy playwright of the period", with eight openings in the West End and three on Broadway.

- Seventeen of his novels (and two short stories) also exist in dramatic versions that he himself wrote, and on four occasions he borrowed (or even bought) plots and dialogue from other writers' dramatic works and incorporated them into his prose.

To complete the audit, we mustn't forget the books that feature theatrical characters or themes (according to Norman Murphy, there are 43 – nearly half the total); his stint as drama critic for US *Vanity Fair* from 1915 to 1917; and, lastly, his highly embroidered theatrical memoir from 1954, *Bring on the Girls*.

So it's hard to justify sidestepping Wodehouse's passion for the theatre if our appreciation of his genius has any pretensions to completeness. Moreover, it is the contention of this book that the perspectives and discipline of live performance helped his prose style cohere faster and far more effectively during the period of 1915 to the mid-1920s than it had done up to that point – so much so that once he understood what was happening and successfully harnessed this new sensibility, the resulting template stayed with him, gently refined but remarkably unaltered, for the rest of his life. Theatre really was that influential, as we can see if we look at the following quotes taken from a scripted interview published in the *Paris Review* magazine in 1975, the year of his death:

> The principle I always go on in writing a novel is to think of the characters in terms of actors in a play.

> For a humorous novel you've got to have a scenario, and you've got to test it so that you know where the comedy comes in, where the situations come in...splitting it up into scenes (you can make a scene of almost anything) and have as little stuff in between as possible...

> I think the success of every novel – if it's a novel of action – depends on the high spots. The thing to do is to say to yourself, "Which are my big scenes?" and then get every drop of juice out of them.

> I like to think of some scene, it doesn't matter how crazy, and work backward and forward from it until eventually it becomes quite plausible and fits neatly into the story.

Actors, scenarios, scenes...the language of theatre (and later the Hollywood movies he worked on) was embedded deep within his creative imagination. In fact, that first quotation was a word-for-word lift from a letter he wrote to Bill Townend half century earlier, indicating that these were abiding metaphors for what he thought he was up to while writing his books. Plum titled the first novel of this new era *Something Fresh*, perhaps because he could feel something that is equally apparent to us, that his writing was now informed by a whole new set of influences, not least of which was an enhanced appreciation of just who he was writing *for*, and how that audience might consume his work to its best advantage.

More than any other genre of theatrical performance, Plum was fascinated by the British 'music hall', a heady and unpredictable mix of popular songs, comedy, speciality acts, and variety entertainment whose heyday, from around 1850 to 1950, coincided with Plum's glory years in the theatre. Chapter 2 of 1909's *The Swoop* opens with the following scene-setting:

Historians, when they come to deal with the opening years

of the twentieth century, will probably call this the Music-Hall Age. At the time of the great invasion the music halls dominated England. Every town and suburb had its Hall, most of them more than one.

Pretty much the same words begin Chapter 5 of the transatlantic rewrite, *The Military Invasion of America* – Plum simply substituted 'vaudeville' for 'music-hall'. On both sets of stages, practically anything went, and his regular musings on this popular phenomenon – and its near cousin, the touring repertory theatre – give us a fascinating insight into why he found live performance so intoxicating. As late as 1961's *Ice in the Bedroom*, he still clearly admired, and was even moved by, whatever it was that drove such artistes as Herpina the Snake Queen, who would fondle her slithery charges "when she could get bookings – which wasn't often" or her son Joe, always "off to play juvenile leads in Wolverhampton and Peebles and places of that kind" to keep going. It was this fascination that had earlier prompted a really rather startling confession. In a 1917 article published in the US *Vanity Fair* (later reworked for 1932's *Louder and Funnier* – I'm cherry-picking from both in what follows), he wrote:

> It is a remarkable proof of my sagacity and good judgment that, while I have never experienced the slightest desire to go on the legitimate stage, it was my earliest ambition to become a vaudeville artist.

"I just wanted to sing", he claims, and there can be little doubt that Plum was absolutely fascinated by the bravery of that solitary figure there in the spotlight, giving his all in front of "that sullen, glowering, set-jawed throng" that could raise the performer's spirit to the rafters or tear his self-esteem to pieces seemingly on a whim. He had given three solo performances at Dulwich School concerts in 1899 and 1900 which all seem to have gone down well (although it's more than likely Plum himself wrote the jaunty reviews that appeared in *The Alleynian*); he had also acted in two school plays, the latter casting him as Guildenstern in W. S. Gilbert's comic take on *Hamlet, Rosencranz and Guildenstern*.

At some point, however, Wodehouse decided that although theatre was very much his 'dish', performing wasn't: it represented 'the supreme test', and as such he bottled it. Harking back to his childhood, he commented in a 1917 essay 'An Appreciation of Vaudeville':

It is the lonesomeness of the job that makes [it] so hard. You have no supports. You remember how you used to feel when they dragged you down to the drawing-room as a child and made you recite that little thing about the Hesperus? Well, that is how vaudeville performers feel all the time.

Being put on the spot in front of an audience, however small, and told to declaim Henry Wadsworth Longfellow's hoary old chestnut 'The Wreck of the Hesperus' was the stuff of nightmares for the young Wodehouse, and he would doubtless have envied Uncle Fred, who somehow managed to solicit "solid applause" for *his* childhood performance of the same poem despite being "rather short on front teeth" ("It was the schcooner Hesperuth that thailed the thtormy thea"). No, Plum was more like the shy and retiring Bertie Wooster, who as a seven-year-old was coerced into reciting Tennyson's 'The Charge of the Light Brigade' in front of a group of his mother's friends. "Bertie recites so nicely", he remembers Ma Wooster saying, "getting her facts twisted, I may mention, because I practically always fluffed my lines" – which he proceeds to do even in his reminiscence:

> "Tum tiddle umpty-pum
> Tum tiddle umpty-pum
> Tum tiddle umpty-pum"

And this brought you to the snaperoo or pay-off which was:

> "Someone had blundered."

I always remember that bit…feeling just as those Light Brigade fellows must have felt.

"Very unpleasant the whole thing was", Bertie concludes, yet in the days before radio and television this domestic version of vaudeville was entirely normal, even obligatory. Everyone, it seems, had to have an act of some kind they could pull out of the bottom drawer for use at Drones Club 'smokers', charity fundraising events in Bottleton East (Plum's fictional East End suburb full of cheery, violent drunks), or 'come all ye' concerts at village halls deep in the English countryside. A cruelly accurate account of such amdram shenanigans can be found in *The Mating Season*, in which Bertie acts as our MC, taking us through a very

English music-hall bill at King's Deverill.

The evening opens with a violin solo by Miss Eustacia Pulbrook, "which seemed to last much longer than it actually did". This is followed by Muriel Kegley-Bassington singing 'My Hero' from Oscar Straus's hugely popular operetta *The Chocolate Soldier*, which she delivers while gurning at a framed photograph of her boyfriend. Next on is her "bullet-headed" younger brother George, who is ordered, possibly under threat of torture, to recite another Victorian parlour favourite, Thomas Hood's poem 'Ben Battle' ("My heart went out to the little fellow", Bertie writes. "I knew just how he was feeling"). Then there's Adrian Higgins ("a man with a face like an anxious marmoset") with his "Impressions of Woodland Songsters Which Are Familiar To You All" before Gussie Fink-Nottle and Claude Catsmeat Potter-Pirbright take the stage in green beards and do their Pat and Mike crosstalk act, which bombs spectacularly, forcing them to exit "like a couple of pallbearers who have forgotten their coffin and had to go back for it". "The whole performance", says Bertie, doubling as our theatre critic, "gave one a sort of grey, hopeless feeling, like listening to the rain at three o'clock on a Sunday afternoon in November".

It was occasions like these that probably persuaded Plum he was not Prince Hamlet, nor was meant to be. It takes an Esmond Haddock ("all boots and pink coat") to lift the King's Deverill show from its knees and bring down the house with a dashing performance of 'Hallo, hallo, hallo, hallo, a-hunting we will go, pom pom', and Plum knew he could never have enough stage presence to do that. So he threw in his lot with the back-room boys and never looked back:

> It was not because I considered authorship a grander pursuit than singing on the Orpheum circuit that I abandoned my boyhood's dreams. It was because I knew that any chump can make a living as an author – and, if you don't believe it, just look at some of our authors – whereas, to be a vaudeville star, you require vim, pep, *espièglerie*, a good singing voice, and a species of indefinable *je-ne-sais-quoi* – none of which qualities I seem to possess.

'Espièglerie' is a word Plum uses time and again in his writing – a quality that comes in handy if you're one of life's performers. Translated from the French, it means something like 'mischievousness' or 'devilment'. We need only say that the red-headed firebrand Bobbie Wickham has it in spades, what with her all-round "oomph…and general outlook on life as a ticking bomb". Plum's schoolboy jabberers have it, too, as do all his characters who carry a sense of the dramatic with them wherever they go. Like the unholy trinity of Gally Threepwood, Psmith and Uncle Fred, these people can be utter liabilities, but they do tend to make life *fun*. They give it edge and an air of unpredictability. Even Lord Emsworth has it in him, if only briefly, when he shoots Rupert Baxter in the backside in 'The Crime Wave at Blandings'. It's a twinkle in the eye, a feeling of daring or a sense of playfulness – all these things. Plum clearly knew it when he saw it, and celebrated it in those of his characters who added life to his plots – even if he felt he didn't belong in their number. When he was seated at the typewriter, however, things took a different turn entirely, and vaudeville's loss was literature's gain; but it seems Plum never ceased to wonder at the peculiar mix of shyness and extroversion, nervousness and self-confidence, despair and joy that feeds those who perform in public, who bring that something extra to the party. "[All] alone in a hard world", they give it their all with no guarantee of getting any of that emotional investment back. A bit like falling desperately in love, as Plum postulates in a fascinating passage from that breakthrough novel *Something Fresh*.

It's a curious conceit that sticks out like a sore thumb, as if Plum simply had to include it no matter what. I would lay a bet there's some autobiography in it somewhere, not least because once more, a child-hood recitation of 'The Wreck of the Hesperus' is involved. At the very second Ashe Marson realizes he and Joan Valentine are soulmates, a distant yet oddly apposite memory suddenly flashes into his mind:

> Years before, when a boy in his father's home in distant Hayling, Massachusetts, those in authority had command-ed that he – in his eleventh year and as shy as one can be only at that interesting age – should rise in the presence of a roomful of strangers, adult guests, and recite The Wreck of the Hesperus. He had risen. He had blushed. He had stammered. He had contrived to whisper: "It was the Schooner Hesperus." And then, in a corner of the room, a little girl, for no properly explained reason, had burst out crying. She had yelled, she had bellowed, and would not be comforted; and in the ensuing confusion Ashe had escaped to the woodpile at the bottom of the garden, saved by a miracle. All his life he had remembered the gratitude he

> had felt for that little timely girl, and never until now had
> he experienced any other similar spasm.

That instantaneous, split-second connection with an audience member clearly left its mark on Ashe; the girl, "for no properly explained reason", had miraculously felt his pain, reacted accordingly, and spared his blushes. He was, if only for an instant, no longer alone, and although his experience is exactly the opposite of the kind of reception an actor usually courts, things had turned out just as he wanted them to. Ashe was not only grateful, but a little in love with his unknown saviour.

Actors often discuss the empathy they experience with an audience of complete strangers; on a good night, it crackles like electricity and powers their performances. And like the (as yet unrequited) electricity Ashe experienced between himself and Joan, it *is* a kind of love. It may be fleeting, yet it's all the more intoxicating for that impermanence, and the performer has to chase that capricious confluence eight times a week in the legitimate theatre, or, if he or she was a vaudevillian, that number of times (and more) *a day*. On one level, it's an act of reckless generosity, putting oneself in a vulnerable position with no guarantee of acceptance and every chance of humiliating rejection. But the rewards of success can be priceless. This pursuit, as many have testified, can develop a narcotic influence while affecting even the most seasoned performer with nervous apprehension prior to a show. No wonder Plum is full of admiration for those who can ride this emotional rollercoaster, and in idle moments I sometimes wonder if this helps explain the high number of chorus girls in his fiction who are invariably upbeat, emotionally generous sorts – and, by Plum's lights, good marriage material. His own wife Ethel had briefly trodden the boards, and even in 1967's *Company for Henry*, by which time chorus girls were an endangered species, he includes ex-hoofer Kelly Stickney in his *dramatis personae* to help gee the plot along and add a note of cheerfulness and practicality to the proceedings.

Sitting in the first-night audience at a play or musical comedy he'd written and witnessing the audience's reaction was the closest Plum would ever get to the thrill of performing; but at least he could write about Archibald's Mulliner's show-stopping routine of a hen laying an egg that wins Aurelia Cammerleigh's heart, and how a ridiculous vaudeville turn somehow metamorphosed into the triumphant coming together of "two jolly old twin souls". Even here, love ups the "gusto" and "brio" Archibald invests in his performance: indeed, "[l]ove thrilled through every 'Brt-t't-t't' that he uttered, animated each flap of his arms" for which he is rewarded with "a look of worship" from his beloved – and no fewer than four encores. A little different from Ashe's experience, maybe, but all part and parcel of the same transactional relationship between a true star and his public.

As with many others who are bitten by the theatre bug, Plum had fallen in love with the experience *as a whole*: what theatre represented, just as much as what it actually was. Yes it was fun, glamour, energy and magic, but at its heart was that fragile and capricious connectedness that would make or break a show. And so his two-year stint as theatre critic at *Vanity Fair* didn't just concern itself with writers and plays; he frequently wrote from the audience's perspective, complaining how cramped and draughty seating, restricted views, stale air, late starts, inadequate theatre bars and even a bad journey to the venue could oh so easily dilute or even kill the magic. On one occasion, he titled his entire column 'Fair Play for Audiences', proposing that there should be a properly constituted society for "the prevention of cruelty to the people who pay money to see plays", even suggesting it call itself "The Amalgamated Union of Ticket Buyers". At just over a dollar for a decent seat (in 1915), musicals were a relatively affordable ticket to heaven that could trump anything the more expensive and higher-browed legitimate theatre had to offer – but only if they were done *well*. Writing in *The Humorist* magazine in 1922, Plum commented:

> [D]oes it not generally happen that, just as the girls come on in bathing-dresses to join in the "Dear Old Deauville" number, you muse wistfully, "If I get out of this alive, me for the legitimate!"

Then again, the legitimate theatre was just as liable to lay an egg:

> How frequently it has happened that, in the middle of one of those tense dramas with strong men in them, you have said to yourself, "After all, there is nothing like musical comedy!"

Plum loved both, and he worked in both, although his preference was for material, like Archibald's hen, "conceived on broad and sympathetic lines". Shakespeare would always be his ultimate hero, but the unalloyed *joy* musicals brought him was something with which he wanted to infect his entire audience, in whatever genre he happened to be writing. Indeed, once we become alerted to the parallels between stage and page in his style, it's possible to experience how the energy, drive, economy and vividness necessary in writing for a live theatre audience was also integral to the way he wanted to communicate with his book readers, and one can begin to distinguish those times when he was imagining his prose stories from the front row of the stalls, rather than sat at his study desk in front of a typewriter.

There can be absolutely no question that Plum's writing was saturated in the disciplines of live performance. Even when it has nothing to do with the theatre at all, much of his prose output aspires to the *condition* of drama, courtesy of the way he wrote it. Because that's how he thought the kind of stories he wanted to write could be told to their best advantage. As early as 1906, in his first 'adult' novel, *Love Among the Chickens*, Wodehouse was already self-consciously framing scenes and stories in terms of staged drama – and letting his readers know exactly what he was up to, for what else is Jeremy Garnet's plot to ingratiate himself with Professor Derrick but a stand-alone playlet? In arranging for the Professor's boat to capsize and then being in the right place at the right time in order to save him from drowning, Garnet (who is, of course, a writer) is producing a structured sequence of events with a desired outcome: the re-establishment of cordial relations between the two men which will ultimately result in Garnet gaining access to the Professor's beautiful daughter, Phyllis. Here's the script in a sort of tableau form:

> I imagined a sudden upset. Professor struggling in water. Myself (heroically): "Courage! I'm coming!" A few rapid strokes. Saved! Sequel, a subdued professor, dripping salt water and tears of gratitude, urging me to become his son-in-law.

Immediately, Garnet begins to have his doubts about all this – he's let his writer's imagination run away with him:

> That sort of thing happened in fiction. It was a shame that it should not happen in real life. In my hot youth I once had seven stories in seven weekly penny papers in that same month, all dealing with a situation of the kind... In other words I, a very mediocre scribbler, had effected seven

times in a single month what the Powers of the Universe could not manage once, even on the smallest scale.

And then, somewhat inevitably, Garnet *does* manage to engineer exactly the same situation in real life – only to see it fail miserably, once again highlighting the gulf between lived experience and what happens on the stage. Nothing daunted, however, he plots and plans a second entertainment: a golf match with the Professor which he deliberately loses by acting the role of a poor player. This time he succeeds, and there's a happy ending, completing the narrative arc. *Just* as it would happen on the stage – and indeed, in the 1906 version of *Love Among the Chickens*, Garnet's wedding to Phyllis *is* cast in the form of a short, three-scene formal play featuring Ukridge in the role of his best man.

But Garnet's amateur dramatics were only the beginning. From this point on, Wodehouse's prose was full of the lore and language of the theatre. Here's a small representative chronological selection from the considerably larger mother lode he created in those early years:

- 'Deep Waters', from 1910, features an "infatuated dramatist" and "the woodenest juvenile in captivity" staging a "performance" of another boating accident to an appreciative and sizeable "audience" gathered on the beach "to which any artist should have been glad to play". This improvised "little drama" cleverly generates press attention for the actual drama they are putting on at the local theatre.

- In 'Helping Freddie' (1911), playwright Jimmy Pinkerton notes that Reggie Pepper's tale of an abandoned child "wouldn't make a bad situation for act two of a farce".

- 'Something to Worry About' (1913) invites the reader: "Throw your mind back to the last musical comedy you saw. Recall the leading lady's song with a chorus of young men, all proffering devotion simultaneously in a neat row? Well, that was how the lads of the village comported themselves towards Sally."

- In 1917's *Uneasy Money*, Plum sets the betrothal of Dudley Pickering to touring company actress Claire

Fenwick to a musical accompaniment (and a telling lyric supplied by himself), just as it might be produced on stage.

- *A Damsel in Distress* (1919) sees George Bevan (who just so happens to be a theatrical songwriter) standing high in a gallery looking down on a glittering coming-of-age ball that uncannily resembles "the second act of an old-fashioned musical comedy (Act Two: The Ballroom, Grantchester Towers: One Week Later)".

- Then we find the estimable Parker – Daniel Brewster's valet from 1921's *Indiscretions of Archie* – "dusting the furniture and bric-à-brac with a feather broom rather in the style of a manservant at the rise of the curtain of an old-fashioned farce".

- In 1927's *The Small Bachelor*, Plum even describes obesity in terms of the theatre: Mrs Sigsbee Waddington is so large that "no theatre, however little its programme had managed to attract the public, could be said to be "sparsely filled" if [she] had dropped in to look at the show".

- Life in an English country house, the narrator of *Money for Nothing* informs us in 1928, often resembles "living in the first act set of an old-fashioned comic opera".

And so on, almost ad infinitum. These are nuggets that lie on the surface of Plum's stories, but if we scratch the ground a bit, it's possible to reveal the deeper stage machinery that makes Wodehouse's writing work. We'll come to this in a moment, but first I'll need to include a brief biographical interlude, which I'll start by returning to those theatre reviews Plum wrote for *The Onlooker* in 1902, since they mark his professional debut into the business we call show, and his introduction to the skewiff version of reality it represents.

The Onlooker was aimed at "well-known people or people who wish to be well-known"; it was run by a Mrs Harcourt Williamson from her home, out of which she also operated a 'social bureau' for members of what she called the "Smart Set". John Dawson, on the Wodehouse website *Madame Eulalie* wonders – as do I – how Plum "came to be introduced to a well-connected society editress who operated a matchmaking service" and speculates whether "he could have met [her] at some social function and offered to write a couple of theater reviews for her". In the absence of further evidence, this must remain our best guess. But however the introduction was affected, at some point around this time Wodehouse started regularly moving in theatrical circles, and Mrs Williamson might plausibly have been his entrée. According to Lady Donaldson's biography of Plum, he had also briefly enrolled in Mrs Marie Tickell's school of dramatic art in London's Victoria district, which may have provided further contacts. Meanwhile, in his notebooks of the period, there are frequent references to the bohemian O'Sullivan family, who lived in the upscale suburb of Holland Park, and whose home Plum seems to have visited quite often (you'll no doubt remember Plum pushing young Biddy around in her pram in Chapter 5). Denis O'Sullivan was a highly accomplished American musician, singer and actor who had risen to prominence in London productions of melodramas by the Irish playwright Dion Boucicault. A highly sociable man and a member of several gentlemen's clubs, he and his artist wife Elizabeth had a wide circle of arty friends bordering on a salon, at which Plum might well have met a number of people who would later prove useful to him. We might even venture that he had become a theatre groupie.

One such crucial figure was Owen Hall (pen name of journalist/playwright James Davis), who invited Plum to contribute a lyric to his 1904 musical *Sergeant Brue*, scheduled to play at the Strand Theatre – and it's from this commission onwards that Plum's professional involvement with the stage slowly started to gather its own momentum. What concerns us about this modest beginning is how Plum hit the ground running: 'Put Me in my Little Cell' is a perfectly efficient pastiche of a music-hall song in which three criminals each take a verse, extolling the "quiet comforts" of English prisons (if you fancy a listen, a commercial recording sung by Billy Murray, released on Victor 4508 in 1905, can be easily tracked down online):

> *There are pleasant little spots my heart is fixed on,*
> *Down at Parkhurst or at Portland on the sea.*
> *And some put up at Holloway or Brixton*
> *But – Pentonville is good enough for me.*
> *And Dartmoor is so breezy and romantic*
> *That you're sorry when they let you out on bail*
> *When you've worked till you are droppin'*

From a week or two of hoppin'
Then you miss the quiet comforts of a jail.

The lyric has many of the merits of Plum's later, better-known work for the stage, with a strong, ingenious central idea, clearly expressed and developed. What's missing is any hint of the pizazz and verbal sophistication he would bring to his work following his exposure to the Broadway musical. No doubt beside himself with excitement and nervous anticipation, he was in the first-night audience on Saturday, 10 December 1904, and again on Monday the 12th, busy noting with pride how his effort was "[e]ncored both times. Audience laughed several times during each verse", before adding the telling comment: "This is fame". Summing up his situation at 12 noon the following day, he wrote: "I have Arrived".

Quite how grateful he was to Hall for this leg up can perhaps be witnessed 18 years later in *The Adventures of Sally*, in which he name-checks *Floradora*, one of Hall's biggest and most often revived hits: Sally's landlady, Mrs Meecher, was in the "first [New York] production" of the show (in 1900), although not one of the original eye-catching 'Sextette' of chorus girls who quickly became the toast of Broadway, each of whom allegedly married a millionaire.

But just as important as being in the right place at the right time, the success of 'Put Me in My Little Cell' considerably broadened Plum's literary outlook, crucially lending him a backstage perspective on the workings of farce. For *Sergeant Brue*'s plot was not entirely dissimilar either in form or casting to those Wodehouse would concoct for the rest of his career. While celebrating his birthday with his family, Sergeant Samson Brue of 'C' Division is visited by a solicitor, who brings the wholly un-expected news that he is heir to a fortune of £10,000 a year – but with one condition: he must be promoted to Inspector. 'Crookie' Scrubbs, who has unsuccessfully tried to rob the barber's shop run by Brue's son, is recruited to set up crimes which Brue can then solve, getting him noticed by his superiors. The ploy fails miserably, succeeding only in getting Brue arrested and sent down [*cue Plum's song*]. Meanwhile, Brue has come to the attention of the gold-digging Lady Bickenhall, who perjures herself in court to get Brue off the hook. She then picks up where Cookie left off, arranging an illegal gambling party which Brue, re-instated in the force, will then raid. All goes well – exceptionally well, in fact, as Brue nets the magistrate who had banged him up (apologies to Barry Day, from whose wonderful book *The Complete Lyrics of P G*

Wodehouse, this plot summary has been freely adapted).

Legacies with awkward codicils, conniving aristos, incompetent crooks, a naïf hero and far-fetched plotting and scheming would all regularly feature in Plum's later work, as would the labyrinthine workings of a plot that is complex, but not *too* complex, for a theatre audience to follow.

But it was in 1906 that Wodehouse came to the attention of two men who would *really* start him off: playwright and novelist Cosmo Hamilton and his actor/impresario collaborator, Seymour Hicks. It was under their patronage, in March of that year, that Plum was given the job of resident lyricist at the Aldwych Theatre. For a second time, we have testimony that Plum was utterly stage-struck: Herbert Westbrook, who had accompanied him to the meeting with Hicks, remembered that "[o]n leaving the stage door, Plum was so stunned with joy and excitement that he walked a mile along the Strand without him knowing where he was or whether he was coming or going". As Plum put it soon afterwards in an article entitled 'Dramatizitis' in *The Pall Mall Magazine*, "I found myself, before I realised what had happened, attached to the staff...as a sort of Hey, Bill! who was expected to turn out topical encore verses every week in exchange for two pounds per and the run of the theatre". This was, of course, almost exactly what he'd been doing at the *Globe* newspaper, churning out, as Barry Day aptly puts it, "literate light verse six times a week". So he was already well prepared for the ad hoc nature of this theatre role; it's just that these verses would end up with tunes and be played before a live audience.

Plum worked hard during his stint at the Aldwych, adapting his style and distilling his experience into practical principles. In many ways, he resembled Dickens's Nicholas Nickleby during his sojourn with the Crummles troupe, being young and eager to please. Hicks's wife, the actress Ellaline Terriss, wrote of him as "like a rather large boy, with an open and happy nature", who was always working. "The Hermit", as he came to be known, got his next big break in the revue *The Beauty of Bath*, on which he collaborated on two (or maybe three) numbers with composer Jerome Kern, with whom, as we'll see in the following chapter, he would enjoy considerable success as a lyricist ten years later across the Atlantic.

The best known of the resulting songs, 'Oh, Mr Chamberlain!', is a satire on a contemporary Conservative politician Joseph Chamberlain, whom we'll be meeting again in Volume 2:

He plays for Aston Villa just by
Way of keeping fit,
He runs the mile in four-fifteen
And wrestles Hackenschmidt
He sleeps a couple of hours a week, and
Works right round the clock
He wrote The Master Christian *and*
Oh! Stop Your Tickling Jock!

One gets the feeling that only a writer of Plum's ingenuity could corral the following landmarks of popular culture in a single eight-line stanza:

- a soccer club of the English Midlands;

- Livonian wrestler/philosopher George Hacken-schmidt (who regularly appears in Wodehouse stories of the period including 'Wilton's Holiday', *Psmith in the City*, and *Mike and Psmith* as a name he simply liked the sound of);

- a book by Queen Victoria's favourite novelist; and

- Harry Lauder's bang-up-to-date 1906 music hall hit.

Plum's Chamberlain, portrayed here as a kind of Edwardian Superman, clearly had the power to tickle the audience's collective funny bone: on opening night (according to Lee Davis, author of the excellent 1993 publication *Bolton and Wodehouse and Kern: The Men Who Made Musical Comedy*), "the song received six encores, much laughter, and a great deal of space in the press".

The Beauty of Bath made it to 287 performances, considered a pretty decent run, and so saturated had his consciousness become in matters theatrical, Plum is perhaps hinting at his own infatuation in an unused lyric he wrote for the show, 'Behind the Scenes', in which the singer can't stop thinking about a performance he has witnessed long after it has ended:

When the curtain has descended
And the comedy is ended,
And the audience to their homes have gone away,
I hate to feel it's finished
For my interest's undiminished

In the doings of the people in the play.
Is the hero still as winning as he was in the beginning
Does the heroine continue to attract?
Is the villain still a nuisance
With his plotting and his sinning
When none of them have really got to act?

Plum contributed songs to further Hicks productions, including *My Darling* and *The Gay Gordons*, before jumping ship in December 1907 to join George Edwardes at the Gaiety Theatre. But then things went a bit quiet until 1914, although Plum continued to write poems and articles about the stage, and to pepper his novels with theatrical references and allusions. To seize on just one example, 1910's 'Deep Waters' has as its backdrop the production of *Fate's Footballs*, a play by first-time writer George Barnert Callender, who is forced to battle those he calls his play's "hired murderers" at every stage of the run-throughs. Remarks such as "rehearsals had just reached that stage of brisk delirium when the author toys with his bottle of poison and the stage-manager becomes icily polite" suggest that his creator was something of an old hand at this game and knew whereof he spoke.

So what did Wodehouse take away from this early burst of theatrical activity? I would argue it was several things: a sense of form, structure and pacing – definitely, as we'll see in a moment. But most important, I think, was an appreciation of how the brain processes language. In his best writing, Plum could quite clearly 'hear' the voices of his characters while he was writing them, as if they were performing in front of him on a stage, delivering their lines for him to transcribe. In fact, this essential skill is the subject of the first substantial reference to theatre in his novels. In 1905's *The Head of Kay's*, when Fenn sneaks out of school to watch a performance of his elder brother's 'opera', he makes the acquaintance of theatre impresario "Mr Higgs" (more than likely a thinly disguised portrait of Seymour Hicks), and it's in the course of this episode that Plum can't resist including some stage lore he must have recently picked up;

> Like every playwright with his first piece, he had been haunted by the idea that his dialogue 'would not act', that, however humorous it might be to the reader, it would fall flat when spoken.

While not at all necessary for the purposes of the plot, this *aperçu* marks the first of several occasions where Plum publicly demonstrates his appreciation that 'read' words and 'spoken' words are 'heard' in different ways by the human brain, making separate sets of demands on writers who straddle the disciplines of literature and drama, just as he was starting to do. These days, the science of 'psycholinguistics' covers this territory in exhaustive complexity, but back in the early years of the 20th century, that term was still three decades away from even being coined. Plum, however, seems to have understood the distinction instinctively, and brought a developed 'double awareness' to his writing from the get-go, such that he was able to make his language on the stage and the page mirror one another as closely as possible. To the benefit of both.

Rather than having me babble on about this at length using polysyllables, why not try a quick experiment: read a passage from just about any Wodehouse novel out loud, and see how easily the language – *and the sense it conveys* – flows out of your mouth and into your mind, as if it was intended not just to be read, but performed. Not just the direct speech or dialogue, but the narrative passages as well.

Easy, isn't it?

Now try that again with just about anything by a Victorian or Edwardian novelist. How many times did you have to go back and start a sentence over again to fully understand its meaning or even get your tongue around its rhythms? Now hold on to that memory in what follows…

1904—1934

Chapter 7
Wodehouse the Lyricist

There is a world of difference between the demeanour of an audience when it merely likes a tune and when it finds the words amusing as well.

The lyrist may rhyme "ships" with "six", and no questions asked.

On Lyric Writing

It was not the money I wanted so much as the fame.

Dramatizitis

In May 1906, high on success, Wodehouse – now the seasoned veteran of just two theatre productions – published an uncredited but magisterial article entitled 'On Lyric Writing' in the London *Evening Standard and St James's Gazette*, from which the following is taken:

> Lyric-writing is like golf—it looks easy, but there is a great deal more in it than the casual spectator would imagine. If the casual spectator doubts this, let him try...

> But there are no second chances on the stage. There is just the instant in which the audience sees or misses a point. Then all is over. And mere toleration is useless. A newspaper reader may feel that a set of verses are passable, though he does not see his way to more than a gentle smile at their humour. But in a theatre the laugh has to be a big one, or it might as well not be laughed at all.

In Plum's theatre rulebook, just as with his prose works, the audience would always be both his point of departure and his top priority, since they were his paying guests who deserved hospitable treatment. As early as the second volume of his commonplace books, which he is thought to have begun in 1904, he tellingly comments: "In writing for the stage you have to frame your dialogue so as to get your points <u>quick</u>" [PGW's underlining]. But once again, as with those leaping Alpine chamois, not *so* quickly that you outpace the audience's ability to process the sense of your words. His long-time collaborator Guy Bolton constantly reminded him to "never give an audience too much to think about at one time". Patrons only have one chance to hear and understand a line before the drama moves on – so the flow of their attention *through* the words shouldn't be needlessly interrupted or get diverted. If it is, they can quite literally lose the plot in the struggle to re-orientate themselves. So excessive verbiage and complex verbal structures should be nixed, as should any form of distraction, however small, whether in the form of a wince-inducing rhyme, a forced rhythm or anything else that draws attention to itself and away from the overall purpose and trajectory of the lyric's sense. In this way, the audience gets things straight in their heads on first (and usually only) hearing, and the point of the piece is free to emerge naturally, in an unforced and orderly exposition. All the words in a Wodehouse lyric, dialogue or narrative are busy pulling their weight, from the humblest indefinite article to the purplest adjective, and are there to do a specific job in partnership with all the rest.

This same attention to detail also applies to structure, timing and flow, particularly when the lyricist wishes to reveal the point of a song – usually in the closing of the refrain – so it can be repeated and re-emphasized to maximum effect. Plum wrote:

> The ideal lyric should give at least two warnings before the point of a verse is reached. Instead of being distributed over eight lines…the point must be concentrated on the last line. Absence of point in the earlier part of [a] stanza is a merit. Absence of point in the latter half of the refrain kills the song.

The refrain – essentially the song's punchline – is typically situated at the close of each verse. By saving it up until the end, the audience is given enough time "to [get] their brains into marching order" using the material leading up to it. If the lyricist plays his hand too early, "the song would be over" before it had finished, either leaving the rest of the lyric with nothing to do, or leaving a confused audience that hasn't yet been given sufficient "warnings" as to what the song is about. Ideally, the writer wants his listeners primed and ready for his knock-out punch, and it's down to the lyricist's sense of pacing to make sure this happens.

Take Plum's best-known song lyric, 'Bill' (what follows is the original version that was written for the 1918 stage musical *Oh, Lady! Lady!!* but dropped prior to its opening):

I used to dream that I would discover
The perfect lover someday,
I knew I'd recognize him if ever
He came 'round my way.
I always used to fancy then
He'd be one of the God-like kind of men
With a giant brain and a noble head
Like the heroes bold
In the books I've read.

But along came Bill
Who's quite the opposite of all
The men in storybooks
In grace and looks
I know that Apollo
Would beat him
All hollow
And I can't explain,
It's surely not his brain
That makes me thrill —
I love him because he's wonderful,
Because he's just my Bill.

He can't play golf or tennis or polo,
Or sing a solo, or row.
He isn't half as handsome
As dozens of men that I know.
He isn't tall or straight or slim
And he dresses far worse than Ted or Jim.
And I can't explain why he should be
Just the one, one man in the world for me.

He's just my Bill, an ordinary man,
He hasn't got a thing that I can brag about.
And yet to be
Upon his knee
So comfy and roomy
Seems natural to me.
Oh, I can't explain,
It's surely not his brain

That makes me thrill –
I love him because he's – I don't know…
Because he's just my Bill.

Deceptively simple, yet there's a lot going on in here. In the song's opening stanza, the singer tells us she once dreamed of "a perfect lover", yet has fallen for a man who is resolutely ordinary in every aspect of his being: looks, intelligence and abilities. The rest of the song is spent listing where he falls short, before concluding that none of this matters: Bill is who he is, and she doesn't need him any other way. Appropriately, the rhyme and rhythms of the words are plain and unassuming – nothing to spook the horses here; any doubts one might entertain when reading the lyric in print (like the rhyming of "knee" with "roomy") evaporate on contact with Kern's music. So we have a proposition and an exposition, leaving the audience ready for the wonderfully understated yet hugely effective final punchline: *I love him because he's – I don't know…/ Because he's just my Bill.*

First time around, Kern's triplet at the end of that first line is conventionally covered by the lingering, slightly sensual trisyllable "won/der/ful". Second time, right before the song's triumphant close, there's a late caesura, a pause that forces the audience's ears to sit up and pay attention, before Plum overlays the same triplet with the throwaway "I don't know". Anticlimactic? Not a bit of it, because in those three words Plum gently emphasizes that this elegant lyric has been about inarticulacy, the state of *not* being able to say what one means – while he, the lyricist, is saying *precisely* what he means.

The enigma that is love's magnetism is a familiar Wodehouse theme that is played out between many of his leading ladies and their chosen men, and in the novels or stories, there's plenty of room for exposition. But watch Ava Gardner singing 'Bill' on the un-overdubbed soundtrack of the 1951 movie *Showboat* (at the time of writing, it's available on YouTube), and that brief hesitation of around one second is a vacancy that speaks volumes. She wants to justify – to herself as much as anybody – *why* she has selected such an unpromising mate; yet her inability to express herself, though frustrating, is an essential part of the mystery of human attraction. So in giving up the fight to say why she feels the way she does, she's also celebrating the strength of her love: after all, if you could itemize love in a set of numbered bullet points, it wouldn't be quite so romantic, would it? And note in the close-up how Gardner's mouth starts silently shaping itself into words that don't come out; hence the resigned impatience of her subsequent "I don't know", which picks up Plum's lyrical hint and sprints off with it. Not only that, her eyes are tearing up at the same time – it's a sublime moment occasioned by what is, when all's said and done, a disarmingly simple set of words.

There – it's taken me umpteen lines to explain what happens in a few short seconds of a performed song lyric. And that is but a single example of what Plum was writing about in that precocious essay of 1906: the lyricist, performer and audience are engaged in a synchronized three-way communication, which, when it's firing on all cylinders, can be magic. But if the song doesn't work, the writer has to face the wrath of the performer: as Seymour Hicks once told him: "When you're singing a rotten verse you see in a sort of mirage the face of the lyrist [sic], and you feel, 'You let me in for this!'" So just as important as the quality of the lyric itself is the lyricist's projection of how his words are going to be (a) performed and (b) listened *to*.

So why, Plum must have asked himself at some point, should this same meticulous care, this courtesy of orderly exposition not be extended to his print readers? As our writer-in-residence Bertie tells us in *The Mating Season*:

> [I]t has been my constant aim throughout to get the right word in the right place and to avoid fobbing the customers off with something weak and inexpressive when they have the right to expect the telling phrase. It means a bit of extra work, but one has one's code.

Similarly, in *Jeeves and the Feudal Spirit*, Florence Craye is described as "a slow, careful worker who mused a good bit between paragraphs and spared no pains to find the exact word… Like Flaubert, she said". To which Bertie replies, "And I said I thought she was on the right lines" since they were "more or less my methods when I wrote that thing of mine for the *Boudoir*". Bertie, of course, hasn't a clue who la Craye is talking about, but Flaubert was to become something of a fixture in Plum's later novels as a writer who always says what he means; in *Company for Henry*, he is dubbed "the exact stylist" and a model to be imitated.

Passing over the multiple ironies in that exchange, Plum would still insist that a bit of extra care will pay dividends, no matter what you're authoring. Back in that article on lyric writing, here's how he pictured a member of his public reading a poem printed in a newspaper – like his earliest efforts were – and not getting its sense first time through:

> [T]here is a certain doggedness, about the average news-paper reader. He argues with himself, after reading a poem which does not seem at first sight to contain any meaning, that the editor would probably not have printed it if there was not a point wrapped up in it somewhere, and he proceeds to attack it again. After that he consults a friend, and they have a dash at it together. And in the end, when the day is far spent, they see the writer's idea.

But isn't that a clumsy process? Isn't it plain *discourteous* of the writer not to make his meaning clear in such a way that the reader has to almost literally mine it out of the text? And so Plum takes care that his prose – practically *all* his prose – is well-mannered: snappy, simple and com-prehensible, as if it were being performed out loud, thus appealing to something we might refer to as 'the mind's ear' as much as the mind's eye.

It's here I'm going to declare a professional interest: as a drama director, it's a joy to work with a Wodehouse text, because his prose doesn't just read beautifully, it can be quickly and painlessly adapted for performance – and this facility is substantially down to Plum's uncanny appreciation of the way words sound. To me, at any rate, it appears he never ceased reminding himself that we 'hear' what we are reading in our heads as we are reading it, just as much as a good writer should 'hear' what he's writing on the page. This awareness benefitted, in dif-ferent ways, both his lyrics and his prose, and for the sake of brevity I'm going to highlight just five of the departments in which it excelled – sound, accent, dialogue, rhythm and rhyme – and which I feel are the most important in helping us to understand Plum's fetish for linguis-tic precision, as well as his writing's 'performativity' (a dreadful recent coinage which is actually quite helpful here, referring to language's ability to encapsulate, express and stimulate action).

First, **sound**: on countless occasions, Plum demonstrates that he was gifted with a kind of osmotic sensitivity to sounds and their signifi-cances, right down to individual syllables; naturally, he has fun with this predisposition. In 'A Slice of Life', Wilfred Mulliner is presented with a visitor, whose card of introduction he reads out loud:

"Sir Jasper Finch-Farrowmere?" said Wilfred.

"ffinch-ffarrowmere", corrected the visitor, his sensitive ear detecting the capital letters.

A recording engineer would refer to the two different 'f' sounds (written here as 'F' and 'ff') as examples of 'attack' – how a sound begins and subsequently varies in volume. In this example, Wilfred gets things wrong when he reads the printed words "ffinch-ffarrowmere" as if each half of the name started with a single, hard capital F, when in fact the double lower-case ff indicates that the attack should be reduced to little more than an exhalation of breath, "ferfinch ferfarrowmere", as if the speaker has a one-beat stutter. Yes, it's a joke – and a good one, too – but it also informs us that here is a writer who was a preternaturally sensitive listener who wants his readers to actually *hear* what he's writing. Similarly in *Big Money*, when Lord Biskerton first hears Kitchie Valentine's voice, he observes that her "intonation" (which is clearly American) dictates that she doesn't say "Yes", but "an observation which was neither 'Yep', 'Yup', nor 'Yop', but a musical blend of all three". How precise is that? Plum has clearly done an audit on verbal affirmation, since in *Money For Nothing* he has Hugo Carmody note that:

> ...the English language provides nearly fifty different methods of replying in the affirmative, including Yeah, Yeth, Yum, Yo, Yaw, Chess, Chass, Chuss, Yip, Yep, Yop, Yup, Yurp...

Tiny little distinctions, maybe – but Plum has noticed them, and the list is only cut short at 13 because Hugo is told in no uncertain terms to zip it. Or how about this from 'The Passing of Ambrose', on the various ways of pronouncing an item of headgear (it's written to be read in a voice that possesses "bluff, sailorly sympathy"):

> Here you are, sir...he's your rat. A little the worse for wear, this sat is, I'm afraid, sir. A gentleman happened to step on it. You can't step on a nat...not without hurting it. That tat is not the yat it was.

Because 'hat' begins with a voiceless pharyngeal fricative (oh yes) – which means in English that the letter 'h' is more a breath than a sound – it tends to get lost in pronunciation, with the rest of the word elided into what has immediately preceded it. Here Plum gives us an object lesson in what happens using five different consonants. He even picks out a character whose accent will make this little party trick work. *There's* an ear for detail if you like. And a nano-vaudeville sketch right there.

In fact, if you are happily leafing through a list of Wodehouse quotations, it's noticeable quite how many of them are descriptions of sounds, vocal or otherwise. For example, most writers' characters would say "Hmmm" or "Huh" when expressing disbelief; but not Angus McAllister, the Blandings gardener from north of the border (the man easily distinguishable from a ray of sunshine when he has a grievance) who employs the utterly unique "mphm". Try it. It's spot on. After me – "m-*phum*" – like a rather diffident sneeze, or a Caledonianized "ahem". Again, most people think cuckoos go "cuckoo", but as Rachel Potter in 'The Nodder' has spotted, they *actually* go "Wuckoo". Listen carefully, and once again, you'll see that Plum is absolutely right: there's no hard 'c' on the front of that distinctive call.

One last example, this time from *The Luck of the Bodkins*: when Monty of that family explains to his former fiancée Gertrude Butterwick that he hadn't been playing around with chorus girl Sue Brown, she punctuates his speech with four variations on a theme of "Oh!" – and once more, Plum goes to great pains to ensure that we read them to ourselves with just the right inflection:

> This was not a sceptical 'Oh', a sneering 'Oh', one of those acid 'Oh's' which, emitted by the girl he loves, makes a man feel as if he has stepped on a tintack. It had relief in it, and kindliness, and remorse. It spoke of misunderstandings cleared away, of grievances forgotten. In fact, it was scarcely an 'Oh' at all, properly speaking. More like an 'Oo!'

Try those four variants out loud, perhaps adding an undertone of breathiness to underscore the element of 'relief' Plum draws our attention to in the final one. What other author takes this trouble to make sure we get things so spot on that his story rings true? Realists make sure they get their facts straight, but Plum is more focused on the space between thought and expression – just like a poet, in fact. Or, of course, a theatre director, who would need to collaborate with the performer to get those tones exactly right when spoken.

Perhaps Plum's most inventive noises are those we experience as

Empress of Blandings happily chows down, which onomatopoeically resemble "a sort of gulpy, gurgly, plobby, squishy, wofflesome sound, like a thousand eager men drinking soup in a foreign restaurant". Transcribed with such care, you can actually hear it for yourself. The same goes for Honoria Glossop's laugh, which sounds like "a squadron of cavalry charging over a tin bridge"; or, my personal favourite, Jeeves's soft cough, which, says Bertie, "reminds me of the very old sheep clearing its throat on a distant mountain top". And although this doesn't strictly fall under the heading of sounds, honourable mention must be made of the correct way to deliver the most famous pig call in literary history (perhaps the *only* pig call in literary history), "Pig-hoo-o-o-o-ey!" Apparently, it's all in the way you "push it over the thorax", and luckily James Belford drops by the Empress's sty to inform Lord Emsworth precisely how it's done:

> You want to begin the "Hoo" in a low minor of two quarter notes in four-four time. From this, build gradually to a higher note, until at last the voice is soaring in full crescendo, reaching F sharp on the natural scale and dwelling for two retarded half-notes, then breaking into a shower of accidental grace notes.

For this vocal feat (the details of which, my esteemed editor tells me, Plum adapted from a newspaper article about a hog-calling champion – Fred Patzel – in Nebraska), you apparently require:

> [A] voice that has been trained on the open prairie and that has gathered richness and strength from competing with tornadoes. You need a manly, sunburned, wind-scorched voice with a suggestion in it of the crackling of corn husks and the whisper of evening breezes in the fodder.

Well…yes. In Belford's delivery it alters transcription slightly, but still resembles "the sound of a great Amen" (Plum quoting from the poetry of little-known Victorian poet Adelaide Anne Procter, by the way):

Pig-HOOOOO-OOO-OOO-O-O-ey!

Which of course does the trick, and the Empress, who has been off her food, begins her gulpy, gurgly, etc., munching straight away. Bless her.

Next we come to **accent**.

When hearing and reproducing accents, Plum's writerly ear will attempt any and all, from the broken English of Russian writer Vladimir Brusiloff, who insists on addressing Cuthbert Banks as "Cootaboot" while scattering half-understood examples of American slang, to jinuwine Bowery slang courtesy of Pugsy Maloney in *Psmith, Journalist*:

> "Sure, dey just butted in… I was sittin' here, readin' me book, when de foist of de guys blew in. 'Boy,' says he, 'is de editor in?' 'Nope,' I says. 'I'll go in an' wait,' says he. 'Nuttin' doin',' says I. 'Nix on de goin' in act.' I might as well have saved me breat'. In he butts, and he's in der now. Well, in about t'ree minutes along comes another gazebo. 'Boy,' says he, 'is de editor in?' 'Nope,' I says. 'I'll wait,' says he lightin' out for de door. Wit dat I sees de proposition's too fierce for muh. I can't keep dese big husky guys out if dey's for buttin' in. So when de rest of de bunch comes along, I don't try to give dem de t'run down. I says, 'Well, gents,' I says, 'it's up to youse. De editor ain't in, but if youse wants to join de giddy t'rong, push t'roo inter de inner room. I can't be boddered.'"

"And what more *could* you have said?" counters Psmith, who, for once, has been silenced by that machine-gun fusillade of hard consonants. Plum reproduces Pugsy's accent and delivery not just phonetically, but complete with the accompanying colloquialisms and tag words necessary for authenticity. But is it accurate? Apparently, yes: at least according to Norman Murphy, who writes that "several American critics have praised [Wodehouse's] writing of New York 'Bowery'". I must confess I haven't been able to track these critics down, but I'm sure he (and they) are right: on one of the few occasions he was accused of being an Englishman with a tin ear for Americanisms (by a *New York Times* reviewer grinding his axe on *Barmy in Wonderland*), Wodehouse took him down by revealing that the offending dialogue was a direct lift from the all-American comic playwright George S. Kaufman, from whom he had bought the rights. For my money, it's the Irish-inflected authenticity of "muh" ("me"), "breat'" and "boddered" that stands out from the more traditional "youse"s, "foist"s and the "dese and dems and dozes" of more actorly Noo Yoik impersonations. Then there's Maloney's authentic Irish slang of "gazebo", (meaning "fool"), which serves to prove that Plum has done his homework and isn't just creating a random idiolect for his character. Also note the "giddy t'rong", the choice of that second word indicating that Pugsy has a little more poetry in his soul and vocabulary in his brain than we might at first suspect. Lastly, we have the verbal assault of the delivery – for this one-man crosstalk exchange was written to be delivered at breakneck speed. A seasoned character actor could have a ball with it, leaping from one mark on the stage to another and back again as he acts out the two-handed exchange single-handedly. Twenty years before the Dead End Kids took the movies by storm, Plum created the big-hearted vaudeville tough that is Pugsy, one of those fabled angels with dirty faces.

A second, rather different favourite of mine is the poshed-up Cockney of Keggs, the butler in *A Damsel in Distress*, who we overhear giving a guided tour round Belpher Castle:

> I will call your attention…to this window, known in the fem'ly tradition as Leonard's leap. It was in the year seventeen 'undred and eighty-seven that Lord Leonard Forth, eldest son of 'Is Grace the Dook of Lochlane, 'urled 'imself out of this window in order to avoid compromising the beautiful Countess of Marshmoreton, with 'oom 'e is related to 'ave 'ad a ninnocent romance… We will now proceed to the Amber Drawing Room, containing some Gobelin tapestries 'ighly spoken of by connoozers.

This is just masterful – the mix of specialized knowledge and linguistic ignorance, high subject and low delivery – yet Wodehouse stops short of simply caricaturing the accent using full-blown stage Cockernee. He knows just when and how to pull back. And because accents are to some degree a window on the speaker's soul, it's important to get them *just* right. I hear this one sounding slightly adenoidal, like Parker, Lady Penelope's slightly disreputable chauffeur in *Thunderbirds* – although Parker tends to add aitches where Keggs drops his. Keggs is an old rogue reeling off his regular script, yet it's clear he takes at least some pride in his ambassadorial role, since it reflects his status and dignity within the household. So he does his best, within his limited capabilities, to raise the tone and content of the tour to match the grandness of his stately surroundings…and fails just enough to let us see what he's up to. Note that instead of saying "1787" he substitutes "seventeen 'undred and eighty-seven", padding like crazy but also trying to make the story sound so much more portentous than a randy toff jumping out of a window with his breeches round his ankles. As a result of his defenestration, note how the Dook suffers "a few 'armless contusions" – far more appropriate injuries for a man of his rank than common "bruises". Then there's the tiny rhythmical shift that makes "an innocent" into "a ninnocent", before Keggs falls at the final fence, betrayed by a treacherous foreign word that he mispronounces as "connoozers".

And talking of Franglais, I can't resist including the classic opening of *The Luck of the Bodkins*, in which Monty requests some stationery from a French waiter in wildly incorrect phonetic French. Said waiter returns with Monty's demands, vocally itemizing them one by one ("[e] enk – pin – pipper – envelope – and a liddle bit of bloddin-pipper") before somehow managing a perfect "Right ho, m'sieur" to round off the exchange.

All good knockabout stuff. But this isn't as easy as it looks. What we're being treated to here is not just a series of vocal impersonations but a gossamer-light treatise on why people choose the words they use, and what's going on in their heads as they're delivering them. And nowhere is this demonstrated more successfully than in *Right Ho, Jeeves*, when that temperamental Provençal and "supreme slinger of roasts and hashes" Anatole lets rip on the subject of the drunken Gussie Fink-Nottle, who has been pulling faces at him through his bedroom window. Three spectacular tirades later, we're left marvelling at Anatole's brilliant but slightly askew grasp of the English vernacular, which he has clearly put a lot of effort into mastering and proudly wants to show off. Plum gives the reader just enough of a clue for us to instantly guess which words the master chef is groping for, but missing or mangling. And so, as Bertie so aptly puts it, the performance that follows is "fluent but a bit mixed":

> *Hot dog! You ask me what is it? Listen. Make some attention a little. Me, I have hit the hay, but I do not sleep so good, and presently I wake and up I look, and there is one who make faces against me through the dashed window. Is that a pretty affair? Is that convenient? If you think I like it, you jolly well mistake yourself. I am so mad as a wet hen. And why not? I am somebody, isn't it? This is a bedroom, what-what, not a house for some apes? Then for what do blighters sit on my window so cool as a few cucumbers, making some faces.*

To which Bertie can only reply, "Quite", before commenting in his narrator's voice: "Dashed reasonable, was my verdict".

There's so much going on here, I'll only unpack it a little, lest too much daylight is let in on the magic. The three main things to remember are that Anatole was once employed by an **American** family who had an **Irish** chauffeur ("one of the Maloneys of Brooklyn", and probably one of Pugsy's blood relatives), before progressing to the very **English** Little household, where he "no doubt picked up a good deal from Bingo" (presumably the "dashed", "blighters" and "what-what"). Wrap the linguistic idiosyncrasies of these three nationalities around Anatole's native tongue, *et voilà!* Speaking in English but thinking first in **French**, he translates "*Fais attention un peu*" literally, which emerges as "make some attention a little", while confusing the English "convenient" for the similar French word "*convenable*", meaning "fitting", or "proper". And so on and so forth.

If any of the above examples were being performed by actors, they simply would not require a director or a voice coach. Plum does both jobs for them: the accent, the delivery and the character are already right there on the page – or, rather, already leaping off it in a 'performative' way. You get the impression, even from that short bit of analysis above, that Plum has sifted and weighed every word of Keggs's tour and Anatole's complaint before signing them off. And even better, in the latter case we're not simply laughing at some silly Frenchman who can't speak English – we're with Anatole all the way because his expression is not a parody but an idiolect, and a damned brilliant one at that.

The same meticulous ear for detail also applies to Plum's **dialogue**: pick just about any novel at random and there are sparkling exchanges to suit just about every occasion that would effortlessly make the journey from the stage to the page – and vice versa. And, in the following example from *Doctor Sally*, actually did:

SIR HUGO: Have you been sleeping there all night?

BILL: Yes. Oo, I'm stiff!

SIR HUGO: But why?

BILL: Well, wouldn't you be stiff if you had slept all night on a hardish sofa?

SIR HUGO: I'm not asking you why you're stiff. I'm asking why you slept on that sofa.

BILL: I gave up my room to a lady.

SIR HUGO: You gave up your room to a lady?

BILL: Yes, I – Oh, heavens! Need we do this vaudeville cross-talk stuff so early in the morning?

Okay, I've helped a bit by inserting the character names, but really, Plum hadn't had to expend much energy on the conversion, because a high percentage of his novelistic dialogue can so easily be cut and pasted directly into a play text, and, of course, vice versa. He absolutely adored vaudeville crosstalk and inserted examples in many of his novels and stories, even between such un-vaudevillian-sounding English toffs as Barmy Fotheringay-Phipps and Pongo Twistleton-Twistleton, who are known for their "sparkling repartee and vigorous by-play":

PONGO: You came here, I see.

BARMY: Yes. I see you came here.

PONGO: Yes. An odd coincidence.

BARMY: Very odd.

PONGO: Well, skin off your nose.

BARMY: Fluff in your latchkey.

Except, of course, that their relationship has been put under a bit of strain by their both courting the same girl, so neither is exactly on form; in fact, one might detect "a touch of constraint" or even "a somewhat stiff manner" in their dialogue. When they're on fire, however, it's a very different story:

BARMY: I've got an aunt who complains of rheumatism.

PONGO: Well, who wouldn't? My father can't meet his creditors.

BARMY: Does he want to? My uncle Joe's in very low water right now.

PONGO: Too bad. What's he doing?

BARMY: Teaching swimming.

And so on. You can find your own favourite examples of Plum's dialogue skills, but another one of mine can be found in the Reggie Pepper short story 'Helping Freddie' from 1911, where, in one brilliantly modulated three-handed exchange, Jimmy Pinkerton, a theatrical type, sketches

196

out the future trajectory of the story's plot [the emboldening is my own, for reasons that will become apparent momentarily]:

> "I might work this up for the stage," **he said**. "It wouldn't make a bad situation for act two of a farce."

> "Farce!" **snarled poor old Freddie.**

> "Rather. Curtain of act one on hero, a well-meaning, half-baked sort of idiot just like — that is to say, a well-meaning, half-baked sort of idiot, kidnapping the child. Second act, his adventures with it. I'll rough it out to-night. Come along and show me the hotel, Reggie."

> **As we went I told him the rest of the story – the Angela part. He laid down his portmanteau and looked at me like an owl through his glasses.**

> "What!" **he said**. "Why, hang it, this is a play, ready-made. It's the old 'Tiny Hand' business. Always safe stuff. Parted lovers. Lisping child. Reconciliation over the little cradle. It's big. Child, centre. Girl L.C.; Freddie, up stage, by the piano. Can Freddie play the piano?"

> "He can play a little of 'The Rosary' with one finger."

> **Jimmy shook his head.**

> "No; we shall have to cut out the soft music. But the rest's all right. Look here." **He squatted in the sand.** "This stone is the girl. This bit of seaweed's the child. This nutshell is Freddie. Dialogue leading up to child's line. Child speaks like, 'Boofer lady, does 'oo love dadda?' Business of outstretched hands. Hold picture for a moment. Freddie crosses L., takes girl's hand. Business of swallowing lump in throat. Then big speech. 'Ah, Marie,' or whatever her name is — Jane — Agnes — Angela? Very well. 'Ah, Angela, has not this gone on too long? A little child rebukes us! Angela!' And so on."

First things to note are the stage directions, which include two appearances of "business of" — signifying those nonverbal cues that help us understand both mood and timing, straight from the theatre playbook. But in this exchange it's the "Boofer" that makes me howl every time, a pitch-perfect rendition of a sickly-sweet Bubbles type of precocious child trying and failing to get his gums round the tricky tri-syllable that is "beau/ti/ful". Then there's the grammatically challenged "does 'oo" and the four alliterative 'd' sounds giving some punctuation to the whole thing. An actor could deliver this line in a stylized baby voice, or in the matter-of-fact tones of a theatre director – for that is the role Jimmy is adopting for this scene. It would get the laugh either way. This is immediately contrasted with the faux seriousness and over-formality of the construction "has not this gone on" (instead of "hasn't this") which is both spot-on accurate and parodic at the same time, followed by the melodramatic repetition of Angela's name.

Now once again read the whole passage – not to yourself, but out loud as a performance, taking out the words I've emboldened as you're going along. And there, with a bit more tweaking, you've got a theatrical scene complete with peerless dialogue on a plate garnished with watercress. Unfortunately, Reggie is once again upstaged by a member of his supporting cast – a problem Wodehouse put right when he rewrote the story as 'Fixing it for Freddie' with Jeeves and Bertie in the two main speaking roles – but it's plain that he was already conflating the needs and demands of book readers with those of theatre audiences to the enrichment of both, because this scene (or perhaps more accurately, comedy sketch) is simply aching to be staged, having the advantages of brevity, punch – and hilarity.

Okay – just one more. There's a fascinating moment in *The Adventures of Sally* when Plum, as narrator, expresses his frustration with the inability of his chosen words, and the way they have to be printed in the book, to carry the precise dialogue rhythm he wants to convey, and he takes time out to set matters straight. First, here's the dialogue, between Bruce Carmyle and his domineering, slightly weird Uncle Donald, who kicks off the exchange:

"You going away?"
"Yes."
"Where are you going?"
"America."
"When you going?"
"Tomorrow morning."
"Why you going?"

Now here is Plum's complaint, and his advice to the reader:

> This dialogue has been set down as though it had been as brisk and snappy as any cross-talk between vaudeville comedians, but in reality Uncle Donald's peculiar methods of conversation had stretched it over a period of nearly three minutes: for after each reply and before each question he had puffed and sighed and inhaled his moustache with such painful deliberation that his companion's nerves were finding it difficult to bear up under the strain.

Plum is concerned that we hear the dialogue as *he* heard it when he dreamed it up, and goes to great pains to instruct us how this might be accomplished. Why? Because if we *do* hear it as snappy musical crosstalk, we will completely misunderstand the relationship that exists between the two men – which is almost unbearably strained rather than crosstalk chummy.

Uncle Donald is a queer fish: mean, embittered, nosy and snobbish – and certainly not one to waste a single word (note he doesn't ask "Why *are* you going?"). Donald, the junior partner in the family hierarchy, is made to sweat in the extended intervals between questions, and Plum reckons it's important that we're aware of this. Uncle Donald's suspicion and mean-spiritedness, squatting menacingly in the silences, now become almost tangible presences in the dialogue as we re-read, re-play and re-hear what's been said as instructed, and the precise time frame of the exchange ("nearly three minutes") is an index of quite how much Uncle Donald has the family in his thrall. Bruce doesn't – and probably daren't – interrupt, and confines his responses to the barest minimum – the economy is catching.

Then – finally – we come to Plum's sense of **rhythm,** his feeling for **rhyme** and how the two interrelate. His stepdaughter, Leonora, once wrote that he was "not a bit interested in music and can't play a note… But in spite of this, at the back of his mind the tune is there; with no knowledge of music he recognizes the rhythm, the short beats and the long beats". From the same source comes the story of the occasion a composer played a melody down the phone to Wodehouse three or four times, who not only finished his lyric the same day, but managed to make it fit the tune perfectly. It's a rare talent, and once again it's dependent on that inner ear that can hear rhythmic possibilities that don't yet exist. But getting *in* the rhythm can make the difference between engaging with art or remaining an uncomprehending outsider, as in this telling passage from *The Adventures of Sally*. Sally has gone back to her old job as a 'dime-a-dance' girl at the Flower Garden club, where most of her clients are what we might call rhythmically challenged, and end up crushing her toes. But then...

> [S]he found herself in the arms of a masterful expert, a man who danced better than she did, and suddenly there came to her a feeling that was almost gratitude, a miraculous slackening of her taut nerves, a delicious peace. Soothed and contented, she yielded herself with eyes half closed to the rhythm of the melody, finding it now robbed in some mysterious manner of all its stale cheapness.

The expert, not named, makes all the difference as he navigates the couple around the floor to the musical accompaniment (men always used to take the lead back in the day), transforming the "cheap" music into something she can work with and not have to fight against. In the same way, Wodehouse demonstrates throughout his writing that reading shouldn't be a struggle with recalcitrant rhythms, and that he should create the conditions for that "delicious peace", that direct engagement, wherever he could, even in his lightest confections. Lightness, that recurring quality in this book, was essential to Plum's whole ethos, and it was no accident that he wrote for the most part in rhythms that reflected this preoccupation, most obviously in the gently jogging rhythms of his comic verse.

Plum had been writing rhyming, rhythmical poetry from the start of his career. In fact, here's his first-ever paid-for poem, 'The Lost Repartee', which appeared in *Fun* magazine on 5 January 1901, when he was just 20:

> Oh! bitter the grief that it causes to me,
> The thought of that wonderful, lost repartee.
> In its youth and its beauty it fled from my brain
> And never, I fear me, ah! never again,
> If I wait all my life, from to-day till I die,
> Shall I find such a chance for a crushing reply.
>
> Its wording was mild, but that rendered it worse.
> It was crisply satirical, bitingly terse.
> And it fled! Yes, it fled! In my hour of need
> From my agonised brain did it coyly recede,

Returning no more with its luminous ray
Till the critical moment had perished for aye.

Oh! let lovers lament of love's terrible pangs,
Let hunters talk darkly of tigers and fangs,
Let the gambler repine o'er the loss of his cash,
Let the banker hold forth on the woes of a smash,
Let the penniless debtor dilate on how ill
He feels, when a dun ambles in with a bill,

Let the footpad explain all the feelings that gnaw
His heart, when he's safe in the hands of the Law,
Let ministers prate of the worries of state,
But none of these woes – though they're all of them great –
Can compare with the grief that is harassing me
For the loss of that priceless, superb repartee.

This was the first of literally hundreds of poems that Wodehouse published throughout his life, often written on the fly and on the most unlikely themes. The first point to note is how regular the metre is, in 11- and 12-syllable lines with the odd enjambement and mid-line caesura for rhythmical variety. There's some pleasing anaphora (the repeated "Let") – and that's pretty much it, other than to remark that the rhymes are all absolutely single and masculine. Couldn't be simpler. One read-through is all it takes for the poem to yield up the vast majority of what meaning it has. And that was pretty much how Plum's verse style remained, although he was perfectly capable of composing in a more adventurous variety of metres and rhyme schemes should he have felt the urge – more of which soon. But the important point to note in all his poems is that sense is never subordinated to sound. Plum is keen for us to *understand* what he's written and makes every effort to ensure he places no obstacles in our way. He will delight us with his rhythmical ingenuity, but once we pick up on the beat we can ride it to the end knowing we're in safe hands. It's verse that was never going to appeal to sophisticated critics or the Bloomsbury set, but it does its job and does it well.

There's a telling scene of poetry criticism in Plum's 1903 school story *A Prefect's Uncle*, in which three members of the Beckford College common room dissect the verses submitted by their pupils for the school poetry prize. Among them is Mr Wells, whom the narrator describes as a "prig", yet who insists on the highest possible standards in writing and reading metre – just as Plum himself would have done had he been the judge. Here's the opening of the winning entry, from one Lorimer of School House:

> Queen of Tyre, ancient Tyre
> Whilom mistress of the wave
> What did fortune e'er deny her?
> Were not all her warriors brave?

Wells has to read "Tyre" as a bi-syllable ("Tye/er") in order that it perfectly rhymes with "deny her" in the third line. As such, he's being perfectly correct, but in being forced to mispronounce the place name, he criticizes this early "flaw...in the gem", remarking that "it was rash of Master Lorimer to attempt such a difficult metre. He should have stuck to blank verse". In suggesting the use of a verse form that scans regularly but doesn't have to rhyme, Lorimer's infelicity would be removed. But while the Headmaster calls out Wells for being "hypercritical", Plum's inner pedant was probably nodding furiously, and he himself would only bend rhythms in the service of rhyme for comic effect; blank verse was not a habit for the serious poet to fall into.

The premium Plum placed on formality, orientation and comprehensibility was reflected in his loathing of slack or absent rhyming, which distracts the reader (or listener) as he wonders if he read (or heard) things right. Even the literary greats weren't immune from the odd duff correspondence, as we discover in *Galahad at Blandings*:

> For an instant Will Allsop's face lit up, as that of the poet Shelley...must have done when he suddenly realized that "blithe spirit" rhymes with "near it", not that it does, and another ode ["To a Skylark"] was off the assembly line.

And it wasn't only Shelley who was guilty of shoddy workmanship: in one of his early pieces for the American version of *Vanity Fair* magazine Plum lamented:

> From an intellectual standpoint, the most interesting thing in *The Passing Show* is that in one of the songs "dance" is made to rhyme with "Spanish". A lyrist [sic] who can do this will go far. It is the biggest thing in its line since Burns, in a moment of inspiration, rhymed "Loch Lomond" with

"before ye", and set a standard which will make modern poets thankful that they took to *vers libre*.

As we'll see later on, Plum hated vers libre for the simple reasons that (a) it didn't have to rhyme or scan, violating his own insistence on strictness of form, which (b) made the reader work too hard to make sense of what he was reading. It was the same with the lyrics of popular songs, even ones Plum admired, but which he thought he could improve with just the odd tweak. Remember 'Bill Bailey' from the previous chapter? Well, in the unlikely figure of Lord Emsworth, who apparently used to sing it as a boy, Plum highlights a jarring mismatch between the words and the tune:

> "[T]he chorus began, 'Won't you come home, Bill Bailey, won't you come home?' Now how did the next line go? Something about 'the whole day long', and you had to make the 'long' two syllables. 'Lo-ong', if you follow me."

And so you do. Lord E is clearly rambling here, but you just know this was something that stuck in the craw of Plum the Songwriter. "Long" is a monosyllable; so why should it suddenly grow an extra one when sung? The very idea...

When this tendency to poetic indiscipline started to infect stage plays, Wodehouse was equally unimpressed. In *Jill the Reckless*, at the first night performance of the aptly titled *Tried by Fire*, the audience reacts with dismay when they discover they're going to be watching a "poetic drama" written "in blank verse". Plum's heart would have sunk, too: in his conservative aesthetic, formal indiscipline usually meant a writer was either big-headed or just plain bad. It was inconsiderate, ill-mannered and lazy, and this was a point he returned to again and again. Rhyming wasn't some bourgeois pastime to be sneeringly dismissed by those whose tastes were more 'advanced'. It *mattered*, and justified the absurd lengths some of his characters go to in order to get the right word to fit – not always successfully:

> There was once a golfer who swore,
> "I will find a rhyme to Skiddaw!"
> He's abandoned the links,
> Smokes excessively, drinks,
> And his handicap's now eighty-four.

That said, one of the joys of Wodehouse's lyrical skill is how he taxes his ingenuity almost to destruction in the creation of what John Dawson has termed "surprise rhymes". Here's a very early example John chose from 1902, on the subject of autumn:

> O, bright is the sun, and oh! blue are the skies,
> And balmy the air, that once froze, is;
> And it's pleasant to watch the thermometer rise,
> And to feel there's a chance for our roses.

And here's another, this time cast as prose from the opening of the 1910 short story 'Deep Waters':

> Historians of the social life of the later Roman Empire speak of a certain young man of Ariminum, who would jump into rivers and swim in 'em. When his friends said "You fish!" he would answer, "Oh, pish! Fish can't swim like me, they have no vim in 'em."

Once again, the ingenuity is mind-boggling, perhaps all the more so for being expended on such a trifling commodity as a throwaway limerick. And yet, almost as soon as Plum started writing verse, the forms and style he was drawn to were rapidly going out of fashion, their appeal confined to the more populist magazines and, of course, their natural and perennial home in musical theatre. But despite the onset of modernism and the various poetic 'isms' that followed it, Plum never lost his love of regular-metred, rhyming verse – and was still writing it at the age of 92 in his preface to *The Golf Omnibus*:

> These are the men whose drives fly far, like bullets from a rifle,
> Who when they do a hole in par regard it as a trifle.
> Of such as these the bard has said: "Hech thrawfu' raltie rorkie,
> wi' thecht ta' croonie clapperhead and fash wi' unco' pawkie."

Still metrically perfect, and with his ear intact even when writing authentic Scottish-inflected jibberish.

So where did Plum's love of formality come from? We don't have to look far since, as has been often remarked, a passion for the theatre wasn't all Wodehouse took away from his 1895 visit to the Crystal Palace: it either inspired or else confirmed him in his love for the work

of William Schwenk Gilbert, the wordsmith of the celebrated Gilbert
and Sullivan partnership, whom we've already met. Gilbert's boot print
(it's far too large and forceful to be called a thumbprint) can be found
everywhere in Plum's writing, not least in the 172 direct allusions to his
writing that pepper Plum's own (that's David Jasen's total, but more are
being discovered all the time). In fact, his influence is so marked, the
paragraphs that immediately follow could be inserted almost anywhere
in this book – for it wasn't just in language, metre and rhyme that we encounter echoes of "England's greatest librettist", as Plum refers to him
in *A Prefect's Uncle*, but in Wodehouse's whole approach to humour, his
public, and literature in general. It's an interesting exercise, but if you
dig out assessments of Gilbert's influence on musical theatre and substitute his surname with "Wodehouse", they tend to be equally applicable.
Try it with this, from an anonymous writer in the London *Times* of
1957, summing up the appeal of the Savoy Operas.

> [T]hey were never really contemporary in their idiom...
> Gilbert and Sullivan's [world], from the first moment was
> obviously not the audience's world, [it was] an artificial
> world, with a neatly controlled and shapely precision
> which has not gone out of fashion – because it was never
> in fashion in the sense of using the fleeting conventions
> and ways of thought of contemporary human society...
> The neat articulation of incredibilities in Gilbert's plots is
> perfectly matched by his language... His dialogue, with its
> primly mocking formality, satisfies both the ear and the in-
> telligence. His verses show an unequalled and very delicate
> gift for creating a comic effect by the contrast between
> poetic form and prosaic thought and wording... How de-
> liciously [his lines] prick the bubble of sentiment... Light,
> and even trifling, though [the operas] may seem upon
> grave consideration, they yet have the shapeliness and
> elegance that can make a trifle into a work of art.

This matches almost point for point some of the praise lavished on
Wodehouse's lyrics (and prose) a generation on from Gilbert's success.
For here also was a shining example of a developed poetic sensibility and
intelligence pressed into service not in the cause of high art, but popular
entertainment. Like Noel Coward's Amanda in *Private* Lives, Plum
really did understand the potency of "cheap music" – only in his view,

just because his work was mainstream and accessible – populist, even – that didn't mean it couldn't be done well. And it's the evident trouble he took, I think, as well as his ingenuity, that endeared Wodehouse to his fellow lyricists like Ira Gershwin, Alan Jay Lerner and all the others who, as we'll see, respected him for having been among the first to up the ante in their profession. It's perfectly possible to criticize Plum for selling his talent short by sticking to songwriting and humorous verse, but it's also possible to celebrate how he helped to introduce higher literary standards into stage musicals, thereby raising the bar within the genre as a whole. Taking care to write in rhythm and paying close attention to rhyme schemes are just two of the ways Wodehouse revealed his deep love and respect both for his métier, his audience – and his literary hero.

Okay, so that's just some of the nuts and bolts that Plum brought from the theatre to his prose. Now it's time to look at how those individual features – an instinct for drama, a good ear, economy, rhythm and rhyme – work within the overall strategy of the play's construction to create a taut, structured whole, and how that coherence was translated into Plum's novels.

1915–1922

Chapter 8
Wodehouse on Broadway

[T]he only known rule governing musical comedy is
that you must imitate the last success.

PGW, writing in (US) Vanity Fair

New York theatrical managers – the lowest order of intelligence,
with the possible exception of the limax maximus *or*
garden slug, known to science...

Jill the Reckless

He said it was an effort to restore the Gilbert and Sullivan tradition.
Say, who are these Gilbert and Sullivan guys anyway?
They get written up in the papers all the time and
I never met anyone who'd run across them.

Jill the Reckless

It's that year again.

In Plum's 1915 story 'Bill the Bloodhound', Henry Pifield Rice can be found strolling backstage at a theatre, and immediately begins "to experience all the complex emotions which come to the layman in that situation". For Henry has strayed, like "a cat...[in] a strange hostile backyard" into "a new world, inhabited by weird creatures, who flitted about in an eerie semi-darkness, like brightly coloured animals in a cavern".

It's not that Henry isn't a fan: theatre had always "fascinated" him. "To meet even minor members of the profession off the boards gave him a thrill". But the musical theatre is one of Plum's many microcosms, a world that exists in its own bubble and governed by rules and behaviour that are often resistant to an outsider's understanding. And so it was with the real thing: up to the time he published this story, Plum, like Henry, had been a comparative outsider as regards the American version, but one soon to be inducted into its deeper mysteries when he was made the drama critic of the upmarket *Vanity Fair* magazine that same year. By the time he had written his two main 'theatre' novels, *Jill the Reckless* and *The Adventures of Sally*, which appeared in 1921 and 1922 respectively, he was sitting pretty at the top of the tree, the master of all he surveyed. So it is with this seven-year period this chapter will mostly concern itself, for it was during this time that Plum overlaid the template of the musical comedies whose book and lyrics he was concocting onto the way he was to approach the craft of novel writing. By the end, both were virtually interchangeable – and it is no coincidence that Plum was entering his long run of mid-season form just as this was happening. For, backstage at the theatre, he found just the kind of reality he could do profitable business with, and a milieu in which he could perfect many of the skills he would need to up his game even further.

All through the years of the First World War, Broadway was booming: The Great White Way was home to between 70 and 80 theatres, many of them hungry for the next great musical comedy. And given that an average musical comedy could end up being home to over 20 songs, that represented an awful lot of songwriting. But quantity did not always equate to quality, and when he started out at *Vanity Fair* in 1915, Plum wasn't a huge fan of much of what was being foisted on the theatregoing public.

Basically, Broadway put on three types of shows that paired comedy with music: vaudeville (which we've already encountered), the revue and the musical play. The first was a series of unconnected, separate acts; the second, a set of sketches with or without a connecting thread; the third, a story with songs, which all too often resembled the second (or even the first) in its lack of cohesion. As Plum complained in one of his early columns, exaggerating only slightly:

> Until this year the only solid idea managers had as regards musical plays was to collect fifteen hundred frocks and a hundred girls and instruct the latter to wear the former and to start making a noise and go on making a noise till somewhere around eleven p.m.

The result? A triumph for chaos and the surreal. These days, with the popularity of fully structured "through-sung" musicals (as are many of Andrew Lloyd Webber's titles, for example), it's difficult for us to witness first-hand what Wodehouse found so clumsy in American musical theatre unless we go to a cabaret or revue, which are, of course, *meant* to be sequences of discreet, separate performances. In 'Bill the Bloodhound', he provides us with a pretty good example when Henry suddenly finds himself at "the centre of a kaleidoscopic whirl of feminine loveliness, dressed to represent such varying flora and fauna as rabbits, Parisian students, colleens, Dutch peasants, and daffodils". And it's true: look at many of the cast photos from productions of the period, and you see a lone male lead drowning at the centre of a sea of frocks and/ or costumes, many of them ill-assorted. This preference for spectacle over content had made musical comedy "the Irish stew of the drama" – a metaphor we'll be meeting again later when Plum, at around the same time, used it to denigrate Modernistic trends in literature. In other words, a musical comedy was a sort of portmanteau into which you can chuck anything, and it will most likely fit. Somehow. With a bit of inge-nuity and perhaps even a crowbar. But this approach had three major disadvantages, as Plum repeatedly informs us in his reviews of the time:

- It was expensive, which discouraged all but the richest investors.

- The show was more a revue than a coherent play, and yet…

- It *still* harboured pretensions to being art rather than pure entertainment.

It's the middle one that will concern us most in this chapter, for it is most closely related to Wodehouse's twin theatrical roles of writing song lyrics and constructing the musical's "book" – the narrative structure that is supposed to keep the score from degenerating into a disjointed medley of songs. We might even call it the 'glue' that holds the show together. As we'll see, internal coherence came to be something of a fetish with Plum, and was perhaps the single important consideration in the way he was to structure his plots, both on and off the stage, for the next 60 years.

Things had gone a bit quiet for him on the musical comedy front since *The Gay Gordons*, a Seymour Hicks production that enjoyed a rea-sonable London run back in 1907. He had contributed around 20 lyrics to a revue, *Nuts and Wine*, in 1914, which closed after a few performanc-es despite being described in the U.K. Government Censor's report as "rather happy in its good-humoured chaff with the crazes of today". Perhaps the most interesting thing about the show was the finale, a song entitled 'We're Clearing out of England', for that's precisely what Plum did a few weeks later, not to return until 1919. The lyric is a litany of annoying gripes, from the inadequacy of the telephone system to the craze for the tango, culminating in the following lines:

And however well I speak
They forget me in a week
What good is that to me?
As far as I can see
Old England simply isn't worth a _____ [*damn*]

Once over the Pond, things moved fast. Now, with his legs under the desk at *Vanity Fair* and busying himself with the debuts of Lord Emsworth and Bertie, there came that fateful night late in 1915 (opinions vary as to the precise month and day) when Wodehouse and Jerome Kern were reacquainted, and Plum was introduced to future lifelong friend Guy Bolton. Bolton and Kern were already collaborators, and Plum, with his reviewer's hat on, had already given his seal of approval to their second joint production, *Nobody Home*. His opening remarks concern the excellence of the male lead, a knut named Freddie Popple, played by the English actor Lawrence Grossmith:

> To get a new angle on the English dude at this late day is much, but to make him the whole evening's entertainment is genius. Freddie, of course, is not, strictly speaking, a dude, for he has spent all his life in the peaceful hamlet of Ippleton (on a branch line; you change at East Wobsley), but, as a comic Englishman, he falls into the dude class and must be considered as such. As Mr. Grossmith presents him, he is a delightful person, always courteous, always half asleep, always slow, but anxious to understand if you will only give him time. He is a creation.

The very same month this review appeared (September 1915), a not entirely dissimilar "creation" (Bertie, not yet surnamed Wooster) was to make his debut in the *Saturday Evening Post* in a story set in New York, 'Extricating Young Gussie'. But then Plum's attention was drawn to weightier matters:

> The undoubted success of *Nobody Home*…suggests…that the time has come when the public is beginning to cry out for something light and restful in the way of musical pieces. If, as has been proved, the public will attend and enjoy a quiet, simple, restful, inexpensive production with one first-class comedian and a small chorus, a new era will

begin. Perhaps as early as next season we shall see musical comedy what it really ought to be—clever coherent farce, depending for its humor on a good central idea and legitimate situations, the whole peppered with attractive music. The idea that the plot of a musical comedy must be inane and its characters like nothing on earth is a purely arbitrary one, due to a quaint old theatrical superstition.

This boded well: Bolton and Kern were thinking along exactly the same lines, and were already involved with a theatre where small-scale shows wouldn't be swallowed up in the echoing void of a cavernous auditorium. The newly built 299-seat Princess Theatre at 104 West 39th Street in Manhattan fitted Wodehouse's prescription exactly: its more intimate space would allow writers to employ a broader palette of vocal effects, making for more nuanced plots, settings and performances. For example, songs could be written that would not require bellowing to playgoers seated miles away at the back of the upper circle. In 'The Pride of the Woosters Is Wounded', Bertie says of Bingo Little: "He always reminds me of the hero of a musical comedy who takes the centre of the stage, gathers the boys round him in a circle, and tells them about his love at the top of his voice". Well, that lack of subtlety would no longer be necessary: a smaller space could allow the intimacy of a love song like 'Bill' to be better appreciated.

Next on Plum's menu was the idea of what he called "restful" entertainment (you'll notice that word crops up twice in the above review), and here he championed the modest demands of the playgoer as rehearsed in *Jill the Reckless*:

> When one considers how full of his own troubles, how weighed down with the problems of his own existence the average playgoer is when he enters the theatre, it is remarkable that dramatists ever find it possible to divert and entertain whole audiences for a space of several hours.

In 'Bill the Bloodhound', the anonymous dramaturge of *The Girl from Brighton* has taken this principle on board, cannily aiming his show at "the Tired Business Man". In fact, this particular class of patron is something of a recurring theme with Wodehouse: in the golf story 'High Stakes', even a swarm of bees viewed in the evening have the air of "tired business men who are about ready to shut up the office and go off to dinner and a musical comedy". All too often, however, writers and/or producers decide that this audience, made weary with work, requires in-your-face spectacle, and lots of it. Plum didn't agree, not least because, artistically, spectacle would always fall victim to the law of diminishing returns: the only way to top a success would be for a bigger or more sensational spectacle (what Plum called "piling situation on situation"), until things got so ridiculously out of hand that some brave soul "was forced to draw the line and shout 'Stop!'" In *Jill the Reckless*, Jill agrees with Wally Mason that this point has been reached in New York musical theatre, both on- and off-stage:

> "There isn't anything that can't happen in musical comedy. Alice in Wonderland is nothing to it."

> "Have you felt that too? That's exactly how I feel. It's like a perpetual 'Mad Hatter's Tea Party'."

Plum had clearly witnessed too much of this sort of thing: his villainous theatre manager Mr Goble's idea of a good show "was something embracing trained seals, acrobats, and two or three teams of skilled buck-and-wing dancers, with nothing on the stage, from a tree to a lampshade, which could not suddenly turn into a chorus girl". Plum's view was rather more refined: musical theatre need not involve hiring a circus, nor a bizarrely costumed chorus. Rather, it was a good old-fashioned story set to good music. The Tired Business Man required something that would serve to mop his fevered brow, not dazzle and excite his already over-stimulated nervous system; and so it was perhaps a better idea to try to gently lure him *into* the show rather than shout *at* him.

Finally, and most importantly on Plum's shopping list, there is that innocent yet incredibly important word 'coherence'. Almost 50 years on from the Princess musicals, Leonard Bernstein would write, "The whole growth of our musical comedy can be seen through the growth of integration" between music, book and lyrics, which is precisely what Plum was saying back in his 1915 review, and had been saying in his column for much of that year. Over three decades later, Gussie Fink-Nottle was still banging on about exactly the same thing in *The Mating Season*. Having read Catsmeat Potter-Pirbright's first draft of a simple crosstalk routine, he comments that it is "absolute drivel", having no "dramatic coherence…motivation and significant form". Slightly lofty ambitions for an encounter between Pat and Mike, but Gussie has his standards and knows what he is looking for. Jeeves, too, is a stickler for structure, similarly criticizing Florence Craye's novel *Spindrift* as "a somewhat juvenile production lacking in significant form" – but which, he tellingly adds, could "quite possibly have its appeal for the theatre-going public" if adapted for the stage.

So there we have it: small-scale, restful, coherent, clever shows were what Plum was looking for, and with a track record in publishing like his, they were just the sort of thing he was hard-wired to deliver. In his April 1915 review of a "Musical-Farcical-Comedy" called *The Only Girl*, he seems to have already found his Holy Grail:

> Here we have a starless cast, inexpensive scenery, and a chorus of six. The music, though by Mr. Victor Herbert, is not remarkably attractive. It is the play with its straight comedy story and its logical situations that has made the success. It contains a real idea, worked out on strictly comedic lines.

And that's precisely what he intended to write. A change of scenery had also helped. England was by now mired in war, but over in New York Bertie, on his debut in 1915's 'Extricating Young Gussie', remarks on the entirely different atmosphere:

> [T]here's something in the air, either the ozone or the phosphates or something, which makes you sit up and take notice. A kind of zip, as it were. A sort of bally freedom, if you know what I mean, that gets into your blood and bucks you up, and makes you feel that—
>
> God's in His Heaven:
> All's right with the world,
> and you don't care if you've got odd socks on.

And so, sometime in that auspicious year, the soon-to-be "trio of musical fame" comprising Bolton and Wodehouse and Kern was formed. Both Plum's collaborators were already singing from the same hymn sheet as he was, with Kern commenting: "It is my opinion that the musical numbers should carry on the action of the play, and should be representative of the personalities who sing them... In other words, songs must be suited to the action and mood of the play". Although Kern was to prove a prickly collaborator, at least he and Plum saw eye to eye on this particular point – as did Bolton, to make up the set – the following Bolton boost for the partnership is taken from Gerald Bordman's 1978 book, *American Musical Theatre: A Chronicle*:

> Our musical comedies…depend as much upon plot and the development of their characters for success as upon their music, and…they deal with subjects and peoples near to the audiences. In the development of our plot… we endeavor to make everything count. Every line, funny or serious, is supposedly to help the plot continue to hold.

Everything boded well, and the team rolled up their sleeves and got to work.

Perhaps the most frequent crime against coherence committed by writers and producers (but mainly producers, if you believe Plum) was to belatedly 'parachute in' songs that had little (or nothing) to do with the original plot trajectory, character development, "the mood of the play" or indeed anything else. "Interpolation" (as it is known in theatrical circles) represented the sworn enemy of integration and coherence, although a producer would claim he was improving the production by weeding out the weak numbers and replacing songs that didn't work with something the audience might actually want to hear. Nonetheless, this prioritization of commercial considerations over artistic integrity was bound to cause disharmony all round, both onstage within the original production team, and backstage among the chancers hoping their song might be given a break. We are informed in *Jill the Reckless* that it was not uncommon during the interval to overhear "a composer who had not got an interpolated number in the show…explaining to another composer who had not got an interpolated number in the show the exact source from which a third composer who had got an interpolated number in the show had stolen the number which he had got interpolated". And *The Girl from Brighton* is a fine example of the perils of this mix-and-match approach, as Plum satirically points out: there is "a crisis in the heroine's life. She meets it bravely. She sings a song entitled 'My Honolulu Queen', with chorus of Japanese girls and Bulgarian officers".

Similarly, Mr Goble's idea of a musical involves "shelv[ing] the plot after the opening number and fill[ing] in the rest of the evening by bringing on the girls in a variety of exotic costumes, with some good vaudeville specialists to get the laugh". It's a lesson that Bingo Little learns from bitter experience in 'The Metropolitan Touch' when he tries to introduce "that Orange-Girl number that's the big hit of the Palace revue" to his village hall entertainment *What Ho, Twing!!* Successful song – wrong audience. It just doesn't work – which makes it slightly ironic that Plum's best-known song 'Bill' (which we encountered earlier), found fame some years later as an interpolated number in *Show Boat*, having been dropped from Plum's *Oh Lady! Lady!!* But that's showbiz for ya. As first-time playwright Otis Pilkington quickly discovers in *Jill the Reckless*, the precious play he has slaved over for years can almost immediately be transformed into something he barely recognizes – and even wishes to disown.

To Plum, theoretically at least, all this mucking about was complete anathema, despite interpolation being a regular (and sometimes necessary) feature of many of the shows he was personally involved with. "Musical comedy", he wrote in a 1917 piece for *Vanity Fair*, "is not dashed off. It grows – slowly and painfully, and each step in its growth either bleaches another tuft of the author's hair or removes it from the parent skull altogether". Once again, he's reinforcing the fact that comedy is the fruit of hard graft. Less obvious but more important, however, is the implication that although any drama is an assembly of different elements, the joints shouldn't show. "It grows" suggests a balanced, organic development from a single point of departure rather than a patchwork of pre-existing pieces. Thought of in this way, the different elements are all mutually dependent: you can't alter one without disturbing its relationship to all the others. It's a principle not unlike that we recently encountered in Plum's views on poetry: a jarring rhyme or rhythm draws the wrong kind of attention to itself, distracting the reader, interrupting his engagement and most likely his enjoyment. And so it is with any stage show. More so, in fact, because in a theatre, the quality of attention is that much more immersive. Unlike the reader, the theatregoer is denied the luxury of travelling back in time and having a second try. Things will have moved on, making incongruity as potentially distracting as the performers forgetting their lines, the lights blowing a fuse, or, in the case of Wally Mason's *Trial By Fire*, the theatre erupting in flames.

Without writing a lengthy essay on mimetic theory, the suspension of disbelief and so forth, it's important to realize that Plum was far from being an idealist in these matters, otherwise he would not have pursued a career in musical theatre at all. As Wally Mason has it, "I don't say a musical comedy is a very lofty form of art, but there's still a certain amount of science about it" – and somewhere in that science is the realization that although a musical comedy *is* a jigsaw assembled from many different pieces, it doesn't, when performed, have to look like that.

Reading his theatrical journalism, it's clear Plum delighted in most of the absurdities of theatrical life. He was – of course he was – fully aware that an audience at a show featuring sea lions and Bulgarian officers hadn't left home expecting to witness an exquisitely crafted, organically structured work of art. But on occasion he did parody the more ridiculous aspects of musical theatre and its insatiable demand for "brainless trash and jingly tunes" – mostly good-naturedly, but sometimes with an evident air of frustration. In *Indiscretions of Archie* he provides us with the full lyric to a perfectly viable song, 'Mother's Knee', which, although the worst possible example of cloying, manufactured sentiment, still goes down a storm with those who hear it. Here's a sample, if you can bear it:

> One night a young man wandered through the glitter of Broadway:
>
> His money he had squandered. For a meal he couldn't pay.
>
> He thought about the village where his boyhood he had spent,
> And yearned for all the simple joys with which he'd been content.
> He looked upon the city, so frivolous and gay;
> And, as he heaved a weary sigh, these words he then did say:

> *It's a long way back to Mother's knee,*
> *Mother's knee,*
> *Mother's knee:*
> *It's a long way back to Mother's knee,*
> *Where I used to stand and prattle*
> *With my teddy-bear and rattle:*
> *Oh, those childhood days in Tennessee,*
> *They sure look good to me!*

"Whether you wanted to or not", says the narrator, "you heard every word". But the audience laps it up, including a hard-bitten labour leader who goes all teary-eyed and calls off a builders' strike, and even the singer herself, who decides to follow its protagonist on the tearful journey back to the simple, homespun values of her midwestern birthplace. "The words, stated [the music publisher] Mr Blumenthal, were gooey enough to hurt, and the tune reminded him of every other song-hit he had ever heard". And so? "There was…nothing to stop this thing selling a million copies".

But even taking into account all the strange, un-naturalistic conventions of the stage musical, Plum was still clearly of the opinion that the audience – though often satisfied with lowest-common-denominator tripe – deserved the kind of total immersion they would experience in a great production of *Hamlet*. Or, to be more precise, that the stage musical should – by its own lights and on its own terms – at least *aim* to create the same quality of illusion Shakespeare managed. Any stage performance in whatever genre is, from curtain up to final bow, a temporary world in miniature, complete with its own laws and customs which, if compromised, instantaneously vanishes like Brigadoon. And just because the musical theatre was populist entertainment didn't give those involved in crafting and delivering a show carte blanche to lower their standards or work beneath their abilities. The show should be as good as any theatre could be; the genre as proud and self-regarding as any other. And that meant taking every possible care to ensure it hung together – *convincingly* hung together, as if everyone involved was engaged in a collective endeavour, guided by a single, overarching vision. So Plum's dream scenario was to be given "a nice little contract by the management to go and sit in his study and evolve a careful and coherent play, in the knowledge that his lines and situations would be acted as written".

Some hope. Here's what he was up against, as detailed in his article 'The Agonies of Writing a Musical Comedy' from March 1917. "Critics", he writes, "are inclined to reproach, deride, blame and generally hammer the author of a musical comedy because his plot is not so consecutive and unbroken as the plot of a farce or a comedy. They do not realize the conditions under which he is working" – which, in a viciously paraphrased nutshell, are these:

Having come up with "a pleasing and ingenious plot", the author begins writing his work, "full of optimism". Almost immediately, he is forced to realign his artistic ambitions with the more practical demands of the theatre manager, the financial backer, and their collective choice of star vehicle, who could just as easily be the producer's current girlfriend as a big-name singer or comedian. Having audited and taken into account the talent (or otherwise) of the performers who have been pencilled in, the writing can begin:

> He takes a stiff bracer, ties a vinegar-soaked handkerchief round his forehead, and sets to work to remodel his piece. He is a trifle discouraged, but he perseveres. With almost superhuman toil he contrives the only possible story which will fit the necessities of the case.

This may have involved changing the character of the pickle manufacturer into a debutante, and casting the talentless but non-negotiable placemen as Trappist monks or deaf mutes, but everything sort of hangs together. Then he remembers, to his considerable chagrin, that he has forgotten "the Gurls", for it is "one of the immutable laws governing musical plays that at certain intervals during the evening the audience demand to see the chorus". This completely throws the structure of the whole piece:

> He cannot possibly shift musical number four, which is a chorus number, into the spot now occupied by musical number three, which is a duet, because three is a "situation" number, rooted to its place by the exigencies of the story. The only thing to do is to pull the act to pieces and start afresh. And when you consider that this sort of thing happens not once but a dozen times between the start of a musical comedy book and its completion, can you wonder that this branch of writing is included among the dangerous trades and that librettists always end by picking at the coverlet?

But even assuming his sanity remains intact and he somehow manages – by means of superhuman ingenuity – to corral everything together again, his troubles are far from over. The ramshackle façade is once more demolished by considerations of billing and status among the different strata of performers:

> Certain scenes are constructed so that A gets a laugh at the expense of B; but B is a five-hundred-a-week comedian and A is a two-hundred-a-week juvenile, and B refuses to "play straight" even for an instant for a social inferior. The original

line is such that it cannot be simply switched from one to the other. The scene has to be entirely reconstructed and further laugh lines thought of. Multiply this by a hundred, and you will begin to understand why, when you see a librettist, he is generally lying on his back on the sidewalk with a crowd standing round, saying, "Give him air."

As late as 1973 in *Bachelor's Anonymous*, Wodehouse was still exercised by this kind of behaviour within a cast, who should all have been pulling together for the good of the show. Joe Pickering's comedy *Cousin Angela* is being wrecked by its temperamental female lead, Miss Vera Dalrymple, who insists on stealing all the best lines for herself, "throw[ing] the whole show out of balance". At rehearsals, Joe complains to journalist Sally Fitch that

> [in] that bit they're doing now, it was supposed to be the man who was scoring. It linked up with something in the next act. The story depended on it. But a lot she cares about the story so long as she gets the laughs. I had to re-write the scene a dozen times before she was satisfied that she had grabbed everything that was worth grabbing.

And it's perhaps because of this selfishness that the show closes after 16 performances. But as Plum tells us repeatedly, all this was par for the course in musical theatre: like it or not, both book and lyrics were infinitely moveable feasts. When writing novels, he was for the most part in control; when writing for the musical stage, just about everything was the result of collaboration and/or a compromise with third, fourth or even fifth parties. Perhaps wisely using the pseudonym 'C. P. West', he complained of this overmanning in a 1916 article, once again for *Vanity Fair*:

> The aggregation contains the author, the part-author, the assistant-collaborator, the man who wrote in additional scenes, the man who contributed extra lines, the man who suggested supplementary business, the man who evolved the central idea, the lyrist, the associate-lyrists, the composer, the man who added extra numbers, the man who contributed supplementary music, the producer, the assistant-producer, the assistant-producer's assistant, the man who helped the assistant-producer's assistant assist

the assistant-producer assist the producer to produce, the
manager, the manager's colleagues, the wardrobe-mistress,
the box-office man, the fireman, the stage-manager, the
stage-manager's assistant, the stage-door keeper, and the
call-boy.

As a cog in this much larger machine, he would win some battles and
lose others, a lesson he learned almost immediately when Bolton/
Wodehouse/Kern's first two properties were turned down flat in
January 1916 by Ray Comstock, the Princess Theatre's manager. In
fact, a BWK musical comedy wouldn't open there until 20 February
1917, 15 months after the partnership was first announced – by which
time it had produced two shows elsewhere.

It's important to note that although writers on Wodehouse sometimes refer to the trio's glorious "Princess Years", what they usually mean
is that Bolton and Wodehouse and Kern were writing shows with the
modest dimensions and budgets of that theatre *in mind* since, for some
reason, it's rarely pointed out that the full team had just two musicals
actually produced there (*Oh, Boy!* and *Oh, Lady! Lady!!*). A maximum of
two sets, 12 "gurls" and 11 musicians sounds pretty lavish now, but at
the time was downright parsimonious, or "lilliputian" as Benny Green
has it. Robert McCrum eloquently described the ethos of a typical
Princess show, whether it ended up playing there or not:

> There was no room for a dull scene, a bad plot or a dud
> lyric. Cast and audience were cheek by jowl. Weaknesses
> that in a larger venue could be disguised by theatrical effects
> would never go unnoticed. The music had to sparkle, the
> comedy had to move like clockwork, and the lyrics had to
> fit into the very tight space between the book and the score.
> So the lyrics had to keep the narrative moving.

These principles, however often they were compromised in the rough
and tumble of bringing a show to the stage, would gradually sublimate
themselves into Plum's literary sensibility. If we wanted to reduce them
to a few key words, 'integration', 'economy', 'impact', 'emphasis', 'pace'
and 'meticulousness' wouldn't be a bad start, and while most of these
were present and correct in some form or other when he started his
'second' theatrical phase in 1915, the time he spent writing and rewrit-
ing books and lyrics would refine and deepen his understanding of the

tools of his trade. Which makes it all the more important to emphasize that in the midst of these theatrical shenanigans, Wodehouse's novelistic output was far from on hold, and that his rapidly developing skillset was a two-way street: in 1917 alone, he published *Piccadilly Jim*, *Uneasy Money*, the story collection *The Man with Two Left Feet*, and two Jeeves and Bertie stories, while completing books and lyrics to two shows (*Kitty Darlin'* and *The Riviera Girl*), writing all the lyrics and part of the book of three more (*Have a Heart*, *Oh, Boy!* and *Leave It to Jane*), and contributing sketches to the extravagantly appointed revue *Miss 1917*.

Nevertheless, as fulsome testimonials from future star lyricists bear witness, Plum was far more than a prolific journeyman. His quiet but far-reaching influence on the American song lyric owed its success to the very same wit, urbanity and technical skills he demonstrated elsewhere in his writing. If you ever think that Wodehouse's reputation in the theatre is overstated, you would have to argue your case with his colleagues Lorenz Hart ("[I was] inspired by Wodehouse"), Richard Rodgers ("Before Larry Hart, only P. G. Wodehouse had made any assault on the intelligence of the song-listening public...the model of light verse in song form"), Howard Dietz ("the lyric writer I most admire"), Johnny Mercer ("One day, in fifty, a hundred years' time, the words of Porter, Hart, Wodehouse, Gershwin, Coward, maybe a few of my own, will be published, recited, analyzed, codified"), Ira Gershwin, and Alan Jay Lerner ("P. G. Wodehouse inaugurated the American Musical...the pathfinder for Larry Hart, Cole Porter, Ira Gershwin and everyone else who followed"). The generous praise of these showbiz titans has been upheld by later critics and theatre historians. Writing in 1985, Gerald Bordman (compiler of the magisterial reference work *The American Musical Theatre*) noted in a learned journal that Wodehouse was "the most observant, literate, and witty lyricist" of his age and that the BWK team "had an influence which can be felt to this day". Cultural critic Gilbert Seldes agreed: Wodehouse's lyrics "say things as simply as you would say them in common speech. There was nothing [he] wanted to say that he couldn't say to music".

This last point is perhaps the most significant of all: Plum had somehow managed to connect song lyrics to their intended audience by developing a shared language that they actually spoke, or perhaps wished they could speak. This stylish new argot was smart, glamorous, attractive and yet not beyond the grasp of anyone listening. But even more than that, it was endlessly versatile and adaptable. It could encompass "breakfast wheaties" while namechecking Sir Galahad ('When a Gent Was a Perfect Gent'); it would cheekily rhyme 'meatless' with 'heatless', 'sweetless' and 'wheatless' and still make sense ('Wheatless Days'); it could poke fun at big-city arty types while appearing tongue-tied ("It's a sort of, sort of, a kind of / It's a sort of kind of something in the air" from 'Greenwich Village'), and deliver a knockout love song which is simultaneously satirizing itself ('Moon Song'). And that's all within the confines of a single show (*Oh, Lady! Lady!!*). Plum's lyrical legacy was profound, yet one that was quickly and brutally eclipsed by the brilliance of those whose talents it set free. He once praised Lorenz Hart in words that could just as easily be applied to his own achievement (and in fact *were*, almost word for word, in the Richard Rodgers quote above): "He was the first to make any real assault on the intelligence of the song-writing public. He brought something new into a rather tired business".

Let's look at a few different aspects of Plum's lyrical skills that unlocked the gates for so many of his successors. The BWK trio's first outing, *Miss Springtime* (which opened on 25 September 1916 at the 1,702-seater New Amsterdam Theatre but with a cast of just seven lead characters), was described in *Vanity Fair* as "a corker" and "the best musical play in years" by a writer who certainly knew what he was talking about – for it was no one other than Plum himself wearing another of his several hats. Fortunately, others agreed, including the *New York Times*, which went as far as to gush that "the occasion became epochal", and *Theatre Magazine*, whose reviewer called it "good all through...as good as anything of its kind and better than anything done for years". Not bad for a first attempt, even though much of the music had been inherited, and Wodehouse only had a hand in seven of the lyrics. But these did include what to my ears is Plum's first classic, 'My Castle in the Air', which I was lucky enough to hear performed impromptu and *a capella* by his great-grandson Hal Cazalet in the unlikely setting of an upstairs room of a scuzzy London pub in 2017. An excellent Kern tune (which is mangled by the operetta-like musical arrangements in early 78 recordings) really takes flight when it's sung as a simple, unadorned ballad. And the lyric closes on a typical Wodehouse sentiment:

> *No one ever worries there, for ev'rything goes right*
> *The sky's always blue and no lover's untrue,*
> *And your life's one long delight.*

A castle in the air indeed, which ambiguity makes the song so much more affecting when delivered dead straight with zero coloratura. And yes, by any standards other than those that govern the stage musical, the lyric *is* mawkish. But this is to take it out of context: this particular castle (a successful performing career in the big city) proves illusory, as the singer's heart remains back home in her provincial town with her long-time lover. It's meant to be trite and sentimental (but not as trite as 'Mother's Knee') because that's what the plot demands, and when set against a breezy, satirical number like 'All Full of Talk', it's all part of a play of light and shade it's difficult to appreciate when you are simply looking at the words of individual lyrics on a page. Here's that latter song's opening premise:

> *I often think how sad and lonesome Adam must have been*
> *Alone inside the Garden till his Eve came on the scene,*
> *It must have made him mad when he went out to take a walk*
> *And couldn't find a single thing that knew the way to talk.*

The animals in Eden don't have much by way of conversation, which reduces Adam to silence. But then Eve appears talking nineteen to the dozen, and the opposite problem arises – her husband remains mute because he can't get a word in edgeways:

> *From the moment when he's waken*
> *For his morning eggs and bacon*
> *Till he put the cat outside last thing at night*
> *She would not stop at all*
> *Talking fashions for the fall,*
> *She said she wished to be correctly gowned*
> *And she's argue whether fig leaves*
> *Should be medium or big leaves.*
> *He was all full of talk*
> *Adam had no chance when Eve was around.*

Once again, it's difficult for those of us raised on the classic stage musical to appreciate quite how sophisticated, fresh and *modern* lyrics like this sounded over 100 years ago in 1916. It was sassy and collo-quial; it contained chummy topical references; and, as the *New York Times* reviewer noted, it was actually funny – the kind of *clever* funny that would characterize the best American show tunes of the next five decades. Note, for example, the tiny but telling ambiguity of "fall" (as in autumn) with the Fall of Man as later enacted by the biblical Adam and Eve (a theme Plum later returned to in a song from *The Riviera Girl* to be sung "with burlesque intensity"). And the abiding images of the Father of All Mankind eating bacon and eggs and putting the cat out is clear evidence that to Plum, (virtually) nothing was lyrically off limits. Perhaps most astounding of all was that he had fallen into this voice almost immediately he started writing in America. It was as if everything he'd written previously, both in prose and verse, had been leading up to this. Buoyed by his success on stage, his novels and stories also gained in confidence and authority during this period, and although he didn't yet have a complete, controlled grasp on what he was doing, he was making giant strides towards a full realization of his style's potential.

Miss Springtime ran for 227 performances in New York, enjoyed even greater success in Chicago, and, as Plum informs us, "went on touring for several years", prompting Comstock to belatedly commission the team's first Princess show that would actually play at the Princess. But before it could oblige, the trio had already been contracted to produce their first full collaboration from soup to nuts. *Have a Heart* (which opened on 11 January 1917) boasts "Book, Guy Bolton and PG Wodehouse; Lyrics, PG Wodehouse; Music, Jerome Kern", and the 16 songs that made it to the final cut include another satirical Wodehouse gem in the form of 'Napoleon' – a pointed dig at *Miss Springtime*'s producer Abraham Lincoln Erlanger, whom he would skewer a second time as the Machiavellian Mr Goble in *Jill the Reckless*. ("He was five feet high / But he was one tough guy".) Further comedy arrived courtesy of a song that was dropped from the original run, despite its obvious excellence: 'Can the Cabaret' details a sequence of annoying interruptions while Henry, the elevator boy and Dolly, "a moving picture star" are trying to canoodle at a nightclub table:

> *When you've picked out a nice little table for two*
> *And you sit just as close as you're able to do,*
> *And you start to impart*
> *All the innermost secrets you have in your heart,*
> *Then the orchestra toots on its flutes,*
> *And the dancers are whirling around,*
> *And the stately soprano beside the piano*
> *Drowns out ev'ry possible sound.*

And when there's a pause in the din
The confounded waiter comes in.

Madame would like more of ze butter?
Monsieur would like more of ze wine?
Ze lobster is utterly utter,
Ze salad exquisite, divine.

Further farcical irritants include a quartet of mature ladies ("singing songs that are eighty years old"), the cigarette boy, Hula dancers and the gypsy fiddler. No wonder the lovers complain that "[o]ur food and our passions grow cold". All the scene lacks is the guy wandering around selling single red roses. And note the highly Gilbertian "utterly utter" – which takes a phrase ("consummately utter") from the epochal production of *Patience* that baptized Plum into the musical theatre, and actually improves on it.

Wodehouse had hit his lyrical stride, and in February 1917 came the triumvirate's biggest success: *Oh, Boy!* As Plum informs us in his unreliable theatrical memoir *Bring On the Girls*, it ran for a total of 475 performances in New York, transferring from the Princess to the 1500-seat Casino Theatre not quite halfway through its run (some claim at the end of its run). No fewer than four (some say five) travelling companies took the show out on the road, one of which hadn't returned over four years later, the whole thing netting a massive profit of $181,000 on an initial investment of $29,000. Among the show's high points are the hardy perennial 'You Never Knew About Me' and a song more commonly linked to its composer than its wordsmith: 'Till the Clouds Roll By' was lifted for the title of MGM's glitzy 1946 biopic of Kern's career, which was to feature no fewer than four Wodehouse lyrics, all of them cruelly uncredited.

The critics concurred with the public: *Oh, Boy!* was a smash. The *New York Times* reviewer summed up the phenomenon when he opined that "you might call this a musical comedy that is as good as they make them if it were not palpably so much better", and said the lyrics "are shrewdly rhymed and have a rare lilt". In fact, it was so well received that the following year, George Grossmith brought the show to London, making it one of the first American musical hits to successfully cross the Atlantic. The retitled *Oh, Joy!* reintroduced Plum the Lyricist to a home audience, including a stage-struck 18-year-old Noël Coward, who would have landed a speaking part in the production were it not for an administrative cock-up and the demands of his massive ego. Recovering from this catastrophe, the show was notable for marking the musical comedy debut of Beatrice Lillie, later dubbed "The Funniest Woman in the World". We should also remark that the song 'Nesting Time in Flatbush' (a bi-syllabic neighbourhood in Brooklyn, New York) translated into 'Nesting Time in Tooting' (a bi-syllabic London suburb) for the duration of the British run.

Listening to Plum's lyrics from this period (and there are several excellent modern recordings of his songs), it's impossible to tell that he was usually handed a finished tune by the composer and told to get on with it. In fact, that was his preferred way of working, and such was his keen sense of rhythm, breadth of vocabulary, and ingenuity that things could just as easily have occurred the other way round. Once again, he seemed to prefer working *inside* a pre-existing framework, however loose and flexible, just to start him off – and, no doubt, as one endowed with a superhuman work ethic, to save time. He explained his preference with mock-belligerence, and for once begged to differ with his hero W. S. Gilbert, who had claimed "that a lyricist can't do decent stuff that way":

> For instance, one of the songs ['Words Are Not Needed'] on *Oh, Boy!* began: "If every day you bring her diamonds and pearls on a string" – I couldn't have thought of that if I had done the lyric first. Why, dash it, it doesn't scan… Another thing… When you have the melody, you can see which are the musical high spots in it and can fit the high spots of the lyric to them. Anyway, that's how I like working, and to hell with anyone who says I oughtn't to.

Fortunately, Kern was the opposite – he liked to compose from a blank sheet of manuscript paper – which meant the two men's opposing preferences actually dovetailed, thus avoiding a potential flashpoint within the writing team. To Kern, allowing the lyricist to start the ball rolling simply resulted in "versifying to music"; in other words, the temptation for the lyricist would be to write entirely regular verses that scanned – which was no fun for a gifted composer when it was *his* turn with the baton. Gilbert's pre-written lyrics had somewhat straitjacketed Sullivan's music, closing down many of the latter's rhythmical options; and Plum – who, as we've already appreciated, was a man of rhythm – had clearly noticed this. In *Jill the Reckless*, Roland Trevis's music for *The Rose of America* is described as having "all Sullivan's melody with a newness of rhythm peculiarly its own" because, presumably, in Otis Pilkington, Trevis has found a librettist with something more rhythmically interesting than a metronome in his head. It's the difference between the predictable jogging rhythm of "rum-ti-tum-ti-tum" and the rather more expressive "rumpty-tiddley-umpty-ay" that brings Bertie's Aunt Julia and Joe Ogden together in 'Extricating Young Gussie'. Or, indeed, "Ta-ra-ra-boom-de-ay", "a pretty good lyric" that Plum claims, in *Louder & Funnier*, he regularly sang in the bath.

With Wodehouse and Kern, there's something more interesting, more genuinely symbiotic happening within the parameters of the song than the words simply following the tune's lead. Going on second encouraged Plum to search far and wide for his verbal rhythms, and paradoxically this additional discipline set his lyrics free. And it seems he did this instinctively whether Kern's music was present or not: in *Bill the Conqueror*, in the unlikely setting of Waterloo Station's Platform 13, the narrator picks up on the rhythm of a hawker's cry, which he "chirrup[s] like a thrush in Maytime" in his "tuneful young voice": "Buns, sweets of all descriptions, chawklit, nut chawklit, sengwidges, oranges, apples, Banbury cikes and bananas!" This, he remarks, "only needed music by Jerome Kern to be a song-hit". Although far from rhythmically regular, Plum evidently heard something useful in it.

Perhaps the most compelling evidence of this enthusiasm for looking for lyrics in the oddest places was Plum's ear for the inventiveness and fresh sounds of American and English slang, together with his facility for coining words and mangling existing words into new forms. I'm sure you won't need reminding of Claud Cockburn's assertion, which I quoted at the end of Chapter 3, that Plum's "heightened sensitivity to the words, syntax and cadences of English" beyond the capabilities of other writers arose from the fact that he had needed to become bilingual in British and American English; and, from Chapter 4, Plum's own 1915 comment in which he predicted that the virtues of American humour would set its English counterpart free. Well, here he was proving both of these assertions absolutely correct and creating a new art form almost single-handedly in the process. Remember the lyrics of 1904's 'Put Me in My Little Cell'? Pure English music hall. In fact, I can easily imagine the wonderful Bernard Cribbins or some such artist performing it in a loud check suit and mutton-chop side whiskers on BBC TV's retro-variety show *The Good Old Days*. The lyrics to just about any song in *Oh, Boy!*, by contrast, are in an entirely different league, for by this time Plum had learned what in *Jill the Reckless* he calls "a certain polish", and educated himself in the vital new forms of American slang.

My visits to Edward Cazalet's private archive revealed a fascinating scrapbook of cuttings his grandfather had excised from American newspapers, including a wonderful column that lists close to a hundred "American Terms for Intoxication" from which Plum borrowed liberally ("stinko", "scrooched" and "woozled" to name but three). Following on from that, there's the six types of hangover he lists in the Mulliner story 'George and Alfred' ("the Broken Compass, the Sewing Machine, the Comet, the Atomic, the Cement Mixer and the Gremlin Boogie"), and in the pages that followed, I came across four examples of a regular feature entitled 'Judge Junior's Dictionary', which lists literally hundreds of contemporary urban neologisms on a wide variety of subjects. These would prove an invaluable resource for Plum's novels, perhaps most notably from the mouth of his regular villainess Dolly Molloy. My personal favourites are "wooden kimono" (a coffin), "hoof and mouth" (one who "craves dances and food"), and a term that was to become the Plum regular, "half pint" ("shrimp, small, undersized", usually referring to women), which he often varied with "half portion".

Although words such as "rannygazoo" and "oompus-boompus" would light up the dialogue in his novels, it is in his song lyrics that we find transatlantic slang in greatest profusion, perhaps because at that stage in his career, Wodehouse had only just discovered it and was keen to lever it in. Returning briefly to the 1917 song 'Napoleon', we're confronted by the following bravura parade of Americanisms: "Little guy", "Shorty", "Ah, fade away!", "take a slant", "the little pill", "mutt", "gink", "doll up", "looked like thirty cents", "goo-goo eye", "booze", "piker", "dough", "gazook", "gee!" – and so on. Many of these have either passed into the language ("dough", "guy", "booze") or have dwindled to period archaisms ("ginger" – in the sense of "pep" or "vitality"); some ("gazook", for example) don't appear in my exhaustive and usually trusty *Crowell's Dictionary of American Slang*, and may well be evidence of Plum's originality (a conflation of the New York Irish "gazebo" we encountered earlier and "mook", a stupid person?); "pill" is wonderfully topical for 1917 ("Kaiser Bill is a pill" was, according to the same volume, "a common WW1 child chant"), while Plum pre-empted the first dictionary-acknowledged use of "goo-goo eye" by a full six years, and "slant" by five.

Perhaps the most wildly gratuitous, over-the-top Wodehouse slang-fest occurs in 1918's *Piccadilly Jim*, in which Jim deliberately overeggs the pudding in order to carry his point:

> You know, Bayliss…life is peculiar, not to say odd. You never know what is waiting for you around the corner. You start the day with the fairest prospects, and before nightfall everything is as rocky and ding-basted as stig tossed full of doodle-gammon.

Top that! Plum's biographer David Jasen has gone so far as to liken Plum's catholic vocabulary and phrasing to the then fashionable 'ragtime' piano playing which, although formally structured, allowed room for the kind of syncopation ("the placement of rhythmic stresses or accents where they wouldn't normally occur") that was already finding a fuller expression in 'hot' jazz. Barry Day correctly adds that breaking away from the formality of regular rhythm allowed Plum to replace lyrical "poeticism" with the "colloquialism of the modern song lyric", and it was the double whammy of these new words and rhythms that helped him catch his audience's ear. How about this fine example of the lyricist's art – the opening of 'Ain't It a Grand and Glorious Feeling!' from *Oh, Boy!*:

> *Some days are bum days, but sometimes there come days*
> *When your luck's in from the start,*
> *Days when the Jinx*
> *Doesn't drive you to drinks*
> *And Old Man Trouble has a heart.*
>
> *When fate doesn't wait 'round the corner with a brick*
> *And your stock goes up to par,*
> *Things aren't this way very much, but say –*
> *"Oh, Joy! Oh, Boy!" when they are!*

The song was inexplicably dropped from the show at some point in the run, but it's certainly not for want of quality. There's absolutely no formality here in any sense: three double rhymes and a colloquialism in the opening line to start things off with a flourish, plus a wayward rhyme scheme (ABCCB/DEFE) and stray syllables flying all over the place – when examined on the printed page it looks like a difficult proposal for any singer. Yet when performed by someone who knows what they're doing, to a tune written by a master (Kern again), these idiosyncrasies lend the song a pally, conversational air that the greater formality of a more regular rhyme, metre and scansion wouldn't. The listener is invited to agree with the title's proposition that although unbroken good luck is a rare commodity, it's the greatest feeling, and the instant suggestion of a shared bonhomie from those first few words prompts him to throw his hat in the ring and celebrate with the performer. It's clever stuff, and, for its time, far from conventional. But then, Plum was always something of the gentle iconoclast.

One of the most celebrated examples of Plum's resourcefulness with rhythm and lyric can be found in *Leave It to Jane*'s 'Cleopatterer', the Egyptian queen's name stretched to five syllables to fit the tune. It wasn't necessary for an American audience to know this was based on the London Cockney pronunciation complete with its median glottal stop where the 'tt' should go; the laughs came courtesy of the lyricist's licence:

> *She danced new dances now and then,*
> *The sort that make you blush,*
> *And when she did them, scores of men*
> *Got injured in the crush.*
> *They'd stand there, gaping, in a line*
> *And watch her agitate her spine;*
> *It simply used to mow them flat,*
> *When she went like this and then like that.*

> *At dancing Cleopatterer*
> *Was always on the spot.*
> *She gave those poor Egyptian ginks*
> *Something else to watch beside the Sphinx.*
> *Mark Antony admitted*
> *That what first made him skid*
> *Was the wibbly, wobbly, wriggly dance*
> *That Cleopatterer did.*

This is a lyric packed with suggestions and opportunities for choreographers; then witness the criminally unimaginative cavorting that accompanies the song in the Kern biopic, albeit led by one of Plum's favourite actresses, June Allyson, who sings it brilliantly. And with "gink", he was once again decades in front of the academics, who didn't credit the general use of the word (meaning "any man or fellow") until 1951, 34 years after Plum used it.

Resourcefulness is also a keynote of Wodehouse's lyrics. A regularly recurring crux in the commercial theatre is that of the formula – something Plum was to exploit with considerable success for the rest of his career. On the one hand, audiences love familiarity, but on the other they can also tire of it quickly. It's the same for writers: while repetition means less work, it doesn't present their creativity with any new challenges. Striking a saleable balance between old favourites and new material is a problem that has no sure-fire solution, but Plum cleverly manages to reconcile both within the confines of a single lyric. 'Where the Good Songs Go' (originally from *Miss 1917* but interpolated into *Oh, Boy!* when the former show divebombed) is, superficially at least, a sappy parade of clichés and motifs. But look a little closer, and it quickly becomes clear that something else is going on beneath the surface…

> *On the other side of the moon,*
> *Ever so far,*
> *Beyond the last little star,*
> *There's a land, I know,*
> *Where the good songs go,*
> *Where it's always afternoon;*
> *And snug in a haven of peace and rest,*
> *Lie the dear old songs that we love the best.*
>
> *It's a land of flowers*
> *And April showers*
> *With sunshine in between,*
> *With roses blowing and rivers flowing,*
> *'Mid rushes growing green;*
> *Where no one hurries*
> *And no one worries*
> *And life runs calm and slow:*
> *And I wish some day I could find my way*
> *To the land where the good songs go.*
>
> *Dear old songs forgotten too soon –*
> *They had their day,*
> *And then we threw them away;*
> *And without a sigh we would pass them by,*
> *For some other, newer tune.*
> *So off to a happier home they flew,*
> *Where they're always loved and they're always new.*

Plum is once again satirizing bad poetry while cunningly and shame-lessly recycling some of its ickier rhymes to suit his purpose. Mind you, having introduced 'moon' at the end of the opening line, he refuses to allow 'June' an appearance – that would be just *too* clichéd – although he did once memorably rhyme it with 'macaroon'. As the Oldest Member informs William Bates in 'Rodney Fails to Qualify':

> You must have known that there is nothing more condu-cive to love than the moon in June. Why, songs have been written about it. In fact, I cannot recall a song that has not been written about it.

One year earlier, in a piece for *Vanity Fair* entitled 'The Alarming Spread of Poetry', Plum had imagined a disappointed father, whose son Willie had expressed the desire to become a poet, trying to persuade his off-spring to take a less taxing job in the family fertilizer factory: "Think", he says, "of having to spend your life making one line rhyme with another! Think of the bleak future, when you have used up 'moon' and 'June', 'love' and 'dove', 'May' and 'gay'! Think of the moment when you have ended the last line but one of your poem with 'window' or 'warmth' and have to buckle to, trying to make the thing couple up in accordance with the rules! What then, Willie?" The next day Willie signs on in the fertilizer factory – where, Plum perhaps implies, all these lazily rhymed "good songs" should end up too. Or, of course, the lyric could be entirely sincere.

As I've already suggested, Plum considered that rhyming was both hard work *and* in a higher creative league than blank verse, which was essentially "chopping prose into bits". But if a lyricist intends to stick with rhyme, he can't keep trotting out the same old pairs of end words, and it's on this score that Ira Gershwin, no slouch with a lyric himself and the only one of the lyrical glitterati from whom I didn't solicit a quote in my earlier list of *encomia*, praised Wodehouse's inventiveness and pioneering spirit:

> Wodehouse once told me that the greatest challenge (and greatest worry) to him in lyric writing was to come across a section of a tune requiring three double rhymes…When I finally wound up with "wings on-strings on-things-on" that was that, and I felt like a suddenly unburdened Atlas.

Like Plum with Kern, Ira worked to pre-existing tunes courtesy of brother George (by coincidence, the rehearsal pianist on *Miss 1917*), whose rhythms suggested the rhyming pattern the lyricist needed to adopt. It's heart-warming to think that the man who somehow managed to come up with words to fit rhythms as complex as those found in 'I Got Rhythm' and 'Fascinating Rhythm' learned a trick or two at the feet of the master. The two remained friends, correspondents and very occasional collaborators for the rest of Plum's life.

Thus, on a tide of originality and brilliance, did the BWK trio quickly graduate to being the toast of the Great White Way. As Plum informs us (perhaps truthfully, perhaps not), he became known as "the Sweet-Singing Thrush of 39th Street…sitting on top of the world and loving it". From this lofty vantage point, he could look down on what was happening and gently take the rise out of the stage musical, its modes and mores. And, of course, he didn't spare the conservatism of his fellow lyricists. In *Oh, Boy!* Jim Marvin sings to Jackie Sampson:

> *I've always liked the sort of songs*
> *You hear so much today*
> *Called "When it's something or other time"*
> *In some place far away.*
> *Oh, "Tulip Time in Holland"*
> *A pleasant time must be*
> *While some are strong for*
> *"Apple Blossom Time in Normandy".*

Sounds like another cue for the girls to come onstage wearing clogs or white peasant aprons, but not in this case: Plum's adoring couple don't wish to be anywhere more exotic than exactly where they are – Brooklyn, where they'll "bill and coo" in their seventh-storey apartment and be perfectly happy.

But it wasn't all jam. Out of the five shows Plum deliberately mis-remembered to have had running simultaneously on Broadway in 1917 (*Oh, Boy!*, *Leave It to Jane*, *The Rose of China*, *The Riviera Girl* and *The Second Century Show* [*Miss 1917*]), the last three were resounding failures financially and, in Plum's view, artistically. For example, *The Rose of China* (which didn't *actually* debut until 1919 and closed after only 47 New York performances) was over-reliant on the very clichés Plum knew he should have avoided, but somehow didn't. "Before you know where you are", he wrote 35 years after the event, "your heroine has gone cute on you, adding just that touch of glucose to the part which renders it unsuitable for human consumption. She twitters through the evening saying 'Me Plum Blossom. Me good girl. Me love Chlistian god velly much' and things of that sort". All that time later, you can almost hear Plum kicking himself for giving her the chance, although the show would later prove popular in the provinces.

The Riviera Girl and *Miss 1917* were cursed with similar short metropolitan runs, the latter because everything was a great big mess which never cohered ("one of those [shows] which starts wrong and never recovers" as Plum has it in *Jill the Reckless*); the former, Barry Day notes, because the plot was simply too complex to care about (interestingly, at exactly this time, Plum was writing a novel – *Piccadilly Jim* – that was similarly overburdened with too many story strands). Although the passage of time would allow Wodehouse to treat these failures light-heartedly in *Bring On the Girls*, there can be little doubt that he would have learned – and quickly – from the team's collective mistakes, an education that would quickly bear fruit in his novels and stories, as we'll see in the next volume.

This book can't pretend to be an exhaustive study of Wodehouse's career in musical theatre, which eventually embraced 40 or so titles, and so we'll use what was advertised as the BWK partnership's fifth and sort-of-final full-scale 'Princess'-style outing (1918's *Oh, Lady! Lady!!*) as a convenient coda, since its plot is an excellent example of how prose and drama were intimately connected within Plum's literary sensibility, being converted into his novel *The Small Bachelor* in 1926 – and back into drama for a silent movie the following year. Plum also sanctions us to end our studies at this point, since he himself also regarded this period as his strongest artistically, referring in 1945 to his songwriting "Muse" being back "in the real 1916–18 form". He would intermittently write song lyrics for the rest of his life, living in perpetual hope that one day someone might take notice and turn them into a show. As the years went by, however, he was gradually forced to admit that he was hopelessly out of step (and out of sorts) with what a modern audience wanted. In 1951, for example, he admitted to "an absolute loathing for the Broadway stage now...everyone raves about *The King and I* and I still can't see what can be the attraction". And having complained in 1917's 'The Agonies of Writing a Musical Comedy' that his muse was frequently being derailed by mandatory appearances from "the gurls", he remarked in 1953 that what principally spoiled *Guys and Dolls* was "this modern practice of *never* bringing on the girls" [italics mine].

Perhaps Plum should have followed the example of the protagonist of a piece he wrote while in detention in Poland in 1940, in which he imagined a songwriter who, while "sipping soda in a gilded cabaret", decides to say "Goodbye Broadway" and head back home to a fictional location not far removed, one imagines at least conceptually – from Mother's Knee:

> America, I love you with your eyes of blue,
> But I'm going back, back, back to the land where dreams
> come true.
> P-n-i-b-w spells Pnibw,
> And, as Ogden Nash would say, what the hell did you think
> it was going to do?

"It's a little rough at present", he confesses, "but the stuff is there. It has the mucus". And because it is a Plum lyric, I don't need to tell you how "Pnibw" is pronounced.

1919–1936

Chapter 9
Wodehouse at Work

[H]e could never understand how fellows thought up ideas for stories or plays.
Sam the Sudden

Literary composition can often be a slow and painful process.
Bill the Conqueror

"I had no notion writing was so easy. The stuff just pours out".
Summer Lightning

*When in due course Charon ferries me across the Styx and everyone is telling
everyone else what a rotten writer I was, I hope at least one voice
will be heard piping up, "But he did take trouble."*
Over Seventy

At the opening of the 1936 novel Laughing Gas, first-time story writer
Reggie Havershot (geddit?) coerces "a literary pal" – who is nursing the
mother of all hangovers – to listen to the few lines he's written so far.
As Reggie reads, the more experienced scribe's face gradually assumes
the expression "of one who has had a dead fish thrust under his nose"
before he demands incredulously: "Is this bilge to be printed?" On
being informed that it is, he testily points out that Reggie has made
the elementary mistake of starting in the middle of the story, thus bewildering the reader who can have no clue who anyone is, or what the
heck's been going on up to that point. "The first rule in telling a story",
he explains as if to a child, "is to make it thoroughly clear at the outset
who's who, when, where and why". So no getting clever-clever with the
plot and no withholding information from the reader. "You wouldn't let
it gradually dawn on him in the course of the narrative?" Reggie asks,
somewhat taken aback. "Certainly not", comes the definitive response.
"You'd better start again from the beginning".

The writer, prior to downing a well-earned bicarbonate of soda,
makes it all sound so easy, and yet when Reggie restarts his narrative
armed with this advice, he flounders even more spectacularly, turning
the confusion of his first attempt into dullness in the second, proving
once more that this writing lark isn't as easy as it can be made to look by
someone who knows what he's doing.

In Plum's world, a similarly basic prescription had recently produced the back-to-back classics *Heavy Weather* (1933), *Thank You, Jeeves* and *Right Ho, Jeeves* (both 1934). Indeed, a straightforward narrative style had always been the North Star of his writing, and it seemed the simpler things got in that department, the better *he* got, even when the complexity of his plots threatened to spiral out of control. By 1938's *The Code of the Woosters* (the book many consider his masterpiece) the frenetic pace of the action resembles a stage farce on acid, yet never is there the slightest confusion in the reader's mind about what is happening. While all around are losing their heads, Plum's style remains calm, measured and admirably expository while somehow holding on to every ounce of energy and humour he can extract from the dizzyingly evolving situations it describes.

Working forwards from the period immediately following the First World War to this golden run in the 1930s, it's possible to witness a steady progression beneath the surface of Plum's writing style as he gradually entered mid-season form. A formula was in the process of being refined, and its watchwords were clarity, economy and discipline. In making his big scenes as big as he could, hitting the dialogue early and cutting out unnecessary interstitial stuff as he'd been forced to do in his stage work to get those all-important big laughs, the redundant stylistic tics he'd acquired, as well as all the literary genres he'd flirted with, either had to earn their place or be ruthlessly shown the door. There needed to be a place for everything, and everything needed to be in that place. It was as (ahem) simple as that – and even in his final completed novel, *Aunts Aren't Gentlemen*, he insisted on having Jeeves "marshal [his] thoughts" for "between twenty and thirty seconds" before telling a story so he can get things straight in his head. "One aims at coherence", he says. It's a word we're going to be meeting a lot in this chapter, for as Bertie comments in the same novel, "it never does, when you're telling a story, to wander off into side issues".

Wodehouse was never one to discuss his style in public, and even when he did it was usually in a self-deprecating manner played strictly for laughs. But in a short but telling preface he wrote for a 1934 anthology entitled *A Century of Humour*, he offers us a useful window onto where his thinking had reached at this comedic high point in his career. Addressing the issue of 'the Spirit of Comedy', he notes:

> Comedy is a game played to throw reflections upon social
> life, and it deals with human nature in the drawing-room

of civilized men and women, where we have no dust of
the struggling outer world, no mire, no violent crashes,
to make the correctness of the representation convincing... The Comic Spirit conceives a definite situation for
a number of characters, and rejects all accessories in the
exclusive pursuit of them and their speech.

The words aren't his but those of Victorian novelist and poet George
Meredith, forming the opening paragraph of his best-known work *The
Egoist*, published in 1879. Having quoted him verbatim, Plum abruptly
states "that is all I have to say about the Spirit of Comedy", implying
that Meredith's definition needs no further elaboration, or that the
whole idea of trying to define comedy is not a brief he would have
chosen willingly. But let's stick with it for a moment. In 1963 fellow
novelist Angus Wilson was to praise *The Egoist* as being a perfectly
crafted theatrical comedy, cast in the form of a novel – and here we get
our first inkling of why Plum might have decided to use it to illustrate
his own ideas.

Now the master both of stage and page, Plum had refined his own
approach to writing comedy in much the same way. Time after time,
he assembled a cast of characters who dance around inside a limited
locality to the tunes and rhythms of a complex plot, during which they
engage in dialogue in various different permutations. And that's it. By
the time he published *The Old Reliable* in 1951, he wasn't even bothering
to conceal the stage mechanics that were left over from the discarded
playscript of *Spring Fever* on which it is based: characters stroll into the
action through the French windows as they would on to the stage set
of a farce. In Robert McCrum's apt words, Plum "had created a world
that was complete, self-sufficient and almost faultless... [T]he man and
the work were one". And by the time he wrote that preface – so they
were. Richard Usborne is less reverential, describing "the theatrical
mincing machine" that Plum's sensibility had become in his later works.
Indeed, by the time *Bachelors Anonymous* and *Pearls, Girls and Monty Bodkin*
came along in the 1970s, the formula was barely clothed. Both men
are correct, yet both manage to underestimate the sheer slog that this
simple formula always demanded to *make* itself look simple.

Plum's meticulousness and dedication to his craft can best be witnessed in the heavily annotated manuscripts he worked on prior to producing his novels' final drafts. For me, having been lucky enough to have
seen one or two in the flesh, it immediately becomes clear that Plum

was an inveterate reviser, re-worker and revisionist. Ideas kept popping into his head and were duly recorded; stray thoughts were jotted down, problems identified, alternatives pondered, several 'good' versions typed out. This is not an academic work, so I don't propose to spend too long on this theme. Two examples are probably sufficient to evidence Plum's habitual modus operandi: one focusing on the specifics of language and telling the story; the second with the actual process of revision itself.

Let's begin by examining the opening page of 1971's *Much Obliged, Jeeves*, whose first typescript copy begins thus:

> As I sat at the breakfast table that morning, digging into the superfine eggs and b. with which Jeeves had provided me, I gave the world a quick glance and liked the look of it. Not a flaw in the set-up, it seemed to me.
>
> "Jeeves," I said, "I am happy."
>
> "I am very glad to hear it, sir."
>
> "How long it will last, I couldn't tell you. Too often, when you're feeling fizziest, disaster steps in and starts doing its stuff. Still, the thing to do is to keep on being happy as long as you can."
>
> "Precisely, sir. As the Roman poet Horace said, *carpe diem*. The English poet Herrick expressed the same sentiment when he suggested that we should gather rosebuds while we may. The toast and butter are at your elbow."

As far as I'm aware, this was the first 'good' copy on which Plum began to scribble his emendations in longhand. Quite how many goes he had before arriving even at this stage is impossible to tell; the earliest surviving notes for the novel date from five years before it was eventually published (on Plum's 90th birthday – 15 October, 1971). In addition, there are at least two sets of handwritten revisions on this particular manuscript, perhaps even three, judging by (a) the different thicknesses of the pens' points or nibs, (b) the variations in pressure and angle Plum applied, and (c) the different shades of ink.

Which is quite bad enough – but there's more. Plum clearly made a few further passes over it before reaching the final printed version [the emboldening is mine, indicating significant revisions that postdate that first typescript.]

As I slid into my chair at the breakfast table and started to deal with the toothsome eggs and bacon which Jeeves had given of his plenty, I was conscious of a strange exhilaration, if I've got the word right. Pretty good the set-up looked to me. **Here I was, back in the old familiar headquarters, and the thought that I had seen the last of Totleigh Towers, of Sir Watkyn Bassett, of his daughter Madeline and above all of the unspeakable Spode, or Lord Sidcup as he now calls himself, was like the medium dose for adults of one of those patent medicines which tone the system and impart a gentle glow.**

"These eggs, Jeeves," I said. "Very good. Very tasty."

"Yes, sir?"

"Laid, no doubt, by contented hens. And the coffee, perfect. Nor must I omit to give a word of praise to the bacon. I wonder if you notice anything about me this morning."

"You seem in good spirits, sir."

"Yes, Jeeves, I am happy today."

"I am very glad to hear it, sir."

"You might say I'm sitting on top of the world with a rainbow round my shoulder."

"A most satisfactory state of affairs, sir."

"What's the word I've heard you use from time to time – begins with eu?"

"Euphoria, sir?"

"That's the one. I've seldom had a sharper attack of euphoria. I feel full to the brim of Vitamin B. Mind you, I don't know how long it will last. Too often it is when one feels fizziest that the storm clouds begin doing their stuff."

"Very true, sir. Full many a glorious morning have I seen flatter the mountain tops with sovereign eye, kissing with golden face the meadows green, gilding pale streams with heavenly alchemy. Anon permit the basest clouds to ride with ugly rack on his celestial face and from the forlorn world his visage hide, stealing unseen to west with this disgrace."

"Exactly," I said. I couldn't have put it better myself. "One always has to budget for a change in the weather. Still, the thing to do is to keep on being happy while you can."

"Precisely, sir. *Carpe diem*, the Roman poet Horace advised. The English poet Herrick expressed the same sentiment when he suggested that we should gather rosebuds while we may. Your elbow is in the butter, sir."

Once again, you'll be glad to know I'm only going to highlight a few of the more significant themes in that slab of prose, some general, some particular, otherwise we'll be here all day.

First, vocabulary: "[s]*uperfine* eggs and b."? Too American for the very English Bertie, although he is at home on both sides of the Pond. And to use one of his habitual abbreviations in the opening sentence might puzzle first-time readers, whom Plum calls "the new customers" a little later, so "bacon" it is, rather than simply "b".

Indeed, a good deal of effort is expended to accommodate any new-comers, as well as "the old gang" who may remember some of this stuff already. Check out that first highlighted passage: Plum will bring us all up to speed with what he calls "the Bertram Wooster Story" on his second page, but here, in the third sentence, he's flagging that what we're about to read is in fact a sequel to his 1963 novel *Stiff Upper Lip, Jeeves*, which in its turn follows on from 1938's *The Code of the Woosters*. A saga indeed, complete with some of its leading characters whom we're going to be meeting again soon. As Bertie goes on to explain, had he begun his story in the middle (as Reggie Havershot had proposed to do), the following dialogue might well have ensued:

> Self: The relief I felt at having escaped from Totleigh Towers was stupendous.
>
> New C: What's Totleigh Towers?
>
> Self: For one thing it had looked odds on that I should have to marry Madeline.
>
> New C: Who's Madeline?
>
> Self: Gussie Fink-Nottle, you see, had eloped with the cook.
>
> New C: Who's Gussie Fink-Nottle?
>
> Self: But most fortunately Spode was in the offing and scooped her up, saving me from the scaffold.
>
> New C: Who's Spode?
>
> You see. Hopeless. Confusion would be rife, as one might put it. The only way out that I can think of is to ask the old gang to let their attention wander for a bit – there are heaps of things they can be doing; washing the car, solving the crossword puzzle, taking the dog for a run – while I place the facts before the newcomers.

"I can't just leave the poor perishers to try to puzzle things out for themselves", concludes Bertie, who considerately puts himself in the position of the Wodehouse newbie before giving a three-paragraph summary of how things got to where they are now. "I think that makes everything clear to the meanest intelligence, does it not?" he asks us. "Right ho, so we can go ahead". And so we will.

Instead of the bald statement "Jeeves, I am happy", we are treated to a much longer slab of crosstalk between the two lead characters, which first explains *why* Bertie is feeling so chipper. He'd earlier stated that "the set-up" looked pretty good while omitting to actually tell us what that set-up was, so in the finished version he itemizes the eggs, coffee and bacon, while informing us where he's doing the eating ("back in the old familiar headquarters" – in other words, on home turf in his Berkeley Street, Mayfair apartment). A frankly lame alternative Plum sketched in above the typewritten section ("the skies are blue, the dicky birds are singing, and everything is the same as mother makes it") is mercifully excised. Or may simply have been a holding position while he came up with something better.

Next, we have the addition of "today" – a small yet significant change, because in a moment, the two men are going to riff on the idea that this happy state of affairs might not last long. While it does, however, Bertie feels as if he has "a rainbow round my shoulder" (the title of a 1928 Al Jolson song). Plum then throws in one of Bertie's regular tropes: his inability to remember individual words, which Jeeves then dutifully supplies. We old timers draw our comfort blankets in tighter around us – but not too tight, since Plum rejects "the stuffed eelskin" and "sleeve across the windpipe" as metaphors he's probably used one too many times in the past. ("Old hat!" Bertie later speculates we'll be shouting into our books, "or, if French, *déjà vu*".) For now, however, Bertie's "euphoria" (the tattered remnants of his classical education coming through) and "fizziness" (a wonderful onomatopoeia) are winning the day.

Jeeves further elaborates the theme of mutability with a generous quotation of the first eight lines from Shakespeare's Sonnet 33, which Bertie ably summarizes in the single sentence "One always has to budget for a change in the weather", prior to introducing the idea that we have to make the most of our happiness while we have it. Jeeves once again picks up the baton as quote generator with lines from Horace and the best-known line from the incredibly obscure English late metaphysical/Cavalier poet Robert Herrick. Plum couldn't quite decide between Bertie's "as long as you can" and "while you can" – he was probably worried about repeating "while" too often, before deciding it read OK. Also, the Horace sentence now begins with the much more arresting "*Carpe diem*" rather than the rather pedestrian "As the Roman poet Horace said".

Finally, we end this feast of reason and flow of soul not with Jeeves informing his employer that the butter is near his elbow, but that his elbow is actually *in* the butter – puncturing all that earlier erudition somewhat. This is Bertie, after all, not a university high table.

One last point – the pacing: the earlier version moves along way too fast, indicating that the manuscript was at the "bare bones" stage I'll elaborate on in a moment. The completed dialogue moves along elegantly, and the rate at which the various ideas are introduced is perfectly judged so they don't hit the reader too hard and fast, allowing him or her to consume the text in a single pass, rather than having to go back repeatedly in order to puzzle things out. It's both thoughtful, polite and practical: perplex the reader too much and the book is likely to be cast aside at a pretty early stage.

That's by no means all of the revisions teased out, but look how much Wodehouse improved what he had written between that first neat copy and the finished product, how much hard graft and detailed thought went into this lightest of confections. And all this at the age of 89… Plum still cared deeply not just about the quality of his writing, but making sure his readers got the most they could from his considerable efforts.

I realize this sleuthing is only addictive to people of a certain persuasion, but if your appetite has been whetted and you want to catch a glimpse of the master forming and shaping his work, a quick and cheap alternative to becoming a bower bird stuck in a library is to pick up any edition of *Sunset at Blandings*, Plum's last and unfinished novel which first saw the light of day in 1977. Here you will find 16 chapters of a first draft, which totalled 90 typewritten pages; then there's a small but well-chosen selection of commentary on what he'd already written and his plans for the remaining six chapters, distilled from no fewer than 183 pages of notes and drafts. Plum may have been 93 and not particularly well when he was working on the novel, but the iron in his soul and the desire to give of his best were still very much present and correct.

The first thing to note about *Sunset at Blandings* is that what is presented as a finished draft is nowhere near finished at all. Those first 90 pages actually represent the stage at which Plum was happy his story 'worked': the plot made sense; the characters hit their marks and successfully delivered what they had to say. Yet to the habitual Wodehouse reader, what we're presented with seems somewhat 'flat' and lacking in sparkle. The prose is what we might call 'efficient' rather than inspired. And no wonder – because Plum was yet to give it the final application of gloss that would add strength and lustre to the primer and undercoats – the so-called nifties that really bring out the shine. Wodehouse's long-serving American editor Peter Schwed called this process "adding the laugh lines". That said, the book opens with the most cracking simile:

Sir James Piper, England's Chancellor of the Exchequer, sat in his London study staring before him with what are usually called unseeing eyes and snorting every now and then like somebody bursting a series of small paper bags.

You can bet Plum wouldn't have edited *that*, although he had used something similar in *Summer Moonshine* nearly 40 years previously. Had he world enough and time, he would have added plenty more of these masterful tropes, given the dialogue greater energy, and sharpened the characterization – among many other tweaks and revisions.

But it was not to be: at this point, Plum had completed what he would have experienced in the theatre as a "technical rehearsal", which ensures that what happens onstage and behind the scenes syncs up. Moving forward, those first 16 chapters were ready for the full "dress rehearsal" treatment; penny plain would have become tuppence coloured as the actors got to perform in their costumes. Even at this late stage, fairly radical changes may still have been made, as the director and cast turn their attention outwards to an audience seeing it for the first time. Plum, ever fascinated by theatrical shenanigans, describes several of these run-throughs in his stories, one of which occurs in 'Startling Dressiness of a Lift Attendant' from *The Inimitable Jeeves*: Blumenfeld, the very model of the superstitious impresario, religiously brings along his obnoxious young son, who, he thinks, "has the amount of intelligence of the average member of the audience, and that what makes a hit with him will please the general public. While, conversely, what he doesn't like will be too rotten for anyone". Well, Plum *was* that talismanic little boy engaged in a dialogue with his father – only in his head – asking awkward and sometimes painful questions of his own writing:

"Pop!"
"Yes, darling?"
"That one's no good."
"Which one, darling?"
"The one with a face like a fish."

Thus does Cyril Bassington-Bassington exit the cast of *Ask Dad.* "You've got to be good to work for my pop", adds the infant. And so it is with Wodehouse's later writing – everything needed to earn its place, to look right and, just as importantly, *sound* right. Like the stage plays he had been involved with, he was always aware that his books were written to be read by an audience who deserved the very best he could deliver. They weren't the product of some kind of divinely inspired afflatus that didn't allow them to be tinkered with. If things didn't work, he would change them – even down to the smallest, most insignificant details that most readers wouldn't even notice had he left them uncorrected.

This meticulousness is reflected early on in 1916's *Uneasy Money*, when the narrator informs us that Dudley Pickering's plan to become an amateur sleuth hadn't been particularly well thought through:

> Like generals, authors, artists and others who, after planning broad effects, have to get down to the detail work, he found that this was where his troubles began.

Plum never believed that the little things didn't matter, or would somehow take care of themselves. Even as he was writing, he typed out reports on how well he thought things were going, and among those 183 pages of notes for *Sunset at Blandings* he left a three-sided set entitled "Scenario. January 19, 1975" which further refines our understanding of his working methods. He had reached the point where he was pretty happy with chapters 1–15 of the novel ("ALL THE ABOVE SEEMS STRAIGHT" he types below his summary) – but there were still small details that niggled away at his professional pride and required further attention. A telling example occurs in Chapter 12, referring to page 67 of the typescript, as Jeff Bennison and Lord Emsworth walk through the rear of Blandings Castle past the servants' quarters, making for the Empress's sty. The sentence under scrutiny reads as follows:

> The route indicated took them past Beach's pantry, and they could hear the butler's fruity laugh, indicating that Gally was telling him some humorous story from his deplorable youth.

Plum writes two telling notes to self: "If Beach is scared of being found out to be Jeff's uncle, he would not be laughing" and "Jeff must hear the rumble of Gally's voice". The first point to note is that men who are nervous or hiding a guilty secret are rarely possessed of a "fruity laugh", as Beach seems to be on this occasion. Fruity laughs are for those with nothing on their mind, and if preoccupied people laugh at all, the sound would be more tentative, perhaps even forced. Beach, in the past, has shown himself to be a nervous individual, so that laughter was going to need some attention. Second, the narrator states that the laughter is occasioned by a biographical anecdote told by Galahad. Yet as things stand, Jeff, from whose perspective this section is told, has no evidence that Galahad is actually *there*: the door to the pantry – presumably – is obstructing his view. So Gally has to somehow announce his presence, even if this is simply a "rumble" that is recognizably his. Both these minor solecisms, occurring in the same sentence, required correction. Unfortunately, Plum didn't get round to making the necessary alterations before he died; but what does survive is his fetish for precision, even as a nonagenarian. With his literary sensibility still sharp as a tack, he is clearly concerned that if he leaves this scene unrevised, the reader may spot it and start asking questions about Beach's sudden-onset devil-may-care attitude or Jeff's ability to see through doors, thus distracting him and breaking the spell the fiction has been busy weaving in his imagination, because, as I've noted before, great comedy is an immersive experience that doesn't suffer interruption gladly. *That's* the level of detail the master craftsman has to bring to his art, and it's to those tolerances that Plum's sensibility was so finely and expertly attuned.

If this kind of close reading isn't your thing, I quite understand, and it is easy to get bogged down in all the detail. Yet Plum didn't have the luxury, as we do, of skipping it if he grew bored. In the end, he would have had to confront "the detail work" and wrestle it to the ground until he had fully convinced himself that the book's mechanism was ticking as smoothly as that of a Swiss watch. And, once more borrowing the language of the theatre, he determined to "play the scene" over and over until it did. In short, Plum tended to build his comedy of quicksilver and gossamer on a foundation of solid concrete, and at the base of this structure was the plot, what for him was the generative underpinning of the entire proceedings.

In creating watertight plots, Plum was the very opposite of Blair Eggleston, the novelist in *Hot Water*, who is the subject of the following exchange between his fiancée Jane Opal and an uncomprehending Packy Franklyn:

> Jane: Blair's novels don't have any plots.
> Packy: No? Why's that?
> Jane: He thinks they're crude.

As a result, Blair writes novels that are "the sort of books that people don't read" despite enjoying considerable critical acclaim (they have "a strange, fearless quality", apparently). Packy promises to tackle them one day, "But not now. Later" – meaning, of course, never. "Tricky devils, these novelists", he ventures. "The ink gets into their heads". Not so Plum, for whom plot wasn't simply the cause-and-effect of what happens in a story but the way those events move within the narrative. For to Wodehouse – as to Aristotle, who had written the rulebook on dramatic theory over 2,000 years earlier – it was important that his stories had a formal structure complete with a beginning, a middle and an end. In this insistence, as in his views on formal structures within rhyme and rhythm we've already looked at, he was an unashamed conservative. It was all part of the courtesy he extended to his audience, and his insistence on authorial control. As the writer, it was his job to make things work. A failure to do so – in the Modernist manner – was a serious dereliction of responsibility.

An overview of Plum's plots reveals a regular Aristotelian pattern: the set-up; the development; and the resolution. We've already looked at quite how hard he laboured at the first, and the last is pretty self-explanatory: at the end of a Plum plot, everything needs to be successfully brought together, and all the loose ends tied up in a bow. But it's in the development – that huge, yawning gap in the middle – that Plum's comedy really shines, being a masterly mixture of motion and stasis, simplicity and elaboration, as summed up in the following two comments, the first from Plum in an article entitled 'The Leisurely Drama' that he wrote for *Vanity Fair* in 1916, the second from Bertie in 'Bingo Has a Bad Goodwood':

> We find ourselves continually wanting to speed things up; with the result that when we encounter one of these leisurely dramatists – the kind that takes a couple of acts to establish the fact that Lord Aubrey is in love with the manicure – there comes the desire to get behind the man and urge him onward with a spiked stick. From the rise of the curtain, we feel, a playwright ought to be as busy as a one-eyed cat in a dairy; and we resent his approaching his job in the detached and dreamy spirit of a plumber who has come to mend the leak in the bathroom.
>
> ~
>
> I never know, when I'm telling a story, whether to cut things down to plain facts or whether to drool on and shove in a lot of atmosphere...and, in a word, what-not.

In Plum's plots, it's the what-not that gets ditched, whether on the stage or the page. He insisted on having his plot outlines and/or framework clear in his mind before he began the work of putting flesh on their bones. From his ruminations in *Performing Flea*, we are regularly given the impression that simply writing a story around a strong character wasn't enough to justify starting work: he had to have some idea of what that character was going to *do* with himself. "[I]n Uncle Fred" he wrote in 1935, "I'm sure I have got a character, but at the moment I simply can't think of another plot for him. I'm just waiting and hoping one will come". It helps, he says, when that character arrives with a job of work – like Sherlock Holmes, who solves mysteries. But so few of Plum's characters have the need or the aptitude to hold down a job that it's an avenue often closed to their creator. This, he continues, led to the downfall of Psmith: "I wouldn't sit down and do a series of *Adventures of Psmith*, because there is no definite line that he would take". Which is why, presumably, a catastrophe in the Psmith family fortunes is the plot generator in *Leave It to Psmith*: with a ready supply of money, our hero doesn't actually *have* to do anything; without one, he's spurred into action.

The older he got, the more Plum seemed to need to plot things through in greater and greater detail before sitting down at his typewriter. This had begun with *Bill the Conqueror*, published in 1924, which he considered "a corker" – even though it bore distinct resemblances to his musical comedy *Sitting Pretty*, first performed that same year. In a letter to Leonora, he claimed to have "got the plot more or less complete" and was "cleaning it up bit by bit". But not, he added, before he'd written "18,000 words of scenario, the equivalent of about three short stories!" by way of "mapping the story out". Note the exclamation mark, as if Leonora might have thought this excessive, or even ridiculous. By the time he told Townend of this "new system" the following year, he had upped the wordage necessary to 30,000 (about *five* short stories, or almost a third of an average novel), and by the time he was writing *Uncle Fred in the Springtime* in 1938, he claimed "[i]t wasn't till I had written three hundred pages of notes that I got the idea of putting Uncle Fred into the story at all". This sounds a little excessive even for Wodehouse, but whichever was the correct total, the advantages of all this preparatory slog were considerable:

> By this means you avoid those ghastly moments when you
> suddenly come on a hole in the plot and are tied up for

three days while you invent a situation. I found that the knowledge that I had a clear path ahead of me helped my grip on the thing. Also, writing a scenario of this length gives you ideas for dialogue scenes and you can jam them down in skeleton and there they are, ready for use later.

More theatrical language ("scenario", "dialogue scenes") and just the sort of detailed treatment Plum the musical writer would have pitched to producers like Ray Comstock or Flo Ziegfeld to interest them in taking a property further. Get the plot straight in your head before you start, and ultimately time is saved and the investment pays off – useful for a writer who regularly over-committed himself and was likely as not working on several projects at once. Notice also how the spine of a plot generates the dialogue scenes that Plum later hangs along its length.

But there was a snag: Plum, by his own admission, was not particularly good at coming up with original plots. Which is ironic, because the intricacy and brilliance of his plotting is one of the features for which his writing is best known. It was Bill Townend who provided Wodehouse with the central idea for his first 'adult' novel, *Love Among the Chickens*, round which Plum wove the scenes that recount Stanley Featherstonehaugh Ukridge's ill-advised entry into the poultry-rearing industry. In one of his first letters to Townend after their correspondence resumed in 1920, he hoped to repeat the wheeze they'd pulled off 14 years earlier: "Listen, Bill, any funny plots you can send me will be heartily welcomed". Plot-begging was a regular feature of their letters, and occasionally Plum would bat one back – but the traffic was usually in the other direction, either from Townend or another source. Even Ethel and Leonora were pressed into service on occasion, and his private scrapbook contains some intriguing paragraph-length press cuttings over which are superscriptions such as "good stuff for Ukridge" and "used in Luck of the Bodkins". These snippets could be anything that caught his eye, of the kind he specialized in dredging up for his *Globe* column. Or something might have come up in conversation, or in his day-to-day business dealings. You can bet that once he'd found out what a 'tontine' was, he recognized that he's been handed a plot on a plate, and rushed off to write *Something Fishy*.

Wodehouse was always more the literary magpie than a great original when it came to plotting, but then again, he knew he was in good company with this particular affliction – didn't William Shakespeare have exactly the same problem? After all, only four (or perhaps five) of

The Man From Stratford's 39 (or so) plays have scenarios that can't substantially be attributed to anyone else. In the April 1916 number of *Vanity Fair* (written under his nom de plume P. Brooke-Haven), Plum informs us that "anybody who had a good plot put it in a steel-bound box and sat on the lid when he saw Shakespeare coming", making him the forerunner of those "dramatizer[s] of novels" who shamelessly recycle the same material in different formats ("dishing up fiction in play form" as he termed it). Having written an entire column in the November 1917 edition of *Vanity Fair* slagging off this modish habit ("[i]f a playwright is incapable of thinking up a plot for himself, he should admit it like a man and return to punching the time-clock at the factory"), it might come as a surprise to discover how often Plum transferred material from one medium to another. Not only had he already recast his novel *A Gentleman of Leisure* as a successful stage show in 1911 starring a young Douglas Fairbanks, it had enjoyed a third outing four years later as a silent movie that credited Cecil B. DeMille as "third scriptwriter". Plum would go on to rework his own prose stories into plays (or vice versa, turning his plays into novels) on around 20 occasions, a body of work that embraces such titles as *Leave It to Psmith, If I Were You, Doctor Sally, The Code of the Woosters, Spring Fever* and *Ring for Jeeves*. Definitely a case of 'do as I say, not as I do', but Plum tried to square this particular circle with the following:

> I would permit, for instance, such dramatizations as that of *Piccadilly Jim*—not only because it is impossible for such a story to have too wide a vogue, but principally because the author, a thoroughly worthy fellow, happens to be furnishing a new apartment at a moment when there is an insistent demand on the part of his family for a new car.

Big-ticket capital goods must have been in steady demand in the Wodehouse household if the figures above are in any way accurate.

Therefore we can argue in general terms that to Plum, plot was a utilitarian element in his writing, in and of itself of lesser importance than dialogue, pacing, characterization, style and structure, even though it necessarily preceded everything else in the act of composition; hence the regular incidence of repetition, formula and plot recycling within both his plays and stories. After all, if the plot is simply an enabling mechanism, why not use one that's tried and trusted? Certainly the incidence of that 'Party A saves Party B from drowning to effect a reconciliation' is such a frequent motif in Plum's work that you occasionally want to throttle him. I fully intend making an exhaustive list one day, but for now I can confirm it pops up in *Love Among the Chickens*, *The Girl on the Boat*, 'The Pride of the Woosters Is Wounded', 'Helping Freddie', *Carry On, Jeeves*, 'Deep Waters', 'Company for Gertrude', *Quick Service*, *Frozen Assets*, *Jeeves in the Offing* and several others. By the time he wrote *Right Ho, Jeeves* in 1934, even he was referring to "that old he-saved-her-from-drowning gag" before summarily dismissing it, even though the suggestion comes from the formidable brain of Jeeves himself.

But even with this wearisome trope, any initial irritation quickly subsides and the long parade of his stock characters, settings and plots turns from a crowd of Ancient Mariners to a family of old friends whose arrival at our reading party we don't just tolerate but welcome. It's this willingness to be seduced by Plum's aesthetic that sorts out the true Wodehouse fan from those who would criticize him for a lack of imagination – at least in my humble opinion. Familiarity, far from breeding contempt, engenders loyalty and even love: we become co-conspirators in creating his unique brand of reality because we trust him to do 'the square thing' by us. And he never lets us down.

À propos of which, have you ever noticed how little suspense there is in a Wodehouse plot? How little he toys with the reader? Very little remains unresolved for long. Particularly in his early novels, even the chapter headings act as spoilers, yet with masterful control, Plum induces just enough curiosity to pique our interest in what is going to happen next. While we're not exactly on the edge of our seats awaiting the next sensational plot development, the pacing of those 'big scenes' manages to keep the narrative momentum going without Plum needlessly tantalising us about what lies in store. It's almost as if he feels such narrative games are somehow disrespectful, or even vulgar. Moreover, the more familiar we become with Plum's world, the more adept we get at guessing what's going to happen way before it actually does. After a while and with a bit of practice, we can tell – usually from their very first appearance – which lead male will end up proposing, and being accepted, by which lead female simply by the way he describes them. For instance, it's very clear at the start of *Hot Water*, even though they are both engaged to other people, that Packy and Jane will eventually end up together, no matter that Jane thinks her novelist beau Blair Eggleston is just her type and that Packy is affianced to the stunning, wealthy and well-connected Lady Beatrice Bracken. And yet, this foreknowledge doesn't ruin our enjoyment of the plot, since Plum's writing offers us far more than simple guessing games strung with red herrings.

In *The Girl on the Boat*, even though Rufus Bennett categorically tells Sam Marlowe that "If you were the last man in the world I wouldn't allow my daughter to marry you!", we can be confident that by the time the book ends in fifty pages' time, Sam and Billie Bennett will end up betrothed.

Yet Plum is so well-mannered, he straight away apologizes for any discomfort Mr Bennett's emotional outburst may have caused the reader:

> As I read over the last few pages of this narrative, I see that I have been giving the reader rather too jumpy a time. To almost a painful degree I have excited his pity and terror; and, though that is what Aristotle says one ought to do, I feel that a little respite would not be out of order.

This, of course, is intended ironically. While there may be cause for pity in a Wodehouse plot, it never hangs around for any length of time. And as for terror…seasoned Wodehouseans need never concern themselves that things won't turn out exactly how we like them. Certainly by 1922, when *The Girl on the Boat* was published, Plum knew that his readers could tolerate his winning brand of comfortable unreality, even at the risk of offending Aristotle and his ill-treated literary principles. As if to rub it in, Plum allows Webster, the valet, to display his peerless knowledge of cheap romantic novelettes (all of whose titles Plum has invented) to find a suitable plot to help Sam and Billie heal their temporary rift. Mercifully rejecting the 'saving from drowning' scenario (which Webster 'discovered' in *The Earl's Secret*), the conspirators settle for a spot of dog-napping (from *Footpaths of Fate*) – which of course goes horribly wrong, and they end up in an even more implausible situation than any writer of novelettes could come up with, involving a china cabinet, an orchestrion and Sam getting himself stuck in a suit of armour. Elsewhere (in *Big Money*), Lady Vera Mace and Lord Hoddesdon respectively inform Ann Moon that life does not resemble "a fairy story" or "a twopenny novelette", yet here is Wodehouse brazenly not only telling us it does, but revelling in the fact that his plots are even more absurd than that.

Plum was to grow yet more shameless as his mid-season style matured, passing off his stories as "chronicles" and on several occasions rebranding himself a "historian", as if what happens in his plots actually *did* happen. We've already encountered one such passage in *Hot*

Water, to which we can add a second, when the narrator again apologizes for introducing distasteful material, but which, having awarded himself the title of "historian", he is "reluctantly" duty-bound to relate. And again in *Big Money*, the narrator of that chronicle informs us that unpleasant though it may prove, "it is the duty of the historian to see life steadily and see it whole" – and so we must endure a full disquisition on the minutiae of T. Paterson Frisby's gastric juices if we want a full and accurate picture of what is taking place. One last one: in *Quick Service* we are told that "the conscientious historian" must neither "scamp" nor "abridge" – "actual words must be placed on the record".

The history or chronicle form – call it what you will – Plum was perfecting in this golden period had started to take shape around 20 years before. As I've already argued, we might consider *Something Fresh* or 'Extricating Young Gussie' (both from 1915) as the most significant points of reference in the genesis of the Wodehouse *ur*-plot, since they feature, respectively, the debuts of the Blandings crowd and Jeeves and Bertie. But we can travel back a little further than that, to *A Gentleman of Leisure*, if we wish to propose another compelling though less-well-known contender. For while the titles above introduce two sets of archetypal and enduring Wodehouse characters, it's the earlier work that first acquaints us with many of the settings and motifs that Plum would keep returning to in his subsequent novels to help him map out his plots.

Before we get stuck in, a word or two about the many extant versions of the story – not just to demonstrate that I've done my homework (and hopefully got it right – bibliography not being my strong suit), but to emphasize just how much Plum was prepared to simultaneously recycle, touch up and monetize his material over and over again:

- *A Gentleman of Leisure* had already seen the light of day as a novella: *The Gem Collector*, published full-length in *Ainslee's* magazine (US) in December 1909 and credited to "G. E. Wodehouse";

- Greatly expanded, this was later reissued as a 14-part serial, *The Intrusions of Jimmy*, starting in the June 11, 1910 edition of *Tit Bits* (U.K.);

- As a novel, the story first materialized in America in May 1910 as *The Intrusion of Jimmy* (note singular noun)...

- ...then six months later in the U.K. as A *Gentleman of Leisure*.

Plum revised the story on each of these four occasions, then more substantially for Herbert Jenkins in 1921, by which time he had pretty much perfected the kind of story he was destined to write for the rest of his life. (Significantly, 1921 also marked the major revision of *The Prince and Betty* we looked at in a previous chapter, as if Plum reckoned the both plots were too good to waste now he had a firmer grasp of what he was doing.) The later the rewrite, the better both stories get – which is no doubt why the editor of the Everyman uniform edition decided to go with the latest versions of both.

Even by Wodehouse's standards, this is a tortuous bibliography. It's as if he had a blueprint for the novel in his head which he wasn't quite getting right and kept needing to tinker with. And as he tinkered, so he was able to find new homes for it. So if we add the theatre and two movie versions I mentioned earlier to the five prose incarnations (and a sixth in 1931), the explosion of new themes even in the basic story must have alerted Plum that he was on to something, both artistically and financially. Although some of the following plot tropes will be familiar from his earlier work, to find them all present and correct in a single story (however many versions there are of it) is worthy of note; and so, rather than slavishly numbering each one, I've simply emboldened them as they occur.

Let's begin with the **transatlantic** nature of A *Gentleman of Leisure*. Indeed, the story's hero switches nationality – from the über-English Sir James Willoughby Pitt to plain American Jimmy Pitt – in the story's transition from (English and American) serial to (American) novel. As if to rub in this twin nations theme, Wodehouse makes his dodgy copper John McEachern an ex-Etonian who, having been expelled from his alma mater, has emigrated to the States, metamorphosing from an English aristo named John Forrest into a New York police captain.

Which brings us to: **characters pretending to be someone else**, of whom there are simply too many to list in Plum's novels, but most notably in the Blandings series.

This in its turn neatly introduces a third theme, our old friend **the stage**. The opening of A *Gentleman of Leisure* consists of topical theatre talk batted around a bunch of actors (all, Plum is at pains to tell us, **clean-shaven**), mainly about the vogue for plays featuring gentleman thieves, inspired by the massive success of E. W. Hornung's *Raffles* stories. Indeed, this group (all members of the Strollers' **Club**) have just witnessed the premiere of one such drama, *Love, the Cracksman*. Prompted by crime-related banter, the germinal incident of *A Gentleman of Leisure* takes shape when Jimmy **bets** he can break into a house just like a real burglar.

And so our next theme, you may not be surprised to learn, is **stealing things**: whether diamonds (as in this case), incriminating letters or memoirs, pigs, or cow creamers, Plum's novels are packed with light-fingered tea-leafs helping themselves to other people's property. Often, these are not **professional larcenists**, but **well-meaning young men doing someone else a service** or being egged on by their peers. And so it is here, leading us to speculate what sort of man would risk his reputation and even his freedom in such a venture.

The answer to that question is **The Archetypal Wodehouse Leading Male (TAWLM)** of whom Jimmy is a good example. As his fellow Stroller, Sutton, informs us, Jimmy has:

> …much more money than any man, except a professional plute, has any right to. He's as strong as an ox. I shouldn't say he'd ever had anything worse than measles in his life. He's got no relations. And he isn't married.

Round off that list with the fact the TAWLM is a "good chap", usually parentless, who is outspoken, dashing, from 26 to 28 years old, and resourceful rather than brilliantly intelligent, and you have most of Wodehouse's leading men in a nutshell. Chances are that, facially, they're not flawlessly attractive and may well have done some boxing at school. Quite why these attributes seem so essential we'll investigate in the next volume. For now, it will suffice to remark that he can go in any direction his creator wants him to. There is literally nothing holding him back. His life is a *tabula rasa* – which it will need to be if Plum's tortuous plot trajectory, packed with motion and **coincidence**, is to stand a chance of working.

While we're here, let's look at **The Archetypal Wodehouse Leading Female (TAWLF)**: these are slightly more varied than the men, particularly physically, but they are all, as Jimmy feels about his in-amorata Molly McEachern, girls "of character". In other words, Molly has spirit and is neither weak, archly romantic, too posh, serious or educated. She is possessed of strong passions and is loyal, fair-minded, generous and kind to animals. What she needs, apparently, is "one of those capable, energetic fellers" (see above) to make her happy.

Next there's **the country house setting**: Dreever Castle is a predecessor of Blandings, being situated in Shropshire, possessed of a lake, and resembling "a glimpse of Fairyland". It is also an archetype of Brinkley Court, Totleigh Towers, Skeldings Hall, Deverill Hall and all the rest, those sylvan locations where **the central characters congregate** to act out the workings of the plot. Among those present are a textbook **knut** (Hildebrand Spencer Poyns de Burgh John Hannasyde Coombe-Crombie, twelfth Earl of Dreever, otherwise known as "Spennie"), who speaks like a low-octane Bertie and confesses to being "a bit of an ass in some ways"; his **henpecked uncle**, Sir Thomas Blunt; and the perpetrator of the henpecking, the formidable chatelaine Lady Julia, Spennie's **aunt**, who is also the forerunner of Connie, Aunt Agatha and the rest of Plum's monstrous regiment of aristocratic women. As a couple, they symbolize **the collision of new and old money**, with Sir Thomas **the bourgeois millionaire** and Lady Julia **the snob**. These country-house gatherings increasingly resembled **staged farces** as Plum's style matured, with doors opening and closing, characters entering and leaving, and different combinations of characters plotting and planning and falling in and out of love, often at **vertiginous speed**.

And so on.

This is by no means an exhaustive list, but there's enough here to carry my point. Even though he might have assembled many of the ingredients of future plots in one place, what Plum hadn't managed to do – and the successive rewrites can't have helped this – was to bring them as seamlessly together as he might have wanted. And he knew it. There's the odd continuity error, and the character of Hargate, the card sharp, does his work within the plot and then instantly vanishes. But most noticeable of all – to Plum as much as anyone – was how *engineered* it all feels. Early in the plot, there is the first of several massive coincidences which, had they occurred in a story written in Plum's mature style, would have passed almost unnoticed because he learned to play our credulity like a finely tuned instrument. Here, by contrast, at a stage when realism still hadn't quite been shown the door, either in his imagination or his writing, we catch Plum virtually apologizing for stretching our disbelief to breaking point:

> [N]ow for the first time…Jimmy was conscious of a sense
> of the unreality of things. It was all so exactly as it would

have happened in a dream. He had gone to sleep thinking
of this girl, and here she was.

Meeting Molly, whom he had only seen from afar on a transatlantic
liner, in the very New York house he had by chance selected to burgle in
order to win a bet is not just a chance in a million but beyond the wildest
dreams of the "optimistic fatalist" Plum tells us Jimmy is. And then,
stone me, it happens again in London, where he bumps into Spike, his
former sort-of sidekick, late one night in the cabman's shelter just shy
of Hyde Park Corner – the same Bowery Boy who, you might expect,
wouldn't stray more than a few blocks from his home turf. Well, here
he is, three thousand miles from it. Just like that. And then it happens a
third time, when in the middle of rural Shropshire, at Dreever Castle,
Jimmy meets Molly completely by chance *again*. And all this in the first
hundred pages. It is, the narrator informs us in Chapter 13, "a series
of the most workmanlike miracles" of a kind that wouldn't have been
out of place in one of Plum's fabulous tales we looked at back in this
book's Chapter 5. Yes, Jimmy is blessed with preternaturally good luck;
indeed, "he was inclined to look upon his luck as a sort of special train
which would convey him without effort to Paradise. Fate had behaved
so exceedingly handsomely up till now!" In drawing our attention to the
artificiality of his plot workings, I could of course claim that Plum was
anticipating the postmodernists by 50 years – but I'm not going to. At
least not now – that's for the Chapter on Fate in Volume 2.

However, whenever Plum mentions "Fate" – which he often does
throughout the canon – it's really a synonym for "the writer" – the
guy who comes up with the plot. In later novels, he's happy to ride
the ambiguity between him and the mysterious workings of the super-
natural, but here one gets the impression he's trying just that little bit
too hard to convince us that he's got nothing to do with it. That's not
to say Jimmy doesn't have to work overtime to get his girl, because he
does; it's simply that Plum's reality isn't quite his own yet. There isn't
sufficient *coherence* – for which you may substitute the word 'confidence'
to force us to accept what happens in his novels *on his terms*. And this
brings us to the second of the big themes in this chapter: as we've
already seen in his musical comedies, Plum was striving for coherence
just as those writers at the cutting edge of literature were abandon-
ing it as a lost cause, and he knew he was swimming against the tide
of those "writing people" whom we now group under the heading of
"Modernists".

Modernism, to Plum, was a racket: in 'The Aunt and the Sluggard', published in 1916, Rockmeteller Todd trousers $400 for a sophomoric poem called simply 'Be!', which allows him "to stay in bed until four in the afternoon for over a month". The narrator on this occasion is Bertie Wooster, who is similarly puzzled that such rubbish could get published:

> I didn't know there was enough money in poetry to support a chappie…but it seems that…American editors fight for the stuff.

Plum's regular targets were the writers who lived out in "the No Man's Land of Bloomsbury", whom he parodies (among many others) in the persons of novelists Stultitia Bodwin (from the story 'Best Seller') and *Hot Water*'s Blair Eggleston, both of whom have coincidentally written works called *Offal*, which suggest their creators are nothing more than "disillusioned, sardonic philanderers". He also likes counterpointing the dizzy heights of aestheticism with the demands of the commercial world: in 'Came the Dawn', Lancelot Mulliner is given the job of coming up with a catchy advertising slogan for Briggs's Breakfast Pickles, but instead turns in a mournful and depressing Modernist lament, the closing lines of which read:

> I am a bat that wheels through the air of Fate;
> I am a worm that wriggles in a swamp of disillusionment;
> I am a despairing toad;
> I have dyspepsia.

Dyspepsia was to become another regular Wodehouse metaphor (cue Volume 2 again), an annoying ailment that sours the mood and makes the sufferer write ill-natured tripe like that above. Modernism was not a heroic challenge to the fragmented reality of the 20th century, but a side effect of poor digestion that a regime of liver salts and regular Swedish exercises (of the kind Plum practised every day) would quickly alleviate. His tissues restored, the writer could then return to creating cheerful stuff that made sense.

But dismissing Modernism and its carefully nurtured aura of complexity didn't mean that Plum didn't understand where it was coming from – he absolutely did. In his June 1914 *Vanity Fair* column 'The Literature of the Future', he goes to some lengths to simplify Futurism, one of Modernism's minor offshoots:

In these complex, hustling days, if authors are to be true to life, they must put far more into their descriptions of every-day life and action than they have dreamed of doing hitherto. The Futurist painters have realized this, and they make it their aim to put everything into their canvases which space will allow them to cram in. It is the old principle of the Irish Stew. Broadly speaking, you cannot go wrong, whatever you put into an Irish Stew; and I, a futurist, hold that this rule applies also to novels.

A spot-on analysis, crystal clear and mercifully free from jargon. Not so the art it describes: as we've already noted, Plum was no fan of Irish Stew as a structural principle, and he imagined what would result if a Futurist were to write a novel. As far as he was aware, this hadn't been attempted, so he made good the deficiency by presenting us with 'The Girl Who Took the Wrong Ferry Boat', featuring a reworking of the "Jones crossed Thirty-third Street" nano-story from the beginning of this book's Chapter 4. Brace yourselves…

> Jones…Zunk…Whoosh…Wow…Now…Ah…
> Clangclangclangclang…Wow…Whew…Woof…
> Kindly look where…Brrrrrrrrrrr…Where do I…
> Ardent gaze…Affinity?…Whoosh…Wow…Wuxtry…
> Brrrrrrrrrrr…Brown's Balsam for the Bilious…Wha-a-a-
> a-a-aaaa…printing-machine…Yipe-yipe-yipe…moving
> pictures…Whoosh…Oo…Affinity…Burning-stare…
> Clangclangclangclang…Hi-yi-yi…Whfff…

Mr Jones's adventure is in there somewhere, barely if at all recognizable (and notice stomach disorders making another guest appearance). But no, Plum admonishes the doubters, this formless jumble of words is not the mess it might at first appear, but a new *improved* Irish Stew, "a compressed soup tablet of literature" that is a whole new way of writing and is going to net him a fortune:

> In a busy age like this it supplies a long-felt want. It is vivid. It grips. It has the punch. It has come to stay. How humanity has got along without it all these years is more than I can understand.

And it can work for you too, he tells us in his best imitation of a snake-oil salesman:

> It is ridiculously easy. Try it yourself. Anybody can see the whole picture.

Not, of course, meaning a word of it. But underneath the buffoonery there's a theme that was clearly exercising him to a great degree around this time, because here it comes again one year later in the June 1915 edition of *Vanity Fair*:

> [W]hat we...resent is the June-bug type of plot, which comes in, disappears, whizzes in again, whizzes off just as we are trying to focus it, and pops up once more just as we have adjusted our minds to its permanent withdrawal.

It's a resentment that would never leave him. In 1936 Plum found a great example of the 'June-bug' plot in an early draft of Bill Townend's novel *Comox*, and the resulting letter is one of the best examples we have of his instinct for creating order and coherence where none previously existed. "PULL THE STORY TOGETHER", he capitalizes as he proceeds to list the many faults of his friend's manuscript.

First off, the novel didn't know what it was meant to be (Plum describes it as an unsatisfactory "hybrid" between "a leisurely, Arnold Bennett sort of novel" and "a story of action"). To solve this identity crisis, he advises Townend to nix "the leisurely note and go for the action". That done, everything will be back in "key". Then he tells him to exercise some "grip". "The stuff is all there", he writes, "but the construction is wrong". Cutting down redundant material, reducing the number of characters, introducing them into the plot as swiftly as possible and focussing on the "high spots" will all serve to make the story "zip along" in an entertaining fashion. "Don't diffuse the interest", he adds by way of gently hinting that Townend had handed him a story that was a dull dog's breakfast in just about every department. Usually the most mild-mannered of men, Plum plays the stern taskmaster in this letter as he makes it clear that, essentially, Townend is going to have to start the thing all over again, just like the hungover writer at the opening of this chapter advises Reggie. But that's a measure of how seriously he took his own writing, and how much effort he was prepared to expend in getting it just right – Do As I Say *And* As I Do.

Back in 1915, the unruliness of reality, and what can be done about it, is a theme that would somewhat incongruously invade the first Blandings novel, *Something Fresh*. Joan Valentine (a magazine writer) remarks to Ashe Marson (a writer of detective fiction):

> Do you ever get moods when life seems absolutely mean-
> ingless? It's like a badly-constructed story, with all sorts of
> characters moving in and out who have nothing to do with
> the plot. And when somebody comes along who you think
> really has something to do with the plot, he suddenly drops
> out. After a while you begin to wonder what the story is
> about, and you feel that it's about – just a jumble.

Imagine if Jean-Paul Sartre had written that in the 1950s: whole forests would have to die as scholars and critics rushed to praise its profundity and tease out its philosophy of alienation and existential angst. Not to mention its daring postmodern perspective. But no – here it is in one of those frivolous P. G. Wodehouse novels. And unlike many of the contemporary Modernists, Plum had the solution to unruly plots. Having listened to Joan's heartfelt complaint, Ashe quickly nips it in the bud with the very unSartrean observation: "There is one thing that knits it together…the love interest". But then, Ashe regularly does Swedish exercises and probably doesn't suffer from dyspepsia that often.

And so it is with just about every Wodehouse plot. Love does not only conquer all, it helps bring order to everything under his sun, as well as being the rather more flighty quality that gives wings to his lightness. It doesn't matter how complicated the plot has been up to that point, how torturous the road has been in order to get the man and woman together in the same place at the same time and with the same attraction for one another. When they agree to marry, all that rambling and chaotic hinterland is immediately forgotten and order established as if by the single touch of a magic wand. Following the couple's declaration of love for one another (which usually consists of a formal proposal of marriage), everyone within their orbit – parents, guardians, friends and even pets and aunts – fall into line around them. Even those few who may not support the union will usually either change their minds, grudgingly admit defeat, or vanish from the scene altogether.

It's the antidote to Modernism. To Plum, things falling apart neither offered exciting artistic possibilities nor represent the death of meaning. Life had simply got a little frantic and needed calming down. Here's

Montrose Mulliner's take on the zeitgeist, taken from the aptly titled 'Monkey Business', published in 1932:

> "I am not a man who often speaks of these deeper things – on the surface, no doubt, I seem careless and happy-go-lucky – but I do hold very serious views on a citizen's duty in this fevered modern age. I consider that each one of us should do all that lies in his power to fight the ever-growing trend of the public mind towards the morbid and the hectic. I have a very real feeling that the body politic can never become healthy while this appetite for sensation persists."

As I've said before, I'm not one to wilfully confuse what a character says with his creator's point of view, and this is borne out when Montrose's principled cultural stand actually turns out to be a brilliant piece of sophistry designed to get him out of having to plight his troth in a gorilla's cage – in which the gorilla is still resident. But I'd be more than a little surprised if some of this didn't ring true for Plum – because that's how he chose to conduct his own life.

Back in 1914, at the age of 32, he had begun setting his own house in order by getting married and thus adding some stabilising "love interest" of his own. After a whirlwind courtship worthy of one of his own plots (it lasted less than eight weeks), Plum and Ethel Wayman got spliced at the absolutely charming Little Church Around the Corner on New York's East 29th Street – and never looked back. Adopting her daughter Leonora soon afterwards, Plum was immediately possessed of a ready-made nuclear family that was to bring order and grounding to his life. Ethel, who outlived him, was renowned for being the organizational brain who allowed Plum to devote himself single-mindedly to the job of writing – and a fine job she made of it. Robert McCrum's biography devotes several pages to the unlikely story of the Wodehouses, so I will not repeat his research here, except to quote the telling remark that Ethel "[gave] his life a new coherence [and] also gave it joy" at almost exactly the same time as Plum would have been busy composing Joan Valentine's lament about the chaos of life's storylines – and Ashe's counter-argument that love is about so much more than mere attraction. A sceptical Joan – like Ethel, also a former chorus girl – fails to see Ashe's point at first, but she is finally won over to his point of view at the novel's close, and all is set fair for the two writers to live happily ever after, their two hearts beating as one. Which is not as clichéd as it first sounds, at least in the case of their creator's partnership. Uncle Fred's description of his own alliance with Jane, Lady Ickenham, also springs to mind when trying to sum up precisely how Plum's marriage was destined to work:

> The only way of ensuring a happy married life is to get it thoroughly clear at the outset who is going to skipper the team. My own dear wife settled the point during the honeymoon, and ours has been an ideal union.

The unity that comes with mutual understanding seems to have been the Wodehouse ideal. And who knows? Maybe if Sartre had taken a leaf out of Plum's book instead of insisting on an open relationship with Simone de Beauvoir, he would have pushed out cheerier stuff. Just a thought.

But did Plum actually believe all this love business worked? Was it a plausible solution to the disorder in life as well as in art? I only pose the question because I'm nearing the end of Volume 1 and I'm in holiday mood, knowing it's an impossible riddle to answer. But here's something from one of Plum's least well-known works that might – just might – provide some food for thought – not that I'm claiming it does, mind.

Immediately prior to Plum's nuptials – just three months before, in fact – he was to publish one of his more untypical works, an oddly prescient story of a marriage blessed with a child, but one that is threatened when the modern world with its fads and fashions is allowed to intrude too far. Both parents, Kirk Winfield (somewhat inevitably a healthy physical specimen and, yes, 26 years old) and his wife, Ruth, seem to have everything going for them. But Ruth's worship of her aunt's faddist philosophy of neurotic personal hygiene and Kirk's inability to focus on what he wants to do with his life drive a wedge between the young couple that even the arrival of their son, Bill, can't heal. Until, that is, Kirk wakes up, banishing all the extraneous baggage that has accumulated in the marriage by the simple expedient of focussing his attention back onto its most important asset. Ruth, deeply unhappy playing the role of society hostess, quickly follows suit, realizing that the answer to her problems has been right under her nose the whole time: the simple expedient of allowing Bill to be a normal child who gets dirty, plays with dogs and gets into fights. This awareness marks "something symbolic...a new order of things" within the family unit.

Here are the closing lines:

> The child…was the real hero of the story, the real princi-
> pal of the drama of their three lives. He was the link that
> bound them together, the force that worked for coherence
> against chaos. He stood between them, his hands in theirs;
> and while he did so there could be no parting of the ways.
> His grip was light, but strong as steel.

"Coherence against chaos" might well have been the legend on Plum's
headstone had not "He gave joy to countless people" made the final
cut. Life and aesthetics are made to meet in this strangely touching
ending to one of his more serious plot lines (actually his *only* serious
plot line). Our individual biographies, he seems to be saying, are, like
the plot trajectory of a drama, continually threatened by the intrusion
of disorder, and we need something that will make sense of them if we
are to feel grounded and fulfilled. Thus armed, he allows the Winfield
family to march into whatever the future might bring, putting an end
to the drifting and chaos that has characterized their relationship up
to this point of recognition. Throwing forward to Volume 2 (again –
sorry), note how Bill's grip is "light" but at the same time "strong as
steel" – it's a metaphor that will become increasingly familiar as our
argument proceeds.

Originally published in May 1914 as a magazine one-parter
entitled *The White Hope*, and later as the novel *The Coming of Bill* (*Their
Mutual Child* in the US), the story represents an experiment Plum
wasn't destined to repeat. But there can be little doubt that its conclusion falls well short of his trademark flippancy, irony or bathos: as
the American press advert for the book puts it, "Literature at its best
is life as we understand it". Once again, I don't think it's too fanciful
to imagine that, here, Plum's life and his art – which represented so
much of his life – have overlapped somewhat. Coherence, order and
structure were essential for literature to work. That single, controlled
vision was paramount and would be steadily refined throughout the
rest of his working life. Plum didn't need to write complex plots if he
didn't want to, but the fact that he chose to do just that in the vast
majority of his books only serves to emphasize the desirability of simplicity, coherence and order when resolution finally *does* arrive – which,
for the characters Plum encourages us to care about, it always does.
Somehow or other. Only then is the complexity of the world swept

away and the true nature of Wodehousean reality restored – making the narrative arc of most of his plots instantly obey Ashe Marson's simple formula.

Which, as reflected in the length of Plum's writing career, and the continuing volume of his sales, was to prove a winning formula.

Continuity Link:
"A Message Short"

Nobody knows what Mr. Wodehouse's philosophy of life is;
or even whether he has one.

J. B. Morton ("Beachcomber")

One never quite forgets a story that has made one laugh.

P. G. Wodehouse, Preface to A Century of Humour

Plum entered mid-season form in the early to mid-1920s – somewhere around the time of *The Inimitable Jeeves* and his golf collection *The Clicking of Cuthbert*. It was only at this point, after two decades as a published author, that he began to write with any consistency in what a 1920 *New York Times* reviewer called "the P. G. Wodehouse manner". He'd finally found the happy place where his talent could give of its best and his comedy resonate the loudest.

This is, of course, an entirely contingent watershed I've dreamed up. To talk about any writer's output in terms of periods and turning points usually represents the triumph of neatness over accuracy, but it does buy us some useful breathing space in which we can take stock of where our argument has reached.

At this point, it's pretty safe to say that the ethos of Plum's created world wouldn't evolve much further. As for his writing style, the majority of the building blocks were now in place and would be further finessed down the years, usually in the direction of simplicity and efficiency, using many of the techniques and criteria explored in Chapter 9 of this book. And so, in a way, most of the hard graft is over: we've hacked our way through the dense undergrowth of his early stylistic dalliances and reached a clearing from which we can glimpse the horizon. All that remains for us in Volume 2 is to do some serious basking in the warmth of his mature vision. But while we anticipate that joyous experience, the question remains of his writing's wider significance – that "something understood" I mentioned right back at the beginning, the whole that is somehow greater than the sum of all the parts. Where are we with that?

Before we start looking at whatever that "exquisite and elusive" quality might be, a necessary caveat: having reached this landing place, we should now leave Wodehouse out of any further amplification of the argument, for he makes it clear that he harboured no conscious aspirations for his work other than keeping his readers amused and himself in tobacco. As he wrote in *Over Seventy*:

> It was not that I had any particular message for humanity. I am still plugging away and not the ghost of one so far, so it begins to look as though, unless I suddenly hit mid-season form in my eighties, humanity will remain a message short.

And so, having done Wodehouse the courtesy of absolving him of all responsibility what follows in these last few paragraphs, we can start seeding a few ideas that can be germinating while we're busy applying the factor 50.

Let's start with a quote from Plum's lifelong friend and fellow author Bill Townend, who, in his introduction to 1953's *Performing Flea*, offers a post–Second World War perspective on what Plum's writing meant to him:

> [O]ne can read in what he has written...an awareness of what life has come to mean, of man's responsibilities and duties in a world beset by fear, of the narrowness of mind that leads to war and the pettiness many men...share in their contacts with other people, and of a tendency to see both sides of a problem at issue.

Whether you agree or not (and let's not forget Plum had okayed these comments prior to *Performing Flea* going to press), Townend's is a significant claim that takes his friend's achievement far beyond 'mere' humour and out into aspects of human experience that are usually off limits when discussing light comedy. And yet comedy, whatever else it may be, undeniably *does* offer that alternative vision, that "tendency to see both sides"; and Wodehouse's comedy, so indivisible from his own personal 'take' on life, offers a set of alternatives so energizing that its pulse still beats strong and steadily in our own age. So what, exactly, is keeping it alive?

To Townend, reading Wodehouse's comedies was to be gently, often inadvertently, reminded of humanity's more worthwhile qualities – if only because its baser instincts are for the most part conveniently absent, or have been sublimated into mere shadows of their former selves. Thus freed by his great good humour, we are allowed to dispense with the "narrowness of mind" that is the essential prerequisite of conflict – for where there is no laughter, there can be no perspective. Because laughter *is* perspective: an instinctive, instantaneous and, in Wodehouse's books, warm-hearted and for the most part *generous* perspective. It's too long and involved an argument to enter here, but those who, down the ages, have thought of laughter as primarily an instrument of repression (when it is used to shame or ungenerously ridicule) can be assured that with Wodehouse, they are in safe hands: almost never in the whole of his oeuvre is there even the slightest scintilla of this kind of mean-spirited amusement at the expense of someone else. As we'll see in the much-trailed Volume 2, Plum liked his characters to be spiritually generous, sympathetic – *em*pathetic, even. And that marked common denominator dispels any suspicion as to what Plum considered laughter was *for*. His comic perspective allows the world to think better of itself, or at least provides a wonderful excuse for it to do so, by heroically sticking to its guns and refusing to lose its faith in laughter's healing – and ultimately levelling – power.

If the previous paragraph gives the impression I'm placing too much weight on a fragile load-bearing surface, I can only apologize because – straight-up honest – it exactly mirrors my own evolving appreciation of Wodehouse over the last 40-or-so years. From being a load of preposterous but hilarious stories with shiny art deco backdrops and a soundtrack crooned by Al Bowlly, I've come to view them as something altogether different – but not a whit less funny for all that. In fact, I now value having Wodehouse in my life more than I have ever done, because he represents something far more than just a good laugh. Bill Townend also remarks that only "with the passage of time" had his appreciation of what his friend had written "grown in depth and understanding". In my own case it took several mighty blows from the stuffed eelskin of Fate before the realization dawned that something highly significant had altered in my own appreciation. Quite what, I wasn't sure, but while doing a feasibility study for this book, I came across comic writer Jonathan Coe's account of *his* late-season blossoming. Although by his own admission he had belonged to the "stupidly snobbish" gang who thought Wodehouse a one-trick pony, Plum nevertheless represented "the elephant in [his] comic room" he would have to stare down at some point. And when he did (after being presented with an award in Wodehouse's name for his comic novel *The Rotters' Club* in 2000), this happened:

It was only then that I realised the pure, unpolluted humour of which he was possessed was the greatest possible gift he could have offered to the world: the same thing, I suppose, that Italo Calvino had in mind when he extolled the virtues of "thoughtful lightness", or "comedy that has lost its bodily weight".

And then, at second remove, it dawned on *me*: the notion of "thoughtful lightness" is a *perfect* description of what typifies Wodehouse's writing, since it seamlessly encapsulates what influenced its composition *and* its most significant effect on those who enjoy reading him – in other words, the conjoining of what he brings to the party and what we must bring so we can join in. Calvino's formulation (via Coe's confession) was one of the last things he wrote prior to his death in 1985, and it finally gave words to what I had long suspected but never managed to articulate.

"Thoughtful lightness" doesn't so much focus on the particulars of Wodehouse's style, language or subject matter. It's more about the comic sensibility that quietly and almost imperceptibly finds its voice *through* them. Here's what Calvino has to say about his choice of terminology:

> After forty years of writing fiction, after exploring various roads and making diverse experiments, the time has come for me to look for an overall definition of my work. I would suggest this: my working method has more often than not involved the subtraction of weight... Whenever humanity seems condemned to heaviness, I think I should fly...into a different space. I don't mean escaping into dreams or into the irrational. I mean that I have to change my approach, look at the world from a different perspective, with a different logic and with fresh methods of cognition and verification. The images of lightness that I seek should not fade away like dreams dissolved by the realities of present and future.

That's just six sentences torn from a long, fascinating and masterful essay, but it's no coincidence that both Townend and Calvino, two writers as alike as chalk and cheese, each speak of the fresh perspectives comedy can offer.

And this is where Calvino's help in defining Wodehouse's message-less message picks up and takes off where Townend's gentlemanly tribute can offer us no further assistance. For while Townend plays the traditional English conservative moralist, Calvino acts as the cerebrally restless Continental polymath. Yet both have something to contribute to our debate about Wodehouse – who was light years away from being either.

The place Calvino wanted his writing to get to, and where I believe Wodehouse's ended up in the 1920s, signifies, to some, a reluctance or an inability on the part of the author to engage with the world's heaviness, which at the very least devalues what he creates. And this (as Wodehouse himself argued in 'A Note on Humorists') is the mindset we fall into when comedy is patronized as escapism. By doing precisely what we ask it to do – to *not* take the world seriously – we've set it up to fail. But throughout history, the greatest comedy never *completely* divorced itself from the world, or we would have forgotten all about it. Its targets may have changed (although many remain reassuringly familiar), but its message and modus operandi have not. The most successful comedy ever written does not involve an ostrich-like avoidance of whatever doesn't fit its brief, but a subtle repositioning of the audience's perspective to one of instinctive subversion – a more mischievous, less principled version of Townend's seeing the other side. This is not the kind of subversion that wants to destroy or even confront, although it might be described as modestly seditious. Rather, it requires its possessor to cultivate an instinct for re-focussing anything that might compromise his or her good nature. And this description fits Wodehouse's comic perspective like a glove.

This is precisely how those mighty ambassadors of well-being, Uncle Fred, Galahad Threepwood and Psmith, go about their work of spreading sweetness and light, confusing those who would resist by smiling in the face of adversity while doing their utmost to find ways round it. Less headline-grabbing are those dozens upon dozens of ordinary Wodehouse men and women – his knuts ("friends of all the world"), his lovers, his chorus girls, his "melodramatic" schoolboys, his mischief makers, even his rogues – who, like Jill Wyvern in *Ring for Jeeves*, are open-minded, open-hearted, "intensely alert and alive", and move, physically and mentally, "with a springy step".

As readers, we somehow find ourselves – without being consulted – on their side and, more importantly, sharing their viewpoints. If we found ourselves taking the part of, say, Connie or Aunt Agatha, we would have already lost patience with Wodehouse, for these are his outsiders who don't 'get' his comic vision and can never be part of it. And yet Wodehouse's lightness even makes it possible for us to sympathize with his 'baddies' if we stop for a moment and think of the asinine behaviour and disruption they have to put up with – a good deal of which they bring on themselves through their inability to embrace anything that smacks of change or playfulness. Connie's inveterate snobbery is one of the most potent symbols of this heaviness in thought and behaviour, and you'd think she might learn that her plots and plans are always destined to be thwarted by those who are lighter in heart and mind (Calvino's ambition), which allows them to embrace "the big, broad, flexible outlook" (Townend's ideal). Only she doesn't: lightness has to have something to float away *from*, and Connie obliges us every time by doggedly refusing to adapt to changing circumstances. And yet even she reveals an unexpectedly human side when she goes all gooey over James Schoonmaker, whom she eventually marries – with our best wishes for her future happiness, and the vain hope that she will finally leave Lord Emsworth alone.

Ultimately, whether any of this would interest Wodehouse is highly doubtful, but he might have been bucked to learn that from Calvino's perspective at least, his own utterly idiosyncratic lightness was the very thing that was keeping his work not just read but relevant to audiences long after his death. Calvino decided to embrace lightness because:

> I felt that the entire world was turning into stone: a slow petrification, more or less advanced depending on people and places but one that spared no aspect of life. It was as if no one could escape the inexorable stare of Medusa.

Only Wodehouse's created world *has* escaped. Lightness is the antidote to the slow petrification that threatens every writer's meaning from the moment he or she gives form to his or her thoughts within the onward flow of time. And somehow, unlike Calvino, who had to theorize like fury to understand his own lightness, Plum happily stumbled on a version that worked for him, even while taking, as we've seen in the course of this book, a long and winding road to his destination. And although he developed and refined it down the years, that lightness remains one reason, in partnership with his comic eloquence, why his books continue to be read and those of many of his contemporaries don't. Somehow, his period trappings don't date. Or, rather, they *do* date – terribly – but it no longer seems to matter.

Wodehouse's future looks bright, even among "the writing people".

Novelist and lecturer Richard T. Kelly has remarked that while his undergraduate students initially have "an instinctual resistance to the idea of comedy as a subject for academic inquiry" (which perhaps should translate as "education isn't usually this much fun"), they are "no more suspicious of Wodehouse than of James Joyce or Chinua Achebe" once they get down to studying what – and how – he wrote. Which does seem to represent progress of a kind.

As for the comic writers of tomorrow, they could do worse than read the conclusion of Plum's essay 'Some Thoughts on Humorists', complete with its quote from Jewish scripture:

> And if any young writer with a gift for being funny has got the idea that there is something undignified and anti-social about making people laugh, let him read this from the Talmud, a book which, one may remind him, was written in an age just as grim as this one...

> ...And Elijah said unto Berokah, "These two will also share in the world to come." Berokah then asked them, "What is your occupation?" They replied, "We are merry-makers. When we see a person who is downhearted, we cheer him up."

Hopefully, the world to come won't be a bad place to end up for those of us who make the trip. But whether it is or not, we can always make the best of our time in the here and now. As Gussie Fink-Nottle, somewhat overdosed on the blushful Hippocrene informs the young blades at Market Snodsbury Grammar School:

> [I]t is a beautiful world. The sky is blue, the birds are singing, there is optimism everywhere... People who say it isn't a beautiful world don't know what they are talking about... [So] you must all use every effort to prevent yourselves becoming pessimists and talking rot.

Attaboy, Gussie. Not bad for a fish-faced teetotaller.

A Practical
BIBLIOGRAPHY

I am not, I think, an irascible man, but after reading a number of recent
biographies and histories I have begun to feel pretty sore about footnotes and not
in the mood to be put upon much longer. It is high time, in my opinion, that this
nuisance was abated and biographers and essayists restrained from strewing
these unsightly blemishes through their pages as if they were ploughing
the fields and scattering the good seed o'er the land.

(Over Seventy)

Well, that is Plum's view on the inclusion of critical apparatus in non-fiction, and I have respected his predilection in compiling this book. Having said that, I have chased dozens of footnotes, endnotes and chapter notes through various publications both in print and online – and mighty useful they have been – so not to include at least *some* help for the bewildered scholar in search of further insight might be accounted somewhat hypocritical. But then, as I noted in the opening sequence, Plum is a bibliographer's nightmare, each novel appearing in a bewildering number of editions and impressions, not to mention under any number of imprints; and that, taken in conjunction with the sheer volume of his output, makes life doubly difficult. In short, this could take forever: by which time you'd be bored out of your mind – and so would I.

So what I've come up with is a compromise: the following is not exhaustive (or, hopefully, exhausting), but it does at least point the seeker after truth in the general direction of what he or she might be looking for. It's a sort of 'Wodehouse Reference Greatest Hits', and to be truthful, I haven't needed much else to get this book written. What's more, I'm guessing most of it will serve for Volumes 2 and 3. Of course, the majority of the titles listed below will already be familiar to the dedicated Wodehouse scholar, but what follows is a concise overview for any general enthusiasts who might wish to dig a little deeper into the mother lode of writing by – or about – Plum.

(ISBN numbers have been provided where available, and all dates are of U.K. publication, except where noted).

BIBLIOGRAPHIES

There are three indispensable bibliographies every Wodehouse scholar really needs to look at:

P.G. Wodehouse: A Comprehensive Bibliography by Eileen McIlvaine (Heinemann, 1990, ISBN 978-087008125-5). At almost 500 pages, this is an absolute monster, and, thanks to a small original print run, ruinously expensive if you wish to buy a copy. Its scholarship, as with all scholarship, has needed updating in the 30 years since its first appearance as new material has come to light, but it remains an awe-inspiring labour of love. However, if you'd like a simplified Plum bibliography, you can do no better than visit The P.G. Wodehouse Society (U.K.)'s website (*www.pgwodehousesociety.org.uk*) and have a gander at Tony Ring's clear and concise listings. Or more concise still, turn to the back of David Jasen's *P.G. Wodehouse, A Portrait of a Master* (see below), where you'll find a decent chronological list of Plum's novels and short stories, complete with date and place of original publication.

If bibliography is your thing, Nick Townend's regular column in the quarterly magazine *Wooster Sauce* is a well-researched, invaluable resource. It's been going donkey's years, and ranges far and wide through Plum's work, introducing new discoveries, correcting errors and generally serving as the forum and diary of record for all matters bibliographic. You have to join the U.K. Society to receive the magazine (once again, see *www.pgwodehousesociety.org.uk* for further details). Nick deserves a gong both for his dedication and painstaking scholarship.

PRIMARY TEXTS
(by which I mean stuff written by Plum himself)

Novels and Stories: In this book, I am among the first writers on Wodehouse to benefit from the existence of a uniform edition of his work, the 99-volume Everyman's Library series which was published from 2000-2015 (Overlook Press in the U.S.) This is my benchmark, and I have quoted both the text and the titles from these editions wherever possible (they follow the English titles throughout). The volumes do not always correspond with what appeared during Wodehouse's lifetime, however: for example, *A Man of Means* is paired with 'The Kid Brady Stories' for the first time. And also note that where more than one edition of a title is available, the editor has been forced to make an agonizing choice about which one to print. He invariably goes with Plum's revised texts, and so, for example, *Love Among the Chickens* is the 1921 revision, not the 1906 original.

Song Lyrics: The last word on Plum's song lyrics arrives courtesy of the following publication:

The Complete Lyrics of P.G. Wodehouse ed. by Barry Day (The Scarecrow Press Inc., 2004, ISBN 978-081084994-1). There they all are, 300+ lyrics from almost 40 shows, complete with insightful commentary. Magisterial. For the biographical background, see also:

Bolton and Wodehouse and Kern: The Men Who Made Musical Comedy by Lee Davis (James H. Heineman Inc. 1993, ISBN 0-87008-145-4)

Poetry: A great place to start is:

What Goes Around Comes Around ed. by Tony Ring (Harebrain Publishing, 2014, no ISBN). A well-chosen and entertaining selection of 100 poems (and the odd song lyric) from Plum's massive oeuvre. Tony is everywhere in Wodehouse scholarship, and he also had a hand in:

P.G. Wodehouse in The Globe Newspaper, 1901-1908 (2 volumes, ed. by John Dawson [Vol. 1] and Tony Ring [Vol. 2] GRP Publishing, 2015, ISBN 978-1943290055). Again: short print run and eye-wateringly expensive (I had to borrow a set!). Volume 1 is an anthology of Plum's columns and topical paragraphs (as identified by an international team of Wodehouse scholars, since most of his work for the newspaper was unsigned); Volume 2 is where you'll find the 200 poems. Of course, Plum wrote poetry intermittently throughout his career, some of his work (usually parodies) dotted throughout his novels and journalism. Which brings us to:

Journalism: For the early stuff, see Vol. 1 of *P.G. Wodehouse in The Globe Newspaper, 1901-1908* immediately above. But for just about every piece of journalism Wodehouse wrote from 1901-1923, visit the spectacularly useful website 'Madame Eulalie's Rare Plums', run by a network of dedicated scholars whose public face is Neil Midkiff. This features just about all Plum's work, in prose and poetry, that is out of (U.S.) copyright, and is endorsed by the P.G. Wodehouse Estate. Fully searchable, it's a boon to the Wodehouse scholar, as it also contains detailed notes and commentary on a number of his early publications. Post-1923 is more of a problem: many of Plum's articles were revised and included in his prose anthologies *Louder & Funnier* (1932); *Performing Flea* (1953); *Bring On the Girls* (1954) and *Over Seventy* (1957). There's also a selection in 1966's *Plum Pie*.

Plays in the 'Legitimate' Theatre: Once again, very little has been published, but Tony Ring rides to the rescue one more time with his:

Second Row, Grand Circle (Harebrain Publishing, 2012, no ISBN). Subtitled: 'A Reference Guide to the Contribution of P.G. Wodehouse to the Legitimate Theatre', this comprehensive book painstakingly picks its way through dozens of plays, many of which were produced, and others that weren't. Packed with useful commentary.

Letters: This is easy. Look no further than:

P.G. Wodehouse, A Life In Letters ed. by Sophie Ratcliffe (Hutchinson, 2015, ISBN 978-009179634-1). Just brilliant, and beautifully edited. But bear in mind not all Plum's surviving letters are included here, or necessarily at full length. Others – though not many – can be found in the various biographies, and (often abridged and doctored) in *Performing Flea*.

Notebooks: *Phrases and Notes: P.G. Wodehouse's Notebooks 1902-1905* ed. N.T.P. Murphy (Popgood & Grooley, 2014). Fascinating glimpses into Plum's early writing career.

BIOGRAPHIES

There is no shortage of material on Plum's life. At the time of writing, there are four main biographies:

P.G. Wodehouse: A Biography by Frances Donaldson (Weidenfeld and Nicolson, 1982, ISBN 978-0749001759-2)

P.G. Wodehouse, A Portrait of a Master by David Jasen (Garnstone Press, 1975, ISBN 0-85511-190-9)

P.G. Wodehouse: A Literary Biography by Benny Green (Pavilion, 1981, ISBN 0-907516-04-1)

Wodehouse: a Life by Robert McCrum (Penguin, 2004, ISBN 0-670-89692-6)

As a rule, we can say the more recent, the more comprehensive: Benny Green's is the most entertaining read, however, and McCrum's mainly excellent account is occasionally marred by unwarranted speculation. Also worthy of a mention in dispatches is:

Wodehouse's School Days by Jan Pigott (Dulwich College Quartercentenary, 2015, ISBN 978-095394933-5)

HANDBOOKS/ MISCELLANIES/ REFERENCE

The daddy of them all is the quite phenomenal:

A Wodehouse Handbook by N.T.P. Murphy (2 vols: Sybertooth, 2013, ISBN 978-192759200-7 and 978-192759201-4). Volume 1, subtitled 'The World of Wodehouse', is arranged into thematic chapters, such as "Family" and "The Clergy"; Volume 2, 'The Words of Wodehouse' is an alphabetical list of vocabulary and themes. Norman's approach was to identify the many occasions when the real world found its way into Plum's created equivalent. As well as being impeccably scholarly, it's wonderfully entertaining. An equally comprehensive survey is attempted in:

The Millennium Wodehouse Concordance by Tony Ring and Geoffrey Jaggard (8 vols: Porpoise Books, various dates, various ISBNs). Another enormous work: each volume deals with a different subsection of Wodehouse World (for example "Blandings Castle" or "Wodehouse Goes to School") and takes the form of an alphabetical list of words, themes and characters which are then idiomatically explained. Sometimes a little *too* idiomatically.

Last but by no means least, we have:

Wodehouse at Work to the End by Richard Usborne (Penguin Books, rev. ed. 1978, ISBN 0-14-004564-3). First cab on the rank back in 1961

(Usborne corresponded regularly with Wodehouse), the revised edition of this pioneering title continues on to Plum's death in 1975. The book takes the form of single essays devoted to each character grouping in Plum's novels. Highly opinionated but hugely enjoyable. Usborne's other major contribution to Wodehouse studies is no less useful, since it contains plot synopses and character indexes of all the novels:

Plum Sauce: A P.G. Wodehouse Companion by Richard Usborne (Overlook Books, 2003, ISBN 978-158567441-1)

CRITICISM

I've tried to use as little Wodehouse criticism as humanly possible, and then only to occasionally buttress an argument or provide historical context. There will be more in Volumes 2 and especially 3 – when I come to examine how Wodehouse has been received and understood down the years – and I will deal with these references then. I don't propose to list all of the Volume 1 entries here, as most were taken from the internet and their URLs might well have changed or disappeared by the time you read this. In the text, however, I have provided sufficient clues as to author, title and publication for you to be able to chase these under your own steam. I will make one honourable exception, however:

Homage to P.G. Wodehouse ed. by Thelma Cazalet-Keir (Barrie & Jenkins, 1973, ISBN 0-214-66880-0). This is a wonderful celebration of Wodehouse by some cracking writers, including Claud Cockburn, Auberon Waugh and Malcolm Muggeridge. Plum's personal favourite was written by Richard Ingrams, then editor of the satirical magazine, *Private Eye*.

INDEX

In keeping with Plum's disdain for footnotes and the like, this volume has eschewed them. However, we have included an index.

INDEX OF WORKS BY P. G. WODEHOUSE

Novels

Short Stories

PELHAM GRENVILLE WODEHOUSE

Lyrics, Musicals and Plays

INDEX

INDEX

THE P.G. WODEHOUSE SOCIETY (U.K.)

The P.G. Wodehouse Society (U.K.) is a friendly and active literary society that exists to promote the enjoyment of the greatest humorous writer in the history of the English language. We hold a number of meetings and events for our members throughout the year, which include lectures, quizzes and performance, and there's a biennial black tie dinner in London. We also publish a quarterly magazine, *Wooster Sauce*, which contains news, reviews and scholarship from correspondents around the world. For further information and details on how to apply for membership, visit *www.pgwodehousesociety.org.uk*.

BOOKS BY P. G. WODEHOUSE (U.K. EVERYMAN EDITIONS)

The Adventures of Sally
Aunts Aren't Gentlemen
Bachelors Anonymous
Barmy in Wonderland
Big Money
Bill the Conqueror
Blandings Castle
Bring on the Girls (non fiction)
Carry On, Jeeves
The Clicking of Cuthbert
Cocktail Time
The Code of the Woosters
The Coming of Bill
Company For Henry
A Damsel in Distress
Do Butlers Burgle Banks?
Doctor Sally
Eggs, Beans and Crumpets
A Few Quick Ones
French Leave
Frozen Assets
Full Moon
Galahad at Blandings
A Gentleman of Leisure
The Girl in Blue
The Girl on the Boat
The Gold Bat
The Head of Kay's
The Heart of a Goof
Heavy Weather
Hot Water
Ice in the Bedroom
If I Were You
Indiscretions of Archie
The Inimitable Jeeves
Jeeves and the Feudal Spirit
Jeeves in the Offing
Jill the Reckless
Joy in the Morning
Kid Brady Stories / A Man of Means
Laughing Gas
Leave it to Psmith
The Little Nugget
Lord Emsworth and Others
Louder and Funnier (non fiction)
Love Among the Chickens
The Luck of the Bodkins
The Luck Stone
The Man Upstairs
The Man with Two Left Feet

The Mating Season
Meet Mr. Mulliner
Mike and Psmith
Mike at Wrykyn
The Swoop! / The Military Invasion of America
Money for Nothing
Money in the Bank
Mr. Mulliner Speaking
Much Obliged, Jeeves
Mulliner Nights
My Man Jeeves
Not George Washington
Nothing Serious
The Old Reliable
Over Seventy (non fiction)
Pearls, Girls and Monty Bodkin
A Pelican at Blandings
Performing Flea (non fiction)
Piccadilly Jim
Pigs Have Wings
Plum Pie
The Pothunters
A Prefect's Uncle
The Prince and Betty
Psmith in the City
Psmith, Journalist
Quick Service
Right Ho, Jeeves
Ring For Jeeves
Sam the Sudden
Service with a Smile
The Small Bachelor
Something Fishy
Something Fresh
Spring Fever
Stiff Upper Lip, Jeeves
Summer Lightning
Summer Moonshine
Sunset at Blandings
Tales of St. Austin's
Tales of Wrykyn and Elsewhere
Thank You, Jeeves
Ukridge
Uncle Dynamite
Uncle Fred in the Springtime
Uneasy Money
Very Good, Jeeves
The White Feather
Young Men in Spats

Forthcoming P. G. Wodehouse titles also by Paul Kent

PELHAM GRENVILLE WODEHOUSE
VOLUME 2: "Mid-Season Form"

In 1915, and for the next decade or so, P.G. Wodehouse's fictional world mushroomed within his imagination. His best-known creations, Jeeves and Bertie, arrived in that year, as did Lord Emsworth and many of the Blandings circle; the Oldest Member teed off in 1919; the Drones Club threw open its doors in 1921; a new, thoroughly improved Stanley Featherstonehaugh Ukridge returned to the fold in 1923, and Mr Mulliner sipped his first hot scotch and lemon at the bar parlour of the Angler's Rest in 1926. Plum would steadily re-visit these characters and locations for another half-century, interspersing his tales with one-off novels, stories and further, less voluminous sub-series until his death in 1975. These were truly golden years, with Plum at the height of what he called his "mid-season form".

Paul Kent continues his groundbreaking study of Wodehouse's imagination by casting a fresh eye over his created world, whose characters and stories have made *our* world feel better about itself for well over a century.

PELHAM GRENVILLE WODEHOUSE
VOLUME 3: "The Happiness of the World"

In 1936, the Mark Twain Society awarded P.G. Wodehouse its highest accolade, the Mark Twain medal, "in recognition of your outstanding and lasting contribution to the happiness of the world". Translated into over thirty languages, and with all his novels and story collections still in print, Plum's work continues to spread sweetness and light around the globe well into the 21st century. But what is the secret of its longevity? How has a world so deeply anachronistic and fantastical managed to sail through the choppy waters of time and geography, manners and modes?

Paul Kent concludes his study of Wodehouse's imagination by getting to the heart of Plum's literary achievement, and how his unique sense of humour and his remarkable facility for writing elegant, memorable and timeless prose still manage to make us laugh into the 21st century.

Forthcoming P.G. Wodehouse titles from Paul Kent

WHAT HO!: P. G. Wodehouse on . . .

In addition to Paul Kent's 3-volume tour of P. G. Wodehouse's creative imagination, TSB is launching a series of Plum-related books by the same author featuring subjects that complement the main trilogy – the first three being 'Food', 'Love' and 'Sport'. Averaging 64 pages each, these will appear approximately every two months and can be bought individually or by annual subscription. Attractively-priced and written in Kent's breezy, no-nonsense style, they are perfect partners to the main books and ideal for gifting. Find out more at www.canofworms.net/whatho

WODEHOUSE AT THE THEATRE

P. G. Wodehouse's love of the American vernacular made him an outstanding lyricist, and along with Jerome Kern, Cole Porter, and George Gershwin (all Wodehouse collaborators), he helped to invent a quintessential American art form, the musical comedy. Mark Steyn makes a convincing case . . . that had Wodehouse died in 1918, he would be remembered not as a novelist, but as "the first great lyricist of the American musical." (Cheryl Miller, Claremont Review of Books)

For many years the toast of Broadway and London's West End, P. G. Wodehouse was bitten by the theatre bug at an early age and stayed bit until the last day of his long life, an influence that also helped to shape his matchless writing style and mighty prose legacy. Former BBC Drama director and commissioning editor Paul Kent lifts the lid on this lesser-known body of Wodehouse's Work, looking at the glittering theatrical worlds of 19th and 20th-century musical comedy, Plum's deep roots in Shakespearean and Classical comedy, and his comprehensive knowledge and understanding of the performing arts.

PLUM'S LITERARY HEROES

It's widely acknowledged that P. G. 'Plum' Wodehouse is the greatest humorous writer England produced in the 20th century. The creator of Jeeves and Bertie, the Blandings saga, Ukridge, Mr Mulliner, Psmith and Uncle Fred, his output totalled almost 100 volumes of peerless comic invention. But where did all that material come from? Not just out of his head, no matter how large his hat size: in Wodehouse's case, much of arrived courtesy of his voracious reading habits, everything from Shakespeare to W.S. Gilbert via the Bible, Tennyson, Sherlock Holmes, gung-ho schoolboy fiction, gory pulp thrillers, the gloopiest romances and literally hundreds of other writers – even T.S. Eliot, who rubs shoulders with a host of authors whose names are now largely forgotten. No other writer can have had a broader range of influences.

In his latest groundbreaking study, Paul Kent, author of the *Pelham Grenville Wodehouse* trilogy of literary biographies (also available from TSB) teases out Plum's literary roots, and how he expertly blended elements from all these writers and genres into the heady cocktail that keeps the world laughing over a hundred years on from when he first created it. It's an alternative history of English Literature that will also make you laugh out loud.